"*School Law and Student Rights: Cases, Controversies, and Practical Guidance* captures the same dynamic, engaging energy I have experienced firsthand in the authors' presentations. Complex legal concepts are brought to life through clear explanations, timely cases, and practical guidance grounded in real school contexts. The book builds legal literacy while reducing anxiety, sharpening professional judgment, and supporting confident decision-making in high-stakes situations. It is an essential, practitioner-friendly resource for every educator and school leader."

Jason A. Pedersen, *Ph.D., Nationally Certified School Psychologist*

"A lack of knowledge of school law can create unnecessary fear or unjustified laxness among educators. This comprehensive text strikes an appropriate balance and encourages a sense of informed alertness to legal issues in the education system. It is a useful resource for educators and other professionals who work with school-aged children."

Samuel Knapp, *Ed.D., ABPP, Former Director of Professional Affairs for the Pennsylvania Psychological Association*

School Law and Student Rights

In this engaging text, prevalent school law topics are presented with interesting cases that help the reader to begin to think about such issues from a legal perspective.

School Law and Student Rights provides information about school law, including relevant statutes and regulations, case law, and hypothetical cases to provide practical examples of implementing the law in the school setting. The legal topics addressed in this book include the federal Family Educational Rights and Privacy Act (FERPA), student First Amendment considerations, educator liability, threat assessment, avoiding common reasons for due process hearings, and Section 504 issues.

Appropriate for educators, administrators, support staff, school psychologists, school counselors, and attorneys and advocates with an interest in school law, this book is an enjoyable and informational read about current and changing school law compared to a typical legal text.

Shirley A. Woika served as a teacher, school psychologist, and administrator before becoming the director of clinical training at Penn State's School Psychology Program. She is currently a psychologist in private practice in State College, Pennsylvania.

Anne M. McGinnis is a partner at Bond Schoeneck & King PLLC in Rochester, New York. She is an attorney who represents schools on legal issues related to students and school board operations. She was previously a school psychologist in a public school district.

School-Based Practice in Action Series

Series Editors

Rosemary B. Mennuti, EdD, NCSP

Department of Psychology, Philadelphia College of Osteopathic Medicine, Pennsylvania, USA

and

Ray W. Christner, PsyD, NCSP, ABPP

Cognitive Health Solutions, LLC

This series provides school-based practitioners with concise practical guidebooks that are designed to facilitate the implementation of evidence-based programs into school settings, putting the best practices in action.

Conducting Student-Driven Interviews: Practical Strategies for Increasing Student Involvement and Addressing Behavior Problems
John Murphy

Single Case Research in Schools: Practical Guidelines for School-Based Professionals
Kimberly J. Vannest, John L. Davis, and Richard I. Parker

Working with Traumatic Brain Injury in Schools: Transition, Assessment, and Intervention
Paul B. Jantz, Susan C. Davies, and Erin D. Bigler

Ecobehavioral Consultation in Schools: Theory and Practice for School Psychologists, Special Educators, and School Counselors
Steven W. Lee and Christopher R. Niileksela

Integrating Structured Literacy Instruction: From Sound to Sentence
Megan Gierka, Nicole Ormandy

School Law and Student Rights: Cases, Controversies, and Practical Guidance
Shirley A. Woika and Anne M. McGinnis

For more information about this series, please visit: https://www.routledge.com/School-Based-Practice-in-Action/book-series/SBPA

School Law and Student Rights

Cases, Controversies, and Practical Guidance

Shirley A. Woika and Anne M. McGinnis

Routledge
Taylor & Francis Group
NEW YORK AND LONDON

Designed cover image: *Original cover art by Savanna Woika*

First published 2027
by Routledge
605 Third Avenue, New York, NY 10158

and by Routledge
4 Park Square, Milton Park, Abingdon, Oxon, OX14 4RN

Routledge is an imprint of the Taylor & Francis Group, an informa business

ISBN: 978-1-041-21789-3 (hbk)
ISBN: 978-1-041-21772-5 (pbk)
ISBN: 978-1-003-72899-3 (ebk)

DOI: 10.4324/9781003728993

Typeset in Galliard
by Deanta Global Publishing Services, Chennai, India

To my husband of over 40 years. Through good times and bad, sickness and health, you have been beside me. A hand to hold in the darkness. A light to guide me home.

– *Shirley*

Dedicated to my son, Joseph, who is my dream come true. Honorable mention to my parents and MVPs of the home team, Laure and Joe.

– *Anne*

Contents

List of Illustrations

Series Editor Foreword

We have long believed that effective school-based practice requires more than technical skill. It requires informed judgment. And informed judgment, in turn, requires clarity about the legal frameworks that shape our daily work. In schools, law is not an abstract discipline reserved for courtrooms and attorneys. It is woven into everyday decisions about confidentiality, discipline, evaluation, free expression, disability rights, and student safety.

The *School-Based Practice in Action* series was built on a simple but demanding premise: research, ethics, and law must not remain theoretical. They must be translated into action. They must guide what professionals actually do in complex, time-pressured, relational environments. This volume embodies that mission in a domain that many educators approach with apprehension – school law.

If we are honest, legal issues in schools often evoke anxiety. Many educators report feeling underprepared, uncertain, or fearful about liability, due process, student rights, and the ever-evolving expectations placed upon them. Yet legal literacy is not optional. It is foundational to ethical and competent practice. Understanding the law is not about defensiveness; it is about clarity. It is about knowing where authority begins and ends, where rights attach, and how professional discretion operates within constitutional and statutory boundaries.

This book arrives at a time when questions of student rights and school authority feel particularly charged. Free speech controversies extend beyond the schoolhouse gate into digital spaces. Threat assessment teams must navigate constitutional protections while prioritizing safety. Section 504 and IDEA distinctions remain misunderstood. Due process hearings continue to shape special education practice. And confidentiality concerns grow more complex as communication increasingly moves into electronic formats.

What makes this volume especially compelling is that it does not treat law as a distant doctrine. Instead, it situates legal principles squarely within the lived realities of schools. Through case analysis, practical illustrations, and clear explanations of foundational statutes such as FERPA, Section 504, and the IDEA, this text bridges legal theory and professional application. The result is neither alarmist nor simplistic. It is grounded, measured, and pragmatic.

The chapters thoughtfully move across critical domains of school law:

- The foundational privacy protections of FERPA and the practical challenges of educational records
- The evolution of student First Amendment rights and the nuanced limits that apply in public schools
- Educator liability and the elements of negligence that shape risk and responsibility
- Threat assessment in the context of constitutional speech protections
- Common pathways to due process and strategies for prevention
- The distinctions and intersections between IDEA and Section 504 protections

Together, these topics form a coherent framework. They remind us that legal compliance is not merely procedural. It reflects deeper commitments to fairness, equity, safety, and dignity.

Importantly, the authors do not present the law as static. They illustrate how precedent evolves, how courts refine standards, and how recent Supreme Court decisions continue to shape interpretation. In doing so, this book reinforces a central truth: competent school-based professionals must remain intellectually curious and responsive to change.

This volume also reinforces an essential value of the series – interdisciplinary relevance. Teachers, school psychologists, administrators, counselors, speech-language pathologists, and related service providers will all recognize themselves in these pages. Legal literacy is not confined to administrators or district counsel. It is shared professional terrain. When teams understand the same legal standards, collaboration becomes more coherent and defensible.

Perhaps most importantly, this book reframes legal knowledge from something to fear into something to understand. When educators grasp the elements of negligence, the meaning of "true threat," the scope of confidentiality protections, or the procedural structure of due process, anxiety often gives way to confidence. Clarity reduces rumors. Precision replaces assumption. And professional judgment becomes stronger.

As series editors, we are proud to include *School Law and Student Rights: Cases, Controversies, and Practical Guidance* in the relaunch of School-Based Practice in Action. This volume exemplifies the spirit of the series: clarity without oversimplification, authority without rigidity, and practical guidance grounded in sound interpretation.

We hope this book does more than increase your knowledge of statutes and case law. We hope it strengthens your professional confidence. We hope it sharpens your decision-making. And we hope it supports you in creating school environments that are legally sound, ethically grounded, and centered on students' rights and well-being.

In a time when legal questions in schools are increasingly visible and consequential, this volume provides both foundation and direction. It reminds us that understanding the law is not peripheral to our work; it is integral to it.

Ray W. Christner, PsyD, NCSP, ABPP & Rosemary B. Mennuti, EdD
Series Editors
School-Based Practice in Action

About the Authors

Shirley A. Woika earned a bachelor's degree in special education, with certificates in Special and Elementary Education, from The Pennsylvania State University. Dr. Woika earned her master's and doctoral degrees in School Psychology from Penn State. She completed additional studies to earn a supervisory certificate in Special Education from Penn State and a superintendent's letter of eligibility from Shippensburg University. Additionally, she is a licensed psychologist.

Dr. Woika has worked in education for over 40 years. She began her career as a teacher and later served as a school psychologist. She was recognized as *School Psychologist of the Year* by her state association (ASPP). She went on to serve as a special education supervisor and a central office administrator. Dr. Woika then accepted the position of Director of Clinical & Field Training in Penn State's APA-accredited School Psychology Program. She served in that role for 16 years before retiring. At present, she continues to engage in private practice and contract work. She enjoys presenting at conferences and inservice trainings, and she is active in state-wide professional organizations.

Dr. Woika and her husband have five adult children and a grandchild. They enjoy spending time with their family. They reside in State College, Pennsylvania, with their rescue dog, Georgette.

Anne M. McGinnis earned dual bachelor's degrees in psychology and music education from the University of Hartford. She then earned her master's and Ph.D. in School Psychology from The Pennsylvania State University (where she was a student of Dr. Shirley Woika). Dr. McGinnis went on to earn her J.D. from St. John's University School of Law. She is a licensed attorney, licensed psychologist, certified school psychologist, and certified music teacher.

Dr. McGinnis has dedicated her career to supporting students and educators. She was a school psychologist at a public school district on Long Island, New York, for five years. Dr. McGinnis has practiced as a school attorney since 2014, and represents public school districts, private schools, and charter schools. Her specialization is in supporting schools with board of education operations and student-related matters, including special education, discipline, homelessness, residency, privacy, bullying, and constitutional rights. She regularly combines her background in school psychology and the law in her practice and enjoys writing and providing trainings on legal best practices for educators.

Dr. McGinnis lives in upstate New York on the shore of Lake Ontario with her family.

Introduction

Anne M. McGinnis

The legal system in the United States is unique in its structure. It relies on the concept of federalism, which distributes power between the federal and state governments. The creators of the Constitution endeavored to establish a balanced system of government that provided significant power to the individual states. This was in part due to the already unique structures within the original colonies that became the states, a desire to avoid the power of the ruling government that was established under British rule, and an effort to compromise. At the same time, there was an understanding that there was a need for a centralized federal government to create unity. Therefore, federalism is a defining feature of U.S. law and a primary source of jurisdictional variation that has resulted in varied laws across the country.

There are several sources of law in the United States that will be discussed in this introduction. Federal and state constitutions establish the framework and powers of the government. There are also statutes and codes that are created at the federal, state, and local levels. Regulations, which are considered to be administrative laws, are created by government agencies under the authority of a statute. There is also case law, known as common law, which establishes law through judicial decisions. These systems operate at different levels and with varying geographic scope.

Understanding U.S. law requires familiarity with substantive legal concepts, including how those concepts are created and applied across jurisdictions. For example, a contract dispute in California may be governed by legal principles that differ significantly from those applicable in New York. The Supreme Court has repeatedly affirmed that federal and state governments are separate sovereigns for many legal purposes (*Heath v. Alabama*, 1985). But federalism also imposes limits: federal law may preempt state law, but only within the scope of federal constitutional authority.

DOI: 10.4324/9781003728993-1

Federal and State Constitutions

Federal Constitution

The United States Constitution, adopted in 1787 and ratified in 1788, applies to every jurisdiction in the United States. The Constitution establishes the structure of the federal government, allocates powers among its branches, and limits governmental authority through the protection of individual rights. The three branches of the federal government include the executive (i.e., the President), the legislative (i.e., Congress, which includes the Senate and House of Representatives), and the judicial (i.e., the Supreme Court). Article VI contains the Supremacy Clause, which provides that the Constitution, federal statutes enacted pursuant to the Constitution, and treaties are "the supreme Law of the Land" and take precedence over conflicting state law.

The Constitution both grants and limits federal power. Congress may legislate only pursuant to powers enumerated in Article I, such as the power to regulate interstate commerce, to tax and spend for the general welfare, and to declare war (U.S. Const. art. I, § 8). Powers not delegated to the federal government are reserved to the states or the people under the Tenth Amendment.

The Bill of Rights was created shortly after the Constitution was ratified and established the Constitution's first ten amendments. The most frequent amendments from the Bill of Rights that apply to school law are the First Amendment (freedom of speech, religion, and other fundamental freedoms) and the Fourth Amendment (the prohibition of unreasonable searches and seizures). An entire chapter of this book is dedicated to First Amendment considerations for students. A foundational U.S. Supreme Court case that applied the Fourth Amendment to student rights is *New Jersey v. TLO* (1985). There, a student was found smoking cigarettes in school and was forced to allow the assistant principal to search the student's purse. The assistant principal found drug paraphernalia in the purse and called law enforcement. The student was charged with several crimes and expelled from school. The student argued her Fourth Amendment rights were violated by the search of her purse. The Supreme Court held that students do have Fourth Amendment protections against unreasonable searches and seizures, but such rights were not violated here because the assistant principal had a "reasonable suspicion" that the student violated the school rules. The search of the student's purse was therefore permissible.

There are now 27 Constitutional Amendments. The authority to amend the Constitution is found in Article V, which allows Congress to propose an amendment that must pass with a two-thirds majority vote in both the House of Representatives or two-thirds of the state legislatures can request Congress to call a national convention to propose an amendment (which has never successfully resulted in an amendment). The Archivist of the United States then carries out the process to ratify the amendment.

The federal government's authority over many laws that apply to public schools is provided by the Fourteenth Amendment, which is also considered the Due Process and Equal Protection Clause. The Fourteenth Amendment provides in part that,

> No State shall make or enforce any law which shall abridge the privileges or immunities of citizens of the United States, nor shall any State deprive any person of life, liberty, or property, without due process of law; nor deny to any person within its jurisdiction the equal protection of the laws.

The Equal Protection Clause has been applied to seminal Supreme Court decisions for public schools, including *Brown v. Board of Education* (1954), which prohibited racial segregation in K-12 public schools. The application of the Fourteenth Amendment in *Brown* found that segregated public schools denied children of color equal protection under the law, and accordingly, "separate educational facilities are inherently unequal" and unconstitutional. This decision overturned the previous "separate but equal" doctrine that allowed for racially segregated public schools in the 1896 Supreme Court decision, *Plessy v. Ferguson.*

The Fourteenth Amendment was applied in another Supreme Court decision impacting schools in *Plyler v. Doe* (1982). That decision found that a state cannot prohibit the children of undocumented immigrants from attending public school absent a substantial state interest. Accordingly, the Texas law that barred undocumented children from attending public school was in violation of the Fourteenth Amendment, as the language in that Amendment also applied to undocumented immigrants. A well-known quote from the decision written by Justice Brennan provided,

> By denying these children a basic education, we deny them the ability to live within the structure of our civic institutions, and foreclose any realistic possibility that they will contribute in even the smallest way to the progress of our nation.

State Constitutions

Each state has its own constitution, which functions as the supreme law within that state, subject to the constraints imposed by the U.S. Constitution. State constitutions typically provide more detailed governance structures than the federal Constitution that frequently include expansive declarations of rights. For example, many state constitutions explicitly guarantee rights to education, labor protections, or environmental quality. These rights are not expressly enumerated in the federal Constitution.

State constitutions may also establish structural requirements on state legislatures, courts, and executive agencies. While federal constitutional rights establish a minimum baseline, states are free to provide greater protections under their own constitutions, a principle recognized by the Supreme Court in cases such as *Michigan v. Long* (1983).

Federal and State Statutes

Statutes, whether federal or state, are codified laws enacted by the legislature. Such statutes may provide for administrative regulations to accompany those statutes – we dedicate a section to regulations later in this introduction. The individual words in statutes make a difference in their interpretation. For example, the word "may" means that something in the statute is permissible, whereas the word "shall" means it is required.

Federal Statutes

Federal statutes are enacted by Congress pursuant to the procedures provided by Article I of the Constitution. A bill becomes law after it passes both the House of Representatives and the Senate in identical form and is signed by the President or enacted over a presidential veto (U.S. Const. art. I, § 7). Once enacted, federal statutes are codified in the United States Code (U.S.C.), which is organized by subject matter into 54 titles. For example, Title 20 governs education. When federal and state statutes conflict, federal law preempts state law under the Supremacy Clause. (*Arizona v. United States*, 2012).

Federal statutes apply nationwide, but their reach depends on the constitutional authority under which they are enacted. For example, public education is not explicitly identified in the Constitution and would typically be left to the states' jurisdictions under the Tenth Amendment. This Amendment establishes federalism and provides that any power not explicitly given to the federal government under the Constitution, and which is not withheld from the states, is automatically provided to the states (or the people). But the Constitution's Spending Clause at Article 1, Section 8, allows Congress to tax and spend for the "general welfare," and is directly invoked to create federal laws related to K-12 public education. Examples of such laws include the Individuals with Disabilities Education Act (IDEA), the Family Educational Rights and Privacy Act (FERPA), Section 504 of the Rehabilitation Act, the Every Student Succeeds Act (ESSA), and the Civil Rights Act (Titles VI and IX). The Spending Clause allows Congress to condition a state's federal funding on its compliance with these laws.

Federal statute 42 U.S.C. Section 1983 is frequently applied in litigation against public school districts that is based on alleged constitutional violations. Section 1983 is a federal civil rights law that provides for a private cause of action (i.e., the right of an individual or organization to sue another party) under the Constitution. A defendant in a Section 1983 action must allegedly violate the rights of the plaintiff while acting "under the color of state law," meaning, acting within their official authority. For example, a public school official who allegedly violates a student's First Amendment rights when disciplining students for their political speech could potentially face a Section 1983 action. For purposes of public schools, such actions are usually also brought against the public school district because individual school employees typically have "qualified immunity." Qualified immunity protects school officials from personal liability in civil lawsuits when they act in good faith in accordance with their position. In plain language, this means public school employees will typically be protected from lawsuits that could result in their personal assets being at risk. With that said, and as we will see in other chapters in this book, individual public school officials are frequently named as defendants in lawsuits. Such lawsuits will typically not be successful against the individual school officials due to qualified immunity unless they operated outside of their position, violated a clearly established law, or acted in a manner that would be considered extreme and/or with malicious intent.

A recent case on school officials' qualified immunity and how it applied to Section 1983 allegations was examined in *K.J. v. Jackson* (2025). There, the Ninth Circuit found that public school administrators were not entitled to qualified immunity for a student discipline matter when they did not comply with the procedural requirements of imposing student discipline under a 1975 Supreme Court decision, *Goss v. Lopez*. The court found that "any reasonable official in the defendant's shoes would have understood" they were violating the student's rights. Accordingly, the court found the administrators should have been aware of the law related to imposing student discipline, and their violation of that law left them vulnerable to personal liability. This is an unusual decision, as most courts will grant public school officials qualified immunity unless their conduct was egregious and/or in clear violation of the law.

State Statutes

States' authorities to enact statutes are far broader than Congress's enumerated powers and thus result in substantial variation among state laws. State legislatures enact laws related to general police powers, family law, and wills, trusts, and estates, among other areas. Like the federal government, most, but not all, states have a bicameral body such as a House and a Senate that pass statutes which are then signed by the Governor. That law then has jurisdictional authority within the state.

State statutory law varies widely across jurisdictions. For example, criminal law, contract law, commercial law, and family law often differ in significant respects, though some uniformity exists through model acts such as the Uniform Commercial Code (U.C.C.), which has been adopted in some form by all 50 states. Education law also varies greatly among the states, including different standards for curriculum, graduation requirements, teacher certification, funding allocations, and the structure of public school systems.

Administrative Regulations

Modern governance in the United States relies heavily on administrative agencies, such as the Education Department. Congress often enacts statutes that establish agencies and delegate to them the authority to promulgate regulations implementing statutory mandates. This delegation has been upheld as constitutional so long as Congress provides an "intelligible principle" to guide agency discretion. (*J.W. Hampton, Jr., & Co. v. United States*, 1928). Accordingly, the legislature enacts statutes, whereas administrative regulations are rules that interpret and expand on those statutes and are drafted by an agency with expertise in that subject matter. These regulations have the force of law and are codified in the Code of Federal Regulations (C.F.R.).

The IDEA is an example of a federal statute that allows the Federal Education Department to develop and enact federal regulations. The regulations are more detailed than the law, and we frequently rely on the regulations when identifying the legal requirements related to special education. Similarly, FERPA has both a statute and regulations that provide parents and eligible students with certain rights regarding educational records and the access, disclosure, and amendment of such records.

States and local governments also maintain extensive regulatory systems. State administrative procedures often mirror the federal regulations, but they vary in important details. Local governments, such as cities, counties, and towns, may adopt ordinances and regulations within the scope of authority granted by state law.

The result is a multilayered regulatory environment in which individuals – and indeed, public schools – may be subject to overlapping federal, state, and local regulations.

Common Law

Common law, which is also called case law, refers to law developed by courts through judicial decisions rather than enacted by legislatures. It originated in England and was adopted by American courts following independence. Every state has a common law legal system with the exception of Louisiana, which relies on a code-based legal system. In the United States, common law governs many areas, particularly where statutes and/or regulations are silent or incomplete. Common law is created in education through lawsuits that are typically brought against the school district.

The doctrine of stare decisis requires courts to follow prior court decisions when the same legal issues arise. This means judicial precedent is created that must be followed in subsequent cases involving similar facts and issues. Therefore, courts within the same jurisdiction are required to apply the same analysis and standards when presented with a case with similar facts and issues from a previous case within that jurisdiction. Stare decisis does not bind courts in other jurisdictions, although courts will frequently borrow an analysis and/or decision from another jurisdiction when that decision is persuasive.

Jurisdiction refers to a court's authority to consider a case. Subject-matter jurisdiction concerns the type of case a court may hear, while personal jurisdiction concerns the court's power over the parties. Federal courts are courts of limited jurisdiction, possessing only the authority granted by the Constitution and federal statutes (28 U.S.C. §§ 1331–1332). State courts generally have broad subject-matter jurisdiction. A state court in California likely would not have personal jurisdiction over parties who reside in Virginia when the dispute also took place in Virginia.

Federal Courts

Federal courts are bound by decisions of the U.S. Supreme Court on matters of federal law. Indeed, Supreme Court decisions apply to every jurisdiction in the United States. Below the Supreme Court are Circuit Courts, and below Circuit Courts are District Courts. A plaintiff may initiate a federal lawsuit when there are issues that fall under federal law. If there are no issues that fall under federal law, then the lawsuit must be initiated in state court. But a federal cause of action is first initiated in the District Court. From there, the decision may be appealed to the Circuit Court. Circuit Court decisions may be appealed to the Supreme Court, but only if the Supreme Court accepts a petition of a writ of certiorari (i.e., agreeing to consider an appeal).

Circuit Court and District Court decisions only create precedent within their jurisdiction. This means the law created by a given court only applies to the geographic area where that court presides. The geographic boundaries of precedent of District Courts are smaller than those of Circuit Courts. There are 11 Circuit Courts with a varying number of District Courts beneath them.

The following provides a hierarchy of federal courts:

- Supreme Court of the United States
  - First Circuit
    - District Courts of Massachusetts, Maine, New Hampshire, Puerto Rico, and Rhode Island

- Second Circuit
  - District courts of Connecticut, New York, and Vermont
- Third Circuit
  - District Courts of Delaware, New Jersey, Pennsylvania, and Virgin Islands
- Fourth Circuit
  - District courts of Maryland, North Carolina, South Carolina, Virginia, and West Virginia
- Fifth Circuit
  - District courts of Louisiana, Mississippi, and Texas
- Sixth Circuit
  - District courts of Kentucky, Ohio, and Tennessee
- Seventh Circuit
  - District courts of Illinois, Indiana, and Wisconsin
- Eighth Circuit
  - District courts of Arkansas, Iowa, Minnesota, Michigan, Nebraska, North Dakota, and South Dakota
- Ninth Circuit
  - District courts of Alaska, Arizona, California, Hawaii, Idaho, Montana, Nevada, Oregon, Washington, Guam, and Northern Mariana Islands
- Tenth Circuit
  - District courts of Colorado, Kansas, New Mexico, Oklahoma, Utah, and Wyoming
- Eleventh Circuit
  - District courts of Alabama, Florida, and Georgia

There are 94 District Courts in the United States. They are divided by state or territory, but some states have more District Courts than others. For example, Utah has one District Court, whereas California has four District Courts. Based on the structure of District Courts, an individual in the Eleventh Circuit would not be bound by decisions issued by the First Circuit, and vice versa. On a more micro level, an educator who is working in the Western District of New York would not be bound by decisions issued in the Southern District of New York, and vice versa. But two District Court decisions in the same state are more likely to have a similar analysis and outcome than two District Court decisions in entirely different geographic areas. This is because, especially for lawsuits involving public schools, there are typically intertwined issues based on state and federal law.

State Courts

State courts apply state law and vary significantly in their structure, but also have a hierarchy of courts and different appeal levels. State courts are bound by their own highest courts on matters of state law. However, state courts are not bound by decisions of other states' courts, though such decisions may be persuasive. Doctrines may differ substantially between states because each state develops its own common law.

Local Laws

Local laws pertain to municipalities, such as cities, counties, or towns, and apply to citizens and entities within the geographic boundaries of those municipalities. Local laws, as related to public school systems, typically apply to issues like building codes, zoning, and environmental requirements. But public school districts themselves have their own governance system through a school board, which establishes policy and oversees the operations of the school district. This includes a Code of Conduct that establishes behavior standards and discipline procedures for students (and frequently for other stakeholders in the school community, such as educators, parents, and visitors to the school). Although not officially "laws," the educators, students, parents, and community members are required to comply with the policies enacted by the School Board. Failure to do so could result in certain consequences.

Guidance Documents

Educators frequently rely on guidance documents that are issued by the state or Federal Education Departments. Such guidance provides the education agency's interpretation of law and regulations in a manner that translates policy into everyday practice. For example, the Federal Education Department's Office for Civil Rights (OCR) issues guidance documents to provide clarity on the Department's interpretation of relevant law and a school's role in complying with the law. OCR has jurisdiction over civil rights laws impacting schools, including those laws that prohibit discrimination on the basis of race, color, national origin, sex, disability, age, or membership in patriotic youth organizations. Guidance sometimes shifts depending on the administration. Take, for example, the guidance on sex discrimination under Title IX. Both the Title IX regulations developed by the Education Department and the OCR guidance related to Title IX have changed considerably over the past few federal administrations. Schools are therefore advised to be aware of any current guidance that is issued to ensure compliance.

Guidance documents assist schools and educators with understanding the expectations of the educational agency and facilitate cohesion across schools within the state or country. Guidance documents do not establish law, and so there is some discretion in how they are applied. But principles from guidance documents are sometimes adopted by courts, and those principles would then become the law through common law.

The Intersection of Ethics and Law

Different professions within a school have different ethical codes. Ethics codes provide aspirational standards specific to a profession and outline the standards those professionals are expected to uphold. For example, the National Education Association's (NEA) Code of Ethics highlights that educators should "recognize the worth and dignity of each human being," promote democratic principles, and maintain "the highest possible degree of ethical conduct." An individual bound by ethical principles is expected to uphold those standards as part of their professional integrity. In contrast, the law governs conduct through enforceable legal principles. The law provides the minimal legal requirements, whereas ethics identify the ideals of a profession.

Ethical codes provide educators with frameworks to navigate complex dilemmas where legal rules may be silent or ambiguous. An educator may face situations involving confidentiality and potential risk where the law does not offer straightforward instructions. The ethical principles help educators identify various interests and the more appropriate course of action.

Take for example, a 16-year-old student who confides that she is pregnant to her school counselor. The counselor may wonder if he is required to notify the student's parents of her pregnancy. The counselor may feel that his ethical duty to the student requires that he keep the information confidential. It is possible, but not likely, that the relevant ethical codes provide explicit guidance on how to manage a student's pregnancy disclosure. But the counselor may also wonder if there is a legal obligation to notify the student's parents due to the student's health and well-being potentially being at risk. In addition to being aware of relevant ethical codes and law, there are other relevant considerations in the analysis, such as the student's age, the circumstances around the student becoming pregnant, the student's plans regarding the pregnancy, the student's access to healthcare, the student's state of mind, and the student's safety.

What should the counselor do? It is advisable to seek out supervision and/or consultation in these ethical dilemmas. Professionals will frequently consult with their colleagues, but they need to take care that no personally identifiable student information is shared if that colleague is not a school official with a legitimate educational interest in knowing that information. But it is also advisable for the counselor to seek out supervision from their supervisor at school. The counselor's ethical code is an important consideration in deciding what to do. There may also be school policy on the issue that should be followed. But perhaps more importantly, there should be an analysis of any relevant laws that impact the counselor's options. The school attorney is well-positioned to consult on this matter. Some states have laws that require the school to affirmatively notify a parent whenever it becomes aware of the student having a condition that could negatively impact their health. Could that include a pregnancy? Perhaps – especially if there is a complication with the pregnancy. There are also states where a student does not have a privileged relationship with their school counselor, meaning the counselor cannot refuse to share information with parents upon their request. Each state is different and there are no federal laws that directly control how to manage a situation of student pregnancy (although federal laws such as FERPA and Title IX are applicable). Relevant law should ultimately control the counselor's actions, but with an awareness of how to do so in consideration of ethical principles. It is advisable that the counselor does not make the decision in a vacuum. There are high stakes, with potential legal liability for both the school and the counselor. This is the reason the decision should be made with the counselor's supervisor and after thoroughly considering the relevant issues.

Regardless of the counselor's decision, best practices in supporting the pregnant student should still be followed. It is generally accepted that in these situations, if the student is not in imminent risk, the counselor should work with the student to help them be comfortable with sharing with their parents on their own, or perhaps with the counselor's support. The student should also be informed prior to the counselor notifying the parents if the counselor believes there is an obligation to notify the parents without the student's agreement.

It is possible different professionals in a school would believe they have different ethical obligations as compared with the counselor. For example, the school nurse may feel there is a stronger need to inform the student's parents due to the potential medical issues that could arise from the pregnancy. It is less likely that school policy or relevant law would make a difference in the nurse's decision-making process as compared with the counselor. Regardless, it is prudent for the nurse to follow the same suggestions above related to seeking out supervision in making the decision and working with the student in a manner that is sensitive to the student's position.

Navigating This Book

This book discusses a number of legal issues encountered by K-12 public schools, including student confidentiality considerations under FERPA, student First Amendment rights, educator liability, threat assessments, frequent issues in special education due process, and Section 504. This book is not all-encompassing of every legal issue that could be faced in public schools – that would require at least a few editions! This book is also not intended to be legal advice. Rather, the book outlines various legal considerations – with examples from case law and hypotheticals – to assist the reader with understanding how to interpret and apply the law, and to use that application to engage in risk management and avoid legal issues.

The discerning reader will understand that not every case or law included in this book applies to every educator in the United States. The jurisdiction of the judicial decision, statute, or regulation determines whether it is applicable law in a given location. Moreover, the cases demonstrate that these issues are fact specific. Even one small change to the facts could result in an entirely different outcome in a case.

The varied laws that pertain to K-12 public educators are complicated and nuanced. This is the reason there are school attorneys, and even school attorneys specialize in certain areas of school law, such as special education and labor and employment. It is advisable for educators to have a familiarity with the laws that impact their area of practice. For example, an effective school administrator is familiar with laws related to student rights and discipline in addition to the school's Code of Conduct and board of education policies. A well-prepared school psychologist is familiar with laws and regulations related to special education, including the procedures for evaluating for certain classifications, the definitional criteria for the 13 special education classifications, and the requirements for developing individualized education programs.

An educator's ability to understand how to access, interpret, and apply law is perhaps even more important than possessing a substantive working knowledge of the law. And accurately applying the law while adhering to relevant ethical practices supports an educator in exercising the highest professional judgment while supporting their students.

List of Cases

Arizona v. United States, 567 U.S. 387 (2012).
Brown v. Board of Education, 347 U.S. 483 (1954).
Goss v. Lopez, 419 U.S. 565 (1975).
Heath v. Alabama, 474 U.S. 82 (1985).
J.W. Hampton, Jr., & Co. v. United States, 276 U.S. 394 (1928).
K.J. v. Jackson, No. 23-3052 (9th Cir. 2025).
Michigan v. Long, 463 U.S. 1032 (1983).
Plessy v. Ferguson, 163 U.S. 537 (1896).
Plyler v. Doe, 457 U.S. 202 (1982).

Laws Cited

28 U.S.C. §§ 1331–1332.
Civil Action for Deprivation of Rights, 42 U.S.C. § 1983.
Every Student Succeeds Act, 20 U.S.C. § 6301 (2015).
Family Educational Rights and Privacy Act of 1974, 20 U.S.C. § 1232g.
Individuals with Disabilities Education Improvement Act of 2004, 20 U.S.C. § 1400 et seq. (2004).
Rehabilitation Act of 1973, Pub. L. No. 93-112, 87 Stat. 355 (1973).
Title VI of the Civil Rights Act of 1964, 42 U.S.C. § 2000d et seq.
Title IX of the Education Amendments of 1972, 34 C.F.R. § 106.
U.S. Const.

Bibliography

American School Counselor Association. (2024). *The School Counselor and Confidentiality.* https://www.schoolcounselor.org/Standards-Positions/Position-Statements/ASCA-Position-Statements/The-School-Counselor-and-Confidentiality.

Bowers, K. R. (2021, April 19). *Agency Use of Guidance Documents.* https://www.congress.gov/crs-product/LSB10591.

Constitution Annotated. (n.d.). *The Constitution of the United States Explained.* https://constitution.congress.gov/.

National Archives. (2025, August 7). *The Bill of Rights: A Transcription.* https://www.archives.gov/founding-docs/bill-of-rights-transcript.

National Archives, Office of the Federal Register. (2016 August 15). *Constitutional Amendment Process.* https://www.archives.gov/federal-register/constitution.

National Education Association. (2020, September 14). *Code of Ethics for Educators.* https://www.nea.org/resource-library/code-ethics-educators.

The United States Government Manual. (n.d.). https://www.usgovernmentmanual.gov/.

United States Courts. (n.d.). *Comparing Federal and State Courts.* https://www.uscourts.gov/about-federal-courts/court-role-and-structure/comparing-federal-state-courts.

USA.Gov. (2025, September 22). *Branches of the U.S. Government.* https://www.usa.gov/branches-of-government.

1 Family Educational Rights and Privacy Act

Anne M. McGinnis

The Family Educational Rights and Privacy Act of 1975 (FERPA) is a federal privacy law that protects student education records and provides requirements for accessing and amending such records. Many states also have their own privacy laws that impact students, but FERPA is a federal law that applies to any educational institution that receives federal funding in the United States. This includes public K-12 schools in the United States.

FERPA was first enacted due to legislators' concerns that educators would keep secret records that could be harmful to students.[1] It permits parents and students who are over the age of 18 (i.e., eligible students) to access the student's education records. An "eligible student" is "a student who has reached 18 years of age or is attending an institution of postsecondary education."[2] FERPA also restricts the access of student education records to third parties, with limited exceptions that will be further discussed in this chapter.

A "parent" under FERPA is "a parent of a student and includes a natural parent, a guardian, or an individual acting as a parent in the absence of a parent or guardian."[3] A parent includes a noncustodial parent unless there is a legal document, such as a court order or other legally binding document, that explicitly revoked parental or FERPA rights. This was considered by the Federal Education Department's Student Privacy Policy Office (SPPO; formerly known as the Family Policy Compliance Office or FPCO) in *Letter to Corr* (2019).[4] There, a noncustodial father requested access to his child's education records. The school contacted the student's mother to inquire about the request, as the school did not have previous interactions with the father. The student's mother provided a family court order that the mother claimed revoked the father's custodial rights and involvement in the student's education. The mother forbade the school from disclosing the student's information to the father. The father then contacted the SPPO and shared that the mother provided outdated documents that were since amended and reinstated the father's custodial rights. The school provided

DOI: 10.4324/9781003728993-2

the father with access to his child's education records upon receiving the updated legal documents. The SPPO advised that school districts use "reasonable methods to...authenticate the identity of parents and eligible students before providing access to avoid improper disclosures."

As stated above, FERPA rights transfer to a student upon becoming an eligible student. However, a parent *may* continue to access their child's education records – even if the child is an eligible student – when the parent claims the child as a dependent for tax purposes.[5] But an educational institution is not required to share a child's education records with the parent when the student reaches the age of 18 and beyond; it is only permissible to do so (assuming the student is claimed as a dependent). There could be different requirements under other relevant laws, such as the Individuals with Disabilities Education Act (IDEA), which allows states to determine whether to transfer special education rights to a student upon turning 18.[6] It is assumed such rights, including rights to access their eligible student's special education records, are retained by the parents if state law does not explicitly transfer special education rights to a student upon turning 18.[7]

What Constitutes an Education Record?

Education records are records that are: "(1) directly related to a student; and (2) maintained by an educational agency or institution."[8] FERPA does not define "information directly related to a student." Education records include, but are not limited to, "grades, transcripts, class lists, student course schedules, health records (at the K-12 level), student financial information (at the postsecondary level), and student discipline files."[9] An education record includes "any information recorded in any way, including, but not limited to, handwriting, print, computer media, video or audio tape, film, microfilm, and microfiche."[10] The definition of an education record is broad because FERPA defaults to granting access to parents and eligible students.

FERPA does not explicitly define what it means for a school to "maintain" a record. "Maintained" does not mean "create." Rather, education records include records related to a student that are originated by a school and those that are obtained by the school and then maintained.[11] For example, a student's report card developed by the school, which is then maintained by the school, would be an education record. But an education record would also include a private evaluation submitted to the school by the student's parent – if the school then maintains that record of the student, it would be an education record under FERPA while in the school's possession. A record is "maintained" by a school even if it is stored off-site by a school official who is providing a service to the school, such as a school attorney. But attorney records would not be education records if they are protected by the attorney-client privilege due to being the attorney's work product.[12]

Is Electronic Mail an Education Record?

Parents sometimes make broad requests to review their children's education records – and such requests may include "all emails sent or received by the school related to my child." These requests can be stress-inducing for educators for a couple of reasons. First, email is typically a more casual communication method than other forms of communication. This can result in emails including information that may not be considered professional or could cause an educator to feel uncomfortable with the parent reviewing the email. For example, an educator may email the following to a colleague: "this parent is totally cuckoo – just like their kid! I guess the apple didn't fall far from the tree." We understand that having an irreverent sense of humor can be a coping mechanism for stressful situations. But a parent seeing an email like that will damage the relationship between the parent and the school. It is also stressful and embarrassing for an educator to have to testify about sending inappropriate emails in forums like special education due process hearings. Parent attorneys are adept at pointing out such emails and cross-examining school witnesses to ask about their intentions when sending such emails.

Second, it is difficult to gather every email that is sent or received about a student. Perhaps the most thorough option is to search the school's email servers for every email related to a student. But what search terms should be used? It is rare that an email would identify a student by their full first and last name, so searching for only the first and last name will not identify all of the responsive emails. Emails frequently identify students by their initials. Searching for only initials across a school district's email servers can yield thousands of emails. Most of those emails would not be related to that particular student, and requires somebody to review each email to identify those that are responsive. This can be time-consuming and expensive. Another option for identifying emails is to ask each individual at the school who may have emails regarding the student to search their own inbox and outbox to identify responsive emails. This is unlikely to produce every email. But are emails even considered to be education records that must be produced? We do not have a standard answer to this question that applies across the country as FERPA is silent on this issue and there are no Supreme Court decisions that have examined whether emails are education records. But the trend for cases across the country suggests that school emails related to a student would *not* be education records under FERPA.

In *S.A. v. Tulare County Office of Education* (2009), the Eastern District of California considered whether email communications regarding the student were education records and thus required to be disclosed to the student's parents upon their request. The court determined that email communications were not education records under FERPA because they were not "maintained" by the school. Rather, the court reasoned that only records in the student's permanent file were maintained, and any emails that were not in the permanent file were not maintained by the school. Therefore, the school complied with its FERPA obligations by providing the parents with access to emails in the student's file, but not all emails related to the student that were sent or received by the district. The court reasoned that Congress did not intend for "education records" under FERPA to be broadly defined to include every record kept by any individual related to the student.

A similar decision was issued by the Northern District of Georgia in *B.F. v. Fulton County School District* (2008). In that case, the court considered whether a school's emails related to a student were "education records" under FERPA. The court ruled that the emails related to the student were not maintained by the district as they were not stored in the student's file. Therefore, the emails were not education records, and the school was not required to provide the parents with access to the emails upon their request.

State education agencies have also opined that emails are not education records. In *Middleton-Cross Plains Area School District* (2015), the Wisconsin Department of Education determined that emails did not constitute an education record under federal or state law. More specifically, the parents of an 18-year-old student with a disability requested access to their child's education records. The parents claimed that this request should have included any emails or personal notes related to the student. The Wisconsin Department of Education disagreed and found that "education records" do not include personal records that are "sole possession records." Moreover, emails related to the student were not education records because they were not "maintained" by the district. Rather, emails may be contained in "multiple in-boxes of many individuals within the school and the school district" and are not kept in a central location. Therefore, they are not maintained by the district.

The Connecticut Department of Education's Bureau of Special Education issued a similar opinion in Complaint No. 19-0486 (2019). There, the parent of a child who received special education services requested the student's complete education records and specifically requested any email communications. The district searched its servers for any relevant emails that resulted in 4,000 pages of potentially responsive documents. This would require a significant review by the district to both identify emails that were responsive to the request and related to the student and to determine whether any of the emails needed to be redacted due to including other students' information. The emails were found in multiple email accounts throughout the district and were not maintained in one location or a physical file. The district did not provide the parents with the complete emails that were identified through the search. The parents complained to the Connecticut Department of Education, which found that the emails retrieved by the district were not "education records" under FERPA or state regulations. The Connecticut Department of Education concluded that the typical definition of "maintain" is "to keep in existence, preserve and retain." This definition would not include emails "that are used as a communication tool and not maintained." Rather, the emails were "merely stored in a public school's computer network system and not treated in a special way, organized or printed." Indiana's Education Department reached a similar decision in *Brownsburg Community School Corporation* (2012), finding that emails referencing a student were a communication tool and were not records that were maintained by the district.

More recently, the Nevada Supreme Court overturned a lower court's decision that concluded student emails are "maintained" under FERPA. In *Clark County School District v. Eighth Judicial District Court* (2025), a school argued a parent was not entitled to emails related to their child because they were stored in Google Vault and thus not maintained by the district. The lower court disagreed, finding that records are "maintained" by a school when they are stored in a "central" and "secure" database, which could include a storage system like Google Vault. The lower court broadly interpreted "maintained" to include any storage format as FERPA's list of included storage formats was not all-inclusive, but rather was intended to be broadly interpreted.[13] But the Nevada Supreme Court reversed and held that "not every email that mentions a student and is stored on a school's email server constitutes an education record under FERPA." An email is only considered to be a student's education record when the school district takes "affirmative and intentional steps" to maintain the email "with a designated individual in a designated space." This decision is consistent with decisions from other jurisdictions related to emails and education records.

Courts and state education departments are consistently finding that emails are not education records unless they are maintained for the student separately from the district's email servers. The cases typically hinge on the meaning of "maintain" in FERPA, and whether emails related to a student are maintained by a school district. But unless and until the Supreme Court provides a definitive decision on this issue (or, less likely, Congress amends FERPA to provide statutory authority related to emails and FERPA), we will not have a federal standard on whether emails are education records.

A school may still be required to produce emails, even if they are not considered to be education records, if the school is presented with a valid subpoena. Therefore, it is important to take care when writing emails and understand that the parent may be able to access that email in the future. It is also easy to accidentally email the wrong person – and this can be especially problematic if the email contains confidential student information. It is suggested that educators take care when writing emails and consider them a formal correspondence. Any correspondence that is particularly sensitive is better to have verbally rather than in writing.

Is Video an Education Record?

Questions arise when a parent or eligible student requests to review a video of a student, such as through surveillance recordings taken at school. A video or photograph of a student would only be an education record in certain circumstances, such as when it is used for disciplinary purposes of a student or if it is a close-up photo of two or three students engaged in an activity (rather than the student being in the background).[14] The Federal Education Department opined that when a video depicts multiple students, a parent or eligible student may access the video if it is an education record of the student. If possible, other students on the video should be redacted. If redaction is not possible or would destroy the record, then the parent or eligible student have the right to inspect the video, or "be informed of" the record, but the parent or eligible student are not entitled to a copy of the video.[15] For example, a parent may request to review the school's surveillance footage that depicts their child engaged in misconduct that led to discipline. The parent would be entitled to review that footage because it was used to impose a consequence on the student; it is therefore an education record of the student's. But the parent would not be entitled to a copy of the video if other students were present and those students could not be redacted.

Video surveillance is frequently used in student disciplinary matters. Here is a scenario when such video surveillance may be used. A student, Maurice, engaged in a fight with another student in the cafeteria, and the school district is holding a disciplinary hearing to consider a long-term suspension of Maurice. The school district intends to use the video surveillance footage from the cafeteria as evidence at that hearing as it depicts Maurice throwing the first punch and continuing the fight after the other student tried to run away. There are many other students on the video as the fight occurred during the lunch period. Maurice's parents request a copy of the video surveillance footage depicting the fight. This footage is considered an education record of Maurice – even though many students are on the video – because it is being used for a disciplinary proceeding for Maurice. Therefore, Maurice's parents are entitled to review the surveillance footage. But they would not be entitled to a copy of the surveillance footage because it shows other students in addition to Maurice. The school is prohibited from providing a copy of the footage to the parent unless it is able to redact the faces and any other identifying information of the other students. But regardless, the school is not required to provide the parent with a copy of their child's education records absent certain exceptions – the school is only required to provide the parent with access to the video. This can be accomplished by inviting the parent to the school to review the video surveillance footage at the school.

A recent case in Pennsylvania, *Easton Area School District v. Miller* (2020), examined whether a video depicting students would be an education record, and if so, whether disclosure was required. A local reporter was engaged in investigative journalism and claimed that an elementary teacher inappropriately physically disciplined a student. The reporter requested a copy of the school bus surveillance video that captured the incident under a state law that provides access to public records. The Easton Area School District denied the reporter's request for the video and argued it was exempt from disclosure under FERPA as the video was an education record of the depicted students. Once denied, the reporter requested an appeal from the Pennsylvania Office of Open Records (OOR). The OOR disagreed with the district's argument and instructed the district to provide the video. The district appealed this decision first to the Court of Common Pleas and then to the Commonwealth Court, both of which upheld the OOR decision. The district then appealed to the Supreme Court of Pennsylvania. The Pennsylvania Supreme Court focused on the question of whether the video was an education record subject to FERPA. The court agreed the video was an education record of the student (in addition to a disciplinary record of the teacher), and thus protected by FERPA. The court reminded agencies responsible for disseminating public records to balance student privacy and the public's right to know interest. Ultimately, the court ordered the video to be released with the students' faces redacted to protect their right to confidentiality under FERPA.

Exemptions to Education Records

Educators frequently wonder if their records need to be disclosed to parents or eligible students upon request. The answer to this depends on whether one of the limited FERPA exemptions applies to a given record. But in general, FERPA is designed to allow for education records to be accessed. Therefore, educators are encouraged to be mindful that in most instances, the records they create or maintain for a student are accessible to parents/guardians or eligible students.

Perhaps one of the most frequent reasons a record is not considered to be an education record is if it is a "sole possession" record. This is narrowly defined as a record of school personnel that is in the sole possession of the maker (with the exception of a substitute) and created only for the purpose of a memory aid. An example of a sole possession record includes personal notes taken at an IEP meeting that are only for the memory aid of the creator of the record and never shared with anybody else (except a temporary substitute). A parent may demand to see those notes, but the school can refuse to provide the parent with access to the notes if they are the sole possession records of the individual who created the notes. This means the notes would not be considered part of the student's education records.

But other notes may be considered education records. For example, notes that are taken to monitor progress toward IEP goals are arguably not sole possession records because IEP goal data is typically considered an education record that a parent is entitled to review. This issue may arise with counseling progress notes taken in school, as such progress notes are sometimes used as IEP goal monitoring data. Counseling notes taken as IEP goal monitoring data cannot be sole possession records because IEP goal monitoring data is considered an education record. Counseling progress notes are therefore not automatically sole possession records that may be withheld from a parent's or eligible student's access; rather, it depends on why the notes were created and who has access to the notes. They would only be sole possession records – and thus exempt from education records and not available to the parent – if they were taken only for the personal memory aid of the creator and not shared with any other individual.

A record is not a sole possession record if it is shared with anybody else at the school, such as with an administrator for supervision purposes or if the record is "moved up" to the next teacher or provider of the student. It is a common practice to send records on to the next teacher or provider of a student so they can build on the student's previous progress – this is a valid reason to create records that are intended to be education records and not sole possession records. But records that are sole possession records should be kept in a separate, confidential file of the individual who created the records and not shared with other teachers or providers.

Employment records are also exempt from FERPA. Such records relate to an individual who is employed by a school, are made and maintained as part of the normal course of business, relate only to the employee, and are not used for another purpose. This exemption does not apply to an employee who is also a student of the school and the student is employed due to their status as a student, such as through work study – these records are education records.

The law enforcement unit exemption applies when they are "(1) created by a law enforcement unit (2) created for law enforcement purposes; and (3) maintained by the law enforcement unit."[16] Such records are not education records, and the FERPA requirements related to access and disclosure do not apply. But the records may not be disclosed absent consent or another FERPA exception if the school's law enforcement receives a student's education records from the school.[17] For example, if a student makes a threat of harm against the school, the school may determine there is a sufficient threat to health or safety to disclose the student's education records to its law enforcement unit without consent. Because this was a disclosure of an education record that was not created by law enforcement or for law enforcement purposes, this record continues to hold its status as an education record and must comply with FERPA requirements for further disclosure. The Federal Education Department recommends that such education records be kept separately from law enforcement unit records.[18]

FERPA also exempts student health records created for students who are over 18 or attending a postsecondary institution. But such health records must be "(1) made or maintained by a physician or other professional acting in that capacity; (2) made, maintained, or used only in connection with treatment of the student; and (3) disclosed only to individuals providing the treatment." The eligible student may have the records reviewed by an appropriate professional of the student's choice. FERPA applies if health records are disclosed for other purposes. Typical student health records maintained by a K-12 school, such as school nurse records, would be education records under FERPA (and, as provided more fully below, would not be protected under HIPAA).

Records are also exempt from FERPA when they were created or received by the school after an individual was no longer a student at that school, and when such records are not directly related to the individual's attendance at that school as a student.

Although not explicitly addressed by FERPA, the Supreme Court of the United States in *Owasso Independent School District v. Falvo* (2002) determined that peer grading is not a disclosure under FERPA and so is exempt under FERPA. The case involved teachers who had students grade their peers' papers and then return the papers to the student. The student could then either call out their score to the teacher or walk to the teacher's desk to quietly share their score. A parent of students in the district challenged both the peer grading system and the practice of calling out scores in front of other students. The parent claimed this practice was embarrassing to her children and asked the school district to instead implement a policy that required teachers to grade papers and keep student grades confidential. The district declined, and the parent brought a class action lawsuit against the district, the superintendent, the assistant superintendent, and the principal. The parent alleged that the grading practice violated FERPA and the Fourteenth Amendment (which grants "equal protection of the laws" to United States citizens), alleging Section 1983 (a federal civil rights statute that allows for lawsuits against government officials for the alleged infringement of constitutional rights) was violated.

The lower District Court for the Northern District of Oklahoma granted the district's motion for summary judgment (meaning, issued a decision without a trial), finding there was no dispute over the material facts, and the district was entitled to a decision in its favor as a matter of law. Specifically, the District Court found that grades on papers were not education records under FERPA because they were not "maintained" by the district. The parent appealed, and the Court of Appeals for the Tenth Circuit reversed, considering whether FERPA provided a private right of action that would allow a parent to sue a school due to an alleged FERPA violation. The Court of Appeals found that the FERPA statute itself was silent about this, but determined it was possible a parent could sue to enforce FERPA. (Note this issue has since been settled by the Supreme Court in *Gonzaga University v. Doe*, discussed later in this chapter, which held there is no private cause of action under FERPA. This means an individual or organization may not sue to obtain damages for an alleged FERPA violation). The Court of Appeals also found that the peer grading practice violated FERPA as it impermissibly disclosed another student's grades to a student grader.

The case made its way to the Supreme Court, which ruled that a student's graded paper is not an education record that is maintained by the school, "at least until the teacher has recorded them." The Supreme Court considered the ordinary meaning of the word "maintain" means to preserve or retain. Peer graders only had possession of assignments for a short period of time, and so they were not maintained. The Court also rejected the lower court's determination that the peer graders were "acting for" the school district when grading papers, as it would be "awkward" to consider students to be acting as teachers when they were instead following teacher directions. Therefore, the Supreme Court found no FERPA violation in the school's practice to engage in peer grading or asking students to call out their grades to the teacher.

Personally Identifiable Information and Disclosures

FERPA protects personally identifiable information (PII) included in student education records. PII includes, but is not limited to:[19]

(a) *The student's name;*
(b) *The name of the student's parent or other family members;*
(c) *The address of the student or student's family;*
(d) *A personal identifier, such as the student's social security number, student number, or biometric record;*
(e) *Other indirect identifiers, such as the student's date of birth, place of birth, and mother's maiden name;*
(f) *Other information that, alone or in combination, is linked or linkable to a specific student that would allow a reasonable person in the school community, who does not have personal knowledge of the relevant circumstances, to identify the student with reasonable certainty; or*
(g) *Information requested by a person who the educational agency or institution reasonably believes knows the identity of the student to whom the education record relates.*

A disclosure is defined as permitting "access to or the release, transfer, or other communication of personally identifiable information contained in education records to any party, by any means, including oral, written, or electronic means."[20] FERPA requires parental or eligible student consent before disclosing PII from student education records.[21] Valid consent under FERPA must: (1) specify the record(s) that may be disclosed; (2) provide the purpose for the disclosure; and (3) identify the individual(s) to whom the disclosure may be made. The written consent must be signed and dated. Verbal consent is insufficient for disclosing education records.

A disclosure may be made without consent if one of the exceptions identified below applies. But a disclosure is unauthorized when personally identifiable information is shared without consent or an applicable exception. This applies regardless of how the disclosure is made. For example, verbally sharing PII about a student without consent and without a valid exception would be an unauthorized disclosure – even if no physical records are shared. Unauthorized disclosures can sometimes happen inadvertently, such as through data breaches. They can also happen due to the negligence of the individual who disclosed the records.

Consider this scenario. Ms. Smith, a sixth-grade math teacher, is concerned about the behavior of one of her students, Marcia. Marcia frequently acts out in class, using inappropriate and aggressive language toward both Ms. Smith and the other students. Ms. Smith emails the following to Marcia's parent:

> Marcia has been struggling with her behavior lately and is bothering and intimidating the other students. She is also very disrespectful to me and frequently swears or shouts at me in class. Can you please talk with her about her behavioral expectations?

Ms. Smith realizes several hours later that she emailed all of the parents in the class rather than just Marcia's parent. Ms. Smith panics and tries to unsend the email, but she is unsuccessful. Marcia's parent calls the principal and is furious that all of the parents in the class now know about Marcia's behavior concerns. Did Ms. Smith engage in an unauthorized disclosure of Marcia's education records? Yes, because she shared private information about Marcia with all of the parents in her class without Marcia's parent's consent. But the actual FERPA statute and regulations do not provide procedures for how to address an unauthorized disclosure or data breach. The Federal Education Department suggests each school have a policy, plan, and procedure to address data breaches.[22] There may also be state requirements for how to address an unauthorized disclosure or data breach. Ethical considerations include taking steps to limit the impact of the unauthorized disclosure and to prevent such disclosures from occurring in the future, such as additional training for Ms. Smith and establishing a system to prevent such unauthorized disclosures from occurring.

PII may be disclosed to third parties without parental consent in certain situations. One such exception to requiring parental consent is for "directory information."[23] This applies to information that would not be harmful to a student if disclosed. Directory information under FERPA includes name, address, telephone listing, date and place of birth, participation in officially recognized activities and sports, dates of attendance, degrees and awards, most recent school attended, and weight and height. But the school district determines what to include in its directory information. Schools are required to disclose to the public on an annual basis their definition of directory information. Schools must also provide parents and eligible students the opportunity to opt out of the student's information being included in directory information. The directory information provision of FERPA is the reason schools can publish a list of graduates, honors, and details about student athletes. But such details may not be disclosed about a particular student without consent if the parent or eligible student opted out of directory information.

Another exception to requiring consent before disclosure is for "school officials."[24] Such school officials include school employees and board members in addition to third-party vendors, consultants, contractors, and volunteers who have a "legitimate educational interest" and perform "institutional services or functions" that would otherwise be performed by employees. This does not mean all student records may be shared with all employees or other individuals who work with the school. Rather, the individual must have a legitimate educational interest in knowing the information to be able to fulfill their obligations to the school. The school official must also be under the "direct control of the school," such as through a contract. And only the records needed for the individual to fulfill their obligations may be disclosed. The school's annual FERPA notification must specify the criteria for an individual to be considered a school official who has a legitimate educational interest in education records. The following are examples of when student PII may or may not be disclosed to school officials:

- A school may disclose a particular student's information to its school attorney when requesting consultation on that student's disciplinary matter. But a school attorney cannot be given full access to all student records. Rather, the attorney may only access the records necessary to provide advice to the school.
- Teachers are only entitled to know PII of students when they have a legitimate educational interest in knowing that information for that particular student (presumably because the teacher is teaching that student or otherwise interacting with the student in a manner that requires the teacher's knowledge).
- School mental health providers may disclose student information to supervisors, administrators, and/or other school staff with a legitimate educational interest when such disclosure is necessary to protect the

safety of a student. For example, it may be prudent to disclose a student's potential to self-harm in school to the student's teachers so they can monitor the self-harm in class.

Disclosures may also be made without consent in health or safety emergencies.[25] This exception applies when a disclosure of a student's education record without consent is necessary to protect the health or safety of the student or others. Only the information necessary for protecting against a health or safety emergency may be disclosed and the disclosure may only be made to those individuals necessary to protect the health and safety of the student or others. This exception applies when the health or safety emergency is current. For example, the school may disclose to law enforcement a student's threat of harm toward the school, but only when it is determined that disclosure is necessary to protect health and safety. The FPCO addressed this issue in 2015 in *Letter to Anonymous*[26] when it opined that a school was permitted to disclose a student's threat assessment to local law enforcement, without parent consent, due to a health or safety emergency. The results of the threat assessment indicated the student was at a "high level of risk," and caused the school principal to disclose the results of the threat assessment to the local police department. The FPCO disagreed with the parents' contentions that this was an unauthorized FERPA disclosure, finding that the school had a legitimate reason to determine whether there was a health or safety emergency that warranted disclosure.

The health or safety exception does not allow the school to continue to share the student's education records without consent over time as part of law enforcement's investigation if the original threat was contained. Rather, law enforcement would need to issue a subpoena, or the school would need to obtain consent from the parent or eligible student, to continue sharing such records when the threat has passed. For example, the Federal Education Department asserted in 2008 in *Letter to Anonymous*[27] that such a health or safety emergency no longer existed when the student was reported and in the custody of law enforcement, thus eliminating any imminent health or safety concern.

Here is a scenario when a school invoked the health and safety exception to FERPA. A school was notified by law enforcement from a city located approximately 100 miles away from the school that a student made a threat of harm against the school principal. The student was in the custody of law enforcement who determined there was not a strong likelihood the student was going to act on the threat. Law enforcement, as part of their investigation, requested the school provide the student's education records, including the student's discipline referrals, counseling records, and report cards. The school provided these records under the health and safety exception. But was this a current health or safety emergency? Likely not because the student was in the custody of law enforcement, and there was no imminent threat of harm. Therefore, it would have been prudent for the school to either obtain parental consent or request law enforcement to issue a valid subpoena prior to disclosing the student's records. But this scenario demonstrates that the determination of whether there is a current threat to health or safety is not always clear.

FERPA allows for records to be disclosed without consent to another school in which a student "seeks or intends to enroll" or to a school in which the student is already enrolled if such records are for "purposes related to the student's enrollment or transfer."[28] Accordingly, there is no federal legal requirement for consent prior to sharing students' education records with a school in which they are enrolling or intending to enroll. The school sending the records must make reasonable attempts to notify the parent or eligible student that the records have been shared.

The exception of sending records to a school in which a student seeks or intends to enroll sometimes arises when an IEP Team recommends applying to an out-of-district placement for a student. FERPA does not require obtaining parent consent prior to sending the student's application to potential placements under the "seeks or intends to enroll" exception. It is possible state law could require such consent. This issue was directly addressed in *W.A. v. Hendrick Hudson Central School District* (2016). There, the parents, as part of their special education due process hearing, alleged that despite at least five written directives to the district not to disclose their son's psychiatric and special education records, the district did just that when it sent their son's records to potential placements as recommended by the IEP Team. The parents argued an alleged violation of their son's right to privacy, due process rights, and rights under the Equal Protection Clause of the Constitution. The parents alleged some details included in the shared records – which they claimed were medical, psychiatric, and neuropsychological records and not education records – were "excruciatingly private and intimate in nature." The Southern District of New York denied the school district's motion to dismiss the Constitutional claims related to the disclosure, finding it was possible there was a protected right of privacy for the medical records. The court posited this claim was separate and distinct from a private cause of action for a FERPA violation, which is not permissible under relevant law. We do not have a final decision on this issue of whether there is a Constitutional claim for the unauthorized disclosure of protected health information when sending a student's records to a school at which the student seeks or intends to enroll. Schools that do not obtain parent consent prior to sending such records should, at a minimum, either make a reasonable attempt to notify the parent in advance of sending the records, or follow the school's policy to forward education records to other agencies and institutions that requested records and in which the student seeks or intends to enroll (which would include an IEP Team applying to a potential placement for a student).

A school can be compelled to share education records without consent upon receipt of a lawful judicial order or subpoena.[29] State law may provide requirements for the type of subpoena. For example, some states require a subpoena duces tecum signed by a judge to disclose certified education records without consent in these circumstances. It is the school's obligation to identify whether the subpoena was "lawfully issued" prior to disclosing the records. A subpoena is lawful if it complies with state law.[30] FERPA requires a school to make a "reasonable effort to notify" the parent or eligible student, although FERPA does not define what such reasonable efforts entail.[31] But the purpose of notifying the parent or eligible student is so they have an opportunity to attempt to quash the subpoena before the education records are shared. The Uninterrupted Scholars Act of 2013 does not require schools to notify parents of the submission of student PII pursuant to a subpoena when the court proceeding related to the order involves suspected child abuse, neglect, or dependency matters, and the parent is a party to the proceeding.[32] Subpoenas frequently have a short deadline to respond, causing schools to need to move quickly to both gather the records to submit and notify the parent or eligible student.

Consider this scenario. Ms. Clark, the school social worker, was subpoenaed to testify at a family court matter involving a custody dispute between two parents regarding their child, Tina. The subpoena called on Ms. Clark to appear at a certain date and time to provide witness testimony and to bring with her any records she has regarding Tina. The school attorney reviewed the subpoena and determined it was lawfully issued. Ms. Clark decided she would not include her sole possession records when she brings her records regarding Tina because she knows they are not considered to be education records under FERPA. Is Ms. Clark correct that she should not bring her sole possession records? No, because even though sole possession records are not considered to be education records under FERPA, they are still subject to disclosure via a lawfully issued subpoena. Therefore, Ms. Clark is obligated under the subpoena to produce her sole possession records regarding Tina when she appears for testimony.

A school may disclose the PII from student education records if the school initiates legal action against the parent or student, or if the parent or student initiates legal action against the school and such records are necessary for the legal action.[33] This is the reason a school may release student education records without consent as part of its exhibit disclosure at a special education due process hearing. Such records are arguably necessary for the school's defense at such a hearing. But the school may only disclose those records that are necessary to defend itself at the hearing, rather than releasing the student's entire education records.

A student's PII may be disclosed to a caseworker or representative of a child welfare agency or tribal organization caseworkers when such agency is responsible for a student's "care and protection."[34] Care and protection are defined by state or tribal law. The disclosure is only permitted if the caseworker or representative has access to the student's "case plan." A case plan is a written document that specifies the care and services provided to children in foster care and also specifies the educational stability of the child.[35]

Education records may be disclosed without consent for purposes of a student applying for or receiving financial aid when such disclosure will assist with determining the eligibility, amount, or conditions of such aid.[36]

There are some permissible disclosures that only apply to postsecondary institutions. A postsecondary institution may disclose to a student's parent, without consent, if a student under the age of 21 has violated a law or policy based on the use or possession of alcohol or a controlled substance.[37] A postsecondary institution may disclose information regarding violent crimes or non-forcible sex offenses made by students, but such disclosures may only include the name of the student who committed the violation, the violation committed, and any sanctions against the student.[38] This provision only applies to disciplinary proceedings that occurred after 1998 in which such allegations are founded. Postsecondary institutions may also disclose the results of disciplinary proceedings for a violent crime or non-forcible sex offense to the victim of the alleged crime or offense, regardless of whether the allegations are founded.[39]

A school may disclose PII without consent to an accrediting organization of the school.[40] Only those records necessary for fulfilling accrediting functions may be disclosed.

When permitted by state law, student education records may be disclosed to juvenile justice authorities.[41] Such disclosure must be related to the juvenile justice authority's ability to address the student's needs prior to adjudication. The juvenile justice authority must certify to the school that it will not share the student's PII with any other party without consent, unless otherwise permitted by state law.

An exception to FERPA consent requirements applies to military recruiters. Schools that receive federal funding under the Elementary and Secondary Education Act of 1965 (ESEA) are required to provide student names, addresses, and telephone numbers to military recruiters unless parents have opted out of such disclosure.[42] In situations in which a school has not designated names, addresses, and telephone numbers as directory information, a school must send a separate notice to parents or eligible students informing them about the information being shared with military recruiters and allowing the option to opt out.[43]

Schools may disclose student PII when such records relate to sex offenders or other individuals required to register for community notification programs. Under the Campus Sex Crimes Prevention Act, a school may provide a list of students who are registered sex offenders pursuant to community notification programs.[44]

PII may be shared without consent with the Secretary of Agriculture or their representative related to the Food and Nutrition Services to conduct program monitoring, evaluations, and performance measurements for schools that receive funding or provide benefits under the National School Lunch Act or the Child Nutrition Act of 1966.[45]

Records may also be disclosed without consent under the "audit and evaluation" exception.[46] This allows the disclosure of PII without consent to authorized representatives to audit or evaluate a federal- or state-supported education program or to enforce or comply with federal requirements related to a program. The educational agency or institution must engage in a written agreement to designate an authorized representative who is not an employee. The educational agency or institution must also take reasonable steps to ensure the PII is only used for an authorized purpose, to protect the PII from further disclosure, and destroy the PII when it is no longer needed.

The final exception is the "studies" exception, which allows the disclosure of PII without consent to organizations or individuals for "studies."[47] Such studies may only be for "developing, validating, or administering predictive tests; administering student aid programs; or improving instruction." This exception also requires a written agreement. The study may not permit the identification of parents and students, and the information must be destroyed when no longer needed for the study's purposes.

FERPA requires educational agencies and institutions to record when PII is released under the studies and audit and evaluation exceptions.[48] Recording disclosures of PII is not required under the directory and school official exceptions.[49]

FERPA allows a school to release education records without consent when any PII included in the record has been redacted and the school determines that a student's identity cannot be identified in the redacted records.[50]

Annual Notice

FERPA requires that every educational agency or institution annually notify parents of students currently in attendance, or eligible students currently in attendance, of their rights under FERPA. This includes the right to: (1) inspect and revise the student's education records;[51] (2) request an amendment of the education record if the record is believed to be inaccurate, misleading, or otherwise in violation of the student's privacy rights;[52] (3) opt out of personally identifiable information;[53] and (4) file a complaint with the Federal Education Department regarding allegations of noncompliance.[54]

The annual FERPA notice must also explain the procedures for inspecting and reviewing education records, for requesting an amendment to the records, and the criteria for determining who constitutes a school official and what constitutes a legitimate educational interest. Schools are required to ensure that parents are effectively notified when the parent has a disability or when the parent's home language is other than English.[55]

The annual notice must include certain required information. For example, if a school discloses without parental consent student education records to school officials who have a legitimate educational interest in knowing that information, then the annual notice must define both "school officials" and "legitimate educational interest."[56] Under FERPA, a "school official" includes teachers; transportation officials; school nurses; interns, student teachers, and practicum students; contractors; volunteers; legal counsel; and other individuals who provide services to the school and perform school functions.[57] But a school may define a school official more broadly. The SPPO found in *Letter to Anderson* (2020)[58] that a school impermissibly disclosed confidential student information to its School Resource Officer (SRO) because the SRO was not included in the school's definition of a "school official" and the parent did not consent to the disclosure. In that case, the SRO was a county sheriff, and the school's assistant principal disclosed the student's written statement regarding an incident that occurred on campus. However, the assistant principal did not obtain parental consent prior to the disclosure, and there were no other applicable exceptions, such as a health and safety exception. The district identified this as being an unauthorized disclosure and took corrective action by providing all staff with additional FERPA training. The SPPO did not require any further corrective action. But interestingly, the SPPO concluded that an SRO could be a school official – and thus have access to student education records when the SRO has a legitimate educational interest in doing so – provided the school includes the SRO in its definition of a "school official."

The annual notice must also inform parents and eligible students of any policy the school has related to disclosing "directory information."[59] This must include (1) the types of PII the school has designated as directory information; (2) the parent's or eligible student's right to refuse the disclosure of the student's directory information; and (3) the time period in which the parent or eligible student must notify the school in writing about refusing the disclosure of the student's directory information.

FERPA does not specify how the annual notice must be provided, but provides that "an educational agency or institution may provide this notice by any means that are reasonably likely to inform the parents or eligible students of their rights." Some educational agencies and institutions publish such notices in their annual calendars. Educational agencies and institutions also typically include FERPA rights on their websites for the public to access.

Managing Parent and Eligible Student Requests to Review Records

Parents may request to review their child's education records if the child is under the age of 18. Parents may also request to review their child's education records if the child is over 18 and the parent claims the child as a dependent on taxes. Eligible students may also request to review their education records. FERPA requires that a school provide access to the education records within 45 calendar days of the request.[60] There may be requirements to provide access prior to 45 days in certain circumstances. For example, under the IDEA, records must be provided upon request prior to 45 calendar days if something special education-related is occurring for the student, such as an IEP meeting, mediation, or due process hearing.[61] In such instances, the records must be provided prior to that special education-related event. Some states may also require that access to records be provided in a shorter period of time.

FERPA generally does not require educational agencies or institutions to provide copies of education records. This means an educational agency or institution complies with a request to review records when allowing the parent or eligible student the opportunity to inspect and review the records. But copies must be provided when circumstances prevent a parent or eligible student from exercising their right to inspect and review a record, and the school does not make other arrangements to inspect and review the record.[62] Examples of this could be a parent who does not live within commuting distance of the school, a parent or eligible student who is too ill to go to the school, or a parent or eligible student who is incarcerated. FERPA allows educational agencies or institutions to charge a reasonable fee for copies unless the fee would prevent the parent or eligible student from exercising their right to inspect and review the student's education records.[63] Fees may not be charged for time spent locating records.[64]

Records may include information about more than one student. FERPA provides that a parent or eligible student may only "be informed of" the information related to the eligible student or the parent's child.[65] Accordingly, PII about other students should be redacted before sharing it with a parent or eligible student.

FERPA does not place an affirmative obligation on school personnel to volunteer disclosure to a parent or eligible student when it is not requested. But other laws – particularly state laws – may require voluntary disclosure under certain circumstances. For example, the well-known *California Supreme Court case of Tarasoff v. Regents of the University of California* (1976) held that mental health professionals are required to notify individuals who were being threatened with bodily harm by a client. This is also referred to as a "duty to warn." Since that case, most states have adopted laws that either require or permit mental health professionals to warn of potential harm.[66]

Parent and Eligible Student Challenges to FERPA

To be clear, there are no "FERPA" police who enforce FERPA against educators. Although it is in violation of the law to make an unauthorized disclosure under FERPA, there is no criminal or civil action that may be initiated against the individual who made the unauthorized disclosure. Indeed, there is no private cause of action under FERPA. This means a parent or eligible student cannot bring a lawsuit for damages against an individual (such as an educator) or entity (such as a school) for an unauthorized FERPA disclosure or alleged FERPA violation. The Supreme Court considered this issue in *Gonzaga University v. John* Doe (2002). That case was related to an undergraduate student, "John Doe," at Gonzaga University, who requested an affidavit of good standing from the University in 1993, as required to become a certified teacher in Washington. The University's "teacher certification specialist" overheard another student mention that John Doe engaged in sexual misconduct against a female undergraduate student at the University. The teacher certification specialist began an investigation into the allegations and called the Washington state agency that issued teacher certifications. During that call, the teacher certification specialist shared John Doe's name and discussed the allegations made against him by the other student. John Doe was unaware of the investigation or the disclosure for approximately five months, at which time he was informed that he would not receive the affidavit of good standing as required for certification.

John Doe sued both the teacher certification specialist and the University in state court, alleging violations of Washington tort and contract law and Section 1983. John Doe argued the defendants violated Section 1983 due to the teacher certification specialist making an unauthorized disclosure under FERPA when she reported the allegations to the Washington teacher certification agency. At the initial state court level, a jury found in favor of John Doe and awarded a total of $1,155,000.00 in damages, which included $150,000 in compensatory damages and $300,000 in punitive damages under FERPA.

The defendants appealed to both the Washington Court of Appeals and then to the Washington Supreme Court. The Court of Appeals reversed the FERPA findings based on the rationale that FERPA does not provide a private cause of action and so cannot be enforced under Section 1983. The Washington Supreme Court reversed that decision and upheld the original damages awarded under FERPA. The rationale was that although FERPA does not explicitly provide for a private cause of action, the FERPA requirement to keep student records confidential "gives rise to a federal right enforceable under Section 1983."[67]

The case made its way to the Supreme Court of the United States. The Supreme Court noted that lower courts were divided regarding FERPA's enforceability under Section 1983, and more specifically, whether a FERPA violation could result in a private cause of action. The Court quoted one of its other FERPA decisions, ruling that "unless Congress 'speak[s] with a clear voice,' and manifests an 'unambiguous' intent to confer individual rights, federal funding provisions provide no basis for private enforcement by Section 1983." Therefore, the Supreme Court held that FERPA does not create "individually enforceable rights" claims under Section 1983, and John Doe was precluded from seeking damages due to an alleged FERPA violation.

The Supreme Court decided Gonzaga in 2002. The alleged FERPA violation was made in 1993. This was a long, drawn-out legal battle that was likely expensive for all parties. But the decision is an important one for FERPA as it establishes that there is no private cause of action related to alleged FERPA violations.

Complaints to the Student Privacy Policy Office

Parents or eligible students may challenge an alleged FERPA violation with the Federal Education Department's Student Privacy Policy Office (SPPO; formerly the Family Policy Compliance Office).[68] Based on personal observation, SPPO investigations are not as commonplace for K-12 schools as other federal investigations, such as Department of Justice or Office of Civil Rights investigations. To initiate a SPPO investigation, a complaint needs to be submitted to the SPPO within 180 days of the date of the alleged violation – or of the date the complainant knew or reasonably should have known of the alleged violation. The complaint must assert specific factual allegations that provide reasonable cause to believe there was a FERPA violation. The SPPO then determines whether to investigate the complaint. The SPPO may also take a more informal approach and provide support to the parties with the intent of assisting them in resolving the conflict. Any founded allegations as a result of such investigations could lead to corrective action. Such correction could result in a school's loss of federal funding, although in experience, this is a rare sanction.[69]

FERPA Amendment Request

A parent or eligible student may request an amendment or correction of an education record that they believe to be inaccurate, misleading, or otherwise in violation of the student's right to privacy.[70] Many schools have written procedures or a policy related to their process of considering a FERPA amendment request. A school is not required to amend a record upon request; however, it is required to consider the request "within a reasonable time" after receiving the request.[71] A school must notify the parent or eligible student of their right to request a FERPA hearing if the school denies their amendment request.

One example of a situation that may warrant a FERPA amendment could be when records are factually inaccurate (e.g., the student's record contains the incorrect birthdate). The SPPO/FPCO has considered parent or eligible student requests to amend education records. The agency repeatedly finds that the FERPA amendment process cannot be used to modify report cards or grades absent proof that the grade or score itself is inaccurate. For example, in the 2007 *Letter to Anonymous*,[72] the FPCO considered a complaint raised by a parent alleging the school improperly denied the parent's request to amend their child's scores generated based on a review of the student's National Honor Society application. The FPCO denied the parent's request because the scores the parent sought to amend were the opinions of the school's National Honor Society reviewers, and such opinions are not subject to a FERPA amendment. The FPCO reasoned that

> while FERPA affords parents the right to seek to amend their child's education records which contain inaccurate information, this right cannot be used to challenge a grade or an individual's opinion, unless the grade or the opinion has been inaccurately recorded.

In the 2016 *Letter to Anonymous*,[73] the FPCO denied a parent's request to amend a teacher's comments on the student's progress report. The FPCO opined that FERPA "does not provide a means to override the accepted standards and procedures for making academic assessments, disciplinary rulings, or placement determinations." Therefore, the FERPA amendment process cannot be used to "challenge grades, an opinion, or other substantive decisions made by a school about a student." This same standard applies to prohibiting parent requests to amend their child's disciplinary records[74] or to exit a student from special education.[75] Rather, the parent is required to challenge special education decisions through the IDEA's due process procedures rather than through a FERPA amendment.

The FPCO determined that the FERPA amendment process cannot be used to amend records that do not fall under the definition of an "education record" in 2015 in *Letter to Anonymous*.[76] In that decision, a student's mother made a complaint to the FPCO and requested to amend her child's homeschool records that were created by the child's father. The FPCO determined that although the homeschool records were maintained by the school, they were not "education records" that were entitled to the FERPA amendment request.

Consider this scenario for a FERPA amendment request. A parent believes the IEP meeting minutes taken by the school related to the parent's child, Sally, do not adequately describe the parent's requests and disagreements with the recommendations of the IEP team. Specifically, the parent believes the minutes should state: "Despite the clear evidence that Sally requires a specially-designed reading program to address her dyslexia, the school members of the IEP Team refused the request because they do not want to spend the money on Sally's needs." The school is left with determining whether the minutes are inaccurate, misleading, or otherwise in violation of Sally's privacy. It is accurate that the IEP Team denied Sally's mother's request for a specially-designed reading program, but the reason for that was due to Sally performing within at least the average range in every area of reading. The IEP team minutes reflect the following regarding the reading conversation:

> The IEP Team considered a request from Sally's mother for a specially-designed reading program to address Sally's dyslexia. The Team determined Sally does not require a specially-designed reading program because all of her reading skills are within the average to high average range. The assistive technology and other programs and services on Sally's IEP address her disability-related needs.

The school has a strong basis for determining a FERPA amendment is not warranted as Sally's mother's request is based more on her own opinion rather than the factual outcome or conversation of the meeting. The amendment request may therefore be denied. The school would need to inform Sally's mother of her right to request a FERPA hearing if it denies her amendment request.

FERPA Hearing

Parents and eligible students may also request an opportunity for a hearing when they believe information contained in the student's education record is inaccurate, misleading, or in violation of the student's privacy rights.[77] FERPA provides a number of requirements for hearings, including:

1. The school shall hold the hearing within a reasonable time after it receives the request for a hearing.
2. The school shall give the parent or eligible student notice of the date, time, and place reasonably in advance of the hearing.
3. The hearing may be presided over by a hearing officer who does not have a direct interest in the outcome of the hearing. This hearing officer may be a school official.
4. The parent or eligible student must be provided a full and fair opportunity to present relevant evidence related to the issues.
5. The parent or eligible student may be represented by one or more individuals of their choice, including an attorney. Such representation is at the expense of the parent or eligible student.
6. The school must issue a written decision within a reasonable time after the hearing concludes.

7. The decision must be based solely on the evidence presented at the hearing and must include a summary of the evidence and the reasons for the decision.

The formal rules of evidence do not apply to FERPA hearings, and the conduct of such hearings may be dictated by state or local rules.

Should the school grant the request to amend the education record as a result of the hearing, the school must amend the record and inform the parent or eligible student in writing of the amendment. Should the school deny the request to amend the education record, the school must inform the parent or eligible student of the right to provide a statement to include in the student's education record that identifies the contested information and states the reason for the disagreement with that record. Schools are required to maintain such statements for as long as that record is maintained and disclose the statement whenever it discloses that portion of the contested record.

Destruction of Education Records

FERPA does not require that a school provide notice to a parent or eligible student upon destroying an education record. However, such notice is required when there is an outstanding request to inspect or review the records.[78] But some states may have their own requirements for maintaining education records of students, including the length of time to maintain such records and/or notification requirements prior to destroying such records.

Intersection with HIPAA

Many school employees who hold qualifications to engage in private practice, such as school nurses, occupational therapists, physical therapists, speech-language pathologists, social workers, psychologists, etc., have been trained in compliance related to the Health Insurance Portability and Accountability Act of 1996 ("HIPAA"). HIPAA is a federal law that applies to health information that is created or maintained by healthcare providers and designed to protect the confidentiality of individually identifiable health information. Healthcare providers who are covered entities must comply with HIPAA. "Covered entities" refers to "health plans, health care clearinghouses, and health care providers that transmit health information in electronic form in connection with covered transactions."[79] A "health care provider" includes institutional providers of health or medical services (e.g., hospitals) and non-institutional providers (e.g., physicians and other practitioners).[80] But HIPAA does not apply to records that are protected by FERPA. There is language explicitly in HIPAA that provides that the term "protected health information" does not include individually identifiable health information in education records that are protected by FERPA.[81]

Based on the above, many schools are not required to comply with HIPAA because the student health records maintained by the school fall under either FERPA's "education records" or "treatment records."[82] Both of these types of records are not health records under HIPAA, but rather FERPA education records.

There are exceptions to the general rule that HIPAA does not apply to schools. For example, a clinic operated by an outside entity at a school is required to comply with HIPAA. Conversely, a school-based health clinic operated by school staff that does not engage in the electronic transmission of health information is not covered by FERPA.[83] Any electronic Medicaid claims filed by a school must comply with HIPAA for any transmissions that are not protected by FERPA.[84]

Although schools are not typically required to comply with HIPAA, a student's private providers are typically required to comply with HIPAA. This means that consent is required to exchange protected information between a school provider and a private provider. Such consent is required under HIPAA for the private provider and under FERPA for the school. There are some circumstances in which private providers may disclose protected health information to school nurses, physicians, or other healthcare providers – without consent – when such disclosure is required for treatment purposes. This issue was considered in a Third Circuit decision from Pennsylvania in *T.F. v. Fox Chapel Area School District.* In that case, a student with a tree nut allergy was starting kindergarten, and his parents disclosed the allergy to the school principal and nurse. The major issue in that case was related to the parents alleging the school failed to adequately accommodate the student's allergies under Section 504. However, another issue was related to the parents' claim that the school nurse improperly contacted the student's physician to obtain clarity regarding the physician's orders for the student. The parents claimed such contact – without their consent – violated both FERPA and HIPAA. The lower court disagreed, citing the Joint Guidance on HIPAA and FERPA, and finding that HIPAA allows a "health care provider to disclose protected health information to school nurses, physicians, or other health care providers for treatment purposes, without authorization." This was affirmed by the Third Circuit.

Consider this scenario. Sammy, a third-grade student, frequently complains about stomachaches to the school nurse, Mr. Santino. Sammy's mother believes the stomachaches could be due to the anxiety Sammy is feeling in school. The school counselor, Mr. Brown, is meeting with Sammy during a lunch-bunch group to help him cope with his anxious feelings. Mr. Brown asks Mr. Santino to share when Sammy is going to the nurse's office with stomachaches to assist Mr. Brown with identifying any patterns to the stomachaches and whether Sammy's symptoms are alleviating. But Mr. Santino refuses to share that information, citing HIPAA and the requirement for parent consent before sharing private medical information with Mr. Brown. Does Mr. Santino have the correct interpretation of relevant law? No, because Mr. Santino's records of Sammy are considered to be education records under FERPA – and not health records under HIPAA. Mr. Brown has a legitimate educational interest as a school official in knowing this information because it is directly related to Mr. Brown's work with Sammy. Therefore, it is legally permissible for Mr. Santino to share information with Mr. Brown regarding Sammy's stomachaches, and there is no requirement for parent consent to do so.

Other Federal Laws with Student Privacy Provisions

There are other federal laws that provide confidentiality provisions for students. The IDEA entitles qualified students with disabilities to special education and related services. Specifically related to records, the IDEA requires schools to keep confidential any records that include personally identifiable information.[85] That same provision also requires every school that must comply with the IDEA to identify an individual who is responsible for ensuring the confidentiality of any PII (this is not expressly required in FERPA). The IDEA also requires any individuals who collect or use PII to have training regarding the relevant policies and procedures related to confidentiality under the IDEA. And finally, the IDEA requires schools to maintain a list of any names and positions of employees who have access to PII.

Like FERPA, the IDEA provides parents the right to amend an education record they believe is inaccurate, misleading, or in violation of the student's privacy rights. These rights under the IDEA reflect those provided by FERPA.[86] But unlike FERPA, the IDEA affords parents the right to request their child's PII be destroyed when it is no longer necessary to provide the student with special education services.[87] However, the school has the discretion to determine whether such records are no longer necessary.[88] The IDEA also requires that parents be notified when a school determines that a student's record is no longer necessary.[89] That notification must include the parent's right to request that the records be destroyed. This notification requirement is not required by FERPA. The IDEA does not require a school to notify a parent when the records are actually destroyed.

FERPA does not expressly allow a parent's representative to inspect and review a student's education records. Therefore, a school is not obligated to allow a third-party representative of the parent to review a child's records under FERPA.[90] The IDEA, however, does allow a third-party representative of a parent to inspect and review the parent's child's education records upon request. This means that an attorney, advocate, or other representative of the parent may review the education records, upon the parent's request and consent, but only to the extent that the student has education records pursuant to the IDEA (e.g., the student is classified with a disability under the IDEA or otherwise has special education records).[91]

The Protection of Pupil Rights Amendment (PPRA) is a federal law that provides parents and students with certain rights related to student surveys. The law requires parents to consent prior to a school that receives federal funding administering surveys regarding (1) political affiliations; (2) mental and psychological problems of the student or the student's family; (3) sexual behavior or attitudes; (4) illegal, antisocial, self-incriminating, or demeaning behavior; (5) critical appraisals of a student's family members; (6) religious practices, affiliations, or beliefs; (7) privileged or similar relationships under the law; and (8) income.[92] Parents must be provided with the option to opt out of such surveys in certain circumstances and to access the instructional materials.[93] The PPRA requires schools to adopt policies related to protecting student privacy and parent rights under the PPRA. The PPRA also requires annual notifications to parents regarding the policy.

The federal Children's Online Privacy Protection Rule (COPPA) provides privacy protections to students. Specifically, COPPA imposes requirements on operators of websites, games, mobile apps, or other online services that are directed at children who are under the age of 13 and also operators of other websites or online platforms that have knowledge they are collecting personal information online from a child who is under the age of 13. The Federal Trade Commission has opined that in certain situations, "schools may act as the parent's agent and can consent to the collection of kids' information on the parent's behalf."[94] But such consent is "limited to the educational context." When consent is obtained from the school, rather than the parent, then the operator of the website or platform should provide direct notice to the school regarding its use of personal information from children, the right to request that such information be deleted, and the opportunity to prevent further use or collection of such personal information. A website or online platform may presume the school obtained the parent's consent when the child's information is only used for educational reasons as approved by the school. The Federal Trade Commission advises that schools should share any relevant COPPA notifications with parents.

Conclusion

FERPA provides considerable rights to parents and eligible students related to education records and also places stringent compliance requirements on schools. It is advisable for school leaders to understand their obligations related to FERPA, including defining directory information and annual notification requirements. School leaders are also tasked with ensuring that any staff who will have access to student education records receive training and ongoing supervision related to FERPA requirements. Educators should be aware of their obligations under FERPA – especially the duty to keep student PII confidential. FERPA compliance ensures student rights are upheld and places schools and their officials in a strong position to both establish trust with families and students while complying with the law.

Notes

1 U. S. Education Department. (2002, June). *Legislative History of Major FERPA Provisions.* https://studentprivacy.ed.gov/sites/default/files/resource_document/file/ferpleghistory.pdf
2 Family Educational Rights and Privacy, 34 CFR § 99.3.
3 Family Educational Rights and Privacy Act of 1974, 20 U.S.C. § 1232g(d) (1974).
4 *Letter to Corr*, 120 LRP 10124 (SPPO 2019).
5 Family Educational Rights and Privacy, 34 CFR § 99.31(a)(8).
6 Individuals with Disabilities Education Improvement Act, 34 CFR § 300.520(a)(1)(ii).
7 Individuals with Disabilities Education Improvement Act, 34 CFR § 300.520(a).
8 Family Educational Rights and Privacy, 34 CFR § 99.2; Family Educational Rights and Privacy Act of 1974, 20 U.S.C. § 1232g(a)(4) (1974).
9 U.S. Education Department. (n.d.). *What Is an Education Record?* https://studentprivacy.ed.gov/faq/what-education-record.
10 Family Educational Rights and Privacy Act of 1974, 20 U.S.C. § 20 U.S.C. 1232g (1974).
11 Family Educational Rights and Privacy, 34 CFR § 99.3.
12 Family Educational Rights and Privacy, 34 CFR § 99.3; *Letter to Anonymous*, 122 LRP 5747 (SPPO 2021).
13 Family Educational Rights and Privacy Act of 1974, 20 U.S.C. § 20 U.S.C. 1232g (1974).
14 U.S. Education Department. (n.d.). *FAQs on Photos and Videos Under FERPA.* https://studentprivacy.ed.gov/faq/faqs-photos-and-videos-under-ferpa.
15 United States Department of Education Office of Management. (2017, December 7). *Letter to Wachter.* https://studentprivacy.ed.gov/sites/default/files/resource_document/file/Letter%20to%20Wachter%20%28Surveillance%20Video%20of%20Multiple%20Students%29_0.pdf.
16 Family Educational Rights and Privacy, 34 CFR § 99.8(b)(1).
17 Family Educational Rights and Privacy, 34 CFR § 99.33.
18 U.S. Education Department. (n.d.). *What Is a "Law Enforcement Unit Record?"* https://studentprivacy.ed.gov/faq/what-law-enforcement-unit-record.
19 Family Educational Rights and Privacy Act of 1974, 20 U.S.C. § 1232g (1974).
20 Family Educational Rights and Privacy, 34 CFR § 99.3.
21 Family Educational Rights and Privacy, 34 CFR § 99.30.
22 U.S. Education Department Privacy Technical Assistance Center (September 2012). *Data Breach Response Checklist.* https://studentprivacy.ed.gov/sites/default/files/resource_document/file/checklist_data_breach_response_092012_0.pdf
23 Family Educational Rights and Privacy, 34 CFR §§ 99.3 and 99.37.
24 Family Educational Rights and Privacy, 34 CFR § 99.31(a)(1)(i)(B).
25 Family Educational Rights and Privacy, 34 CFR §§ 99.31(a)(10) and 99.36.
26 *Letter to Anonymous*, 115 LRP 3314 (FPCO 2015).
27 *Letter to Anonymous*, 53 IDELR 235 (U.S. Department of Education 2008).
28 Family Educational Rights and Privacy, 34 CFR § 99.31(a)(2).
29 Family Educational Rights and Privacy, 34 CFR § 99.31(a)(9).

30 U.S. Education Department Family Policy Compliance Office (1998, June 22). *Letter to Ms. Linda C.T. Simlick from LeRoy S. Rooker*. https://studentprivacy.ed.gov/sites/default/files/resource_document/file/california.pdf.
31 U.S. Education Department Family Policy Compliance Office (1999, February 16). *Letter to Cochran*. https://studentprivacy.ed.gov/sites/default/files/resource_document/file/youngstownoh.pdf.
32 Family Educational Rights and Privacy Act of 1974, 20 U.S.C. § 1232g(b)(2)(B) (1974).
33 Family Educational Rights and Privacy, 34 CFR § 99.31(a)(9)(iii).
34 Family Educational Rights and Privacy Act of 1974, 20 U.S.C. § 1232g(b)(1)(L) (1974).
35 Adoption Assistance and Child Welfare Act, 42 U.S.C. § 675(1).
36 Family Educational Rights and Privacy, 34 CFR § 99.31(a)(4).
37 Family Educational Rights and Privacy, 34 CFR § 99.31(a)(15).
38 Family Educational Rights and Privacy, 34 CFR §§ 34 CFR 99.31(a)(14) 99.39; and Appendix A to Part 99, Title 34.
39 Family Educational Rights and Privacy, 34 CFR §§ 99.31(a)(13) and 99.39.
40 Family Educational Rights and Privacy, 34 CFR § 99.31(a)(7).
41 Family Educational Rights and Privacy, 34 CFR §§ 99.31(a)(5) and 99.38.
42 Elementary and Secondary Education Act, 20 U.S.C. § 8528.
43 U.S. Education Department Office of Management. (2016, November 1). *Dear Colleague Letter*. https://studentprivacy.ed.gov/sites/default/files/resource_document/file/military-recruiter_.pdf.
44 Family Educational Rights and Privacy Act of 1974, 20 U.S.C. § 1232g(b)(7) (1974).
45 Family Educational Rights and Privacy Act of 1974, 20 U.S.C. § 1232g(b)(1)(K) (1974).
46 Family Educational Rights and Privacy, 34 CFR §§ 99.31(a)(3) and 99.35.
47 Family Educational Rights and Privacy, 34 CFR § 99.31(a)(6).
48 Family Educational Rights and Privacy, 34 CFR § 99.32.
49 Family Educational Rights and Privacy, 34 CFR §§ 99.32(d)(4) and 99.32(d)(2).
50 Family Educational Rights and Privacy, 34 CFR § 99.31 (b)(1).
51 Family Educational Rights and Privacy, 34 CFR § Section 99.10.
52 Family Educational Rights and Privacy, 34 CFR §§ 99.20, 99.21, and 99.22.
53 Family Educational Rights and Privacy, 34 CFR §§ 99.30 and 99.31.
54 Family Educational Rights and Privacy, 34 CFR § 99.7.
55 Family Educational Rights and Privacy, 34 CFR §§ 99.7(b)1) through (b)(1)(2).
56 Family Educational Rights and Privacy, 34 CFR § 99.7(a)(3)(iii).
57 Family Educational Rights and Privacy, 34 CFR § 99.31; 73 Fed. Reg. 74,815 (2008).
58 *Letter to Anderson*, 121 LRP 4902 (SPPO 2020)
59 Family Educational Rights and Privacy, 34 CFR § 99.31(a)(11).
60 Family Educational Rights and Privacy, 34 CFR § 99.10(b).
61 Individuals with Disabilities Education Improvement Act, 34 CFR § 300.613.
62 Family Educational Rights and Privacy, 34 CFR § 99.l0(d).
63 Family Educational Rights and Privacy, 34 CFR § 99.11.
64 Family Educational Rights and Privacy, 34 CFR § 99.11(b).
65 Family Educational Rights and Privacy Act of 1974, 20 U.S.C. § 1232g(a)(l)(A) (1974); and Family Educational Rights and Privacy, 34 CFR § 99.12(a).
66 National Association of Social Workers. (2009). *Social Workers and "Duty to Warn" State Laws*. https://www.traumahealth.org/wp-content/uploads/2017/07/Section-9-Social-Workers-and-Duty-to-Warn-Article.pdf.

67 *Doe v. Gonzaga*, 143 Wash. 2d 687, 24 P. 3d 390 (2001), at 400.
68 U.S. Education Department. (n.d.). *File a Complaint*. https://studentprivacy.ed.gov/file-a-complaint.
69 Family Educational Rights and Privacy, 34 CFR §§ 99.66(c) and 99.67(a).
70 Family Educational Rights and Privacy, 34 CFR § 99.20.
71 Family Educational Rights and Privacy, 34 CFR § 99.20(b).
72 *Letter to Anonymous*, 107 LRP 52770 (FPCO 2007).
73 *Letter to Anonymous*, 116 LRP 48415 (FPCO 2016).
74 *Letter to Anonymous*, 121 LRP 32141 (SPPO 2021).
75 *Letter to Anonymous*, 121 LRP 32151 (SPPO 2021).
76 *Letter to Anonymous*, 116 LRP 17292 (FPCO 2015).
77 Family Educational Rights and Privacy, 34 CFR § 99.22.
78 *Letter re: Keystone Central School District*, 105 LRP 25813 (FPCO 2005).
79 U.S. Education Department and U.S. Department of Health and Human Services. (2019, December 19). *Joint Guidance on the Application of HIPAA and FERPA Student Health Records*. https://studentprivacy.ed.gov/resources/joint-guidance-application-ferpa-and-hipaa-student-health-records.
80 U.S. Education Department and U.S. Department of Health and Human Services. (2019, December 19). *Joint Guidance on the Application of HIPAA and FERPA Student Health Records*. https://studentprivacy.ed.gov/resources/joint-guidance-application-ferpa-and-hipaa-student-health-records.
81 Health Insurance Portability and Accountability Act, 45 CFR § 160.103.
82 U.S. Education Department and U.S. Department of Health and Human Services. (2019, December 19). *Joint Guidance on the Application of HIPAA and FERPA Student Health Records*. https://studentprivacy.ed.gov/resources/joint-guidance-application-ferpa-and-hipaa-student-health-records; and U.S. Department of Education (2023, April). *Family Educational Rights and Privacy Act: Guidance for School Officials on Student Health Records*. https://studentprivacy.ed.gov/resources/family-educational-rights-and-privacy-act-guidance-school-officials-student-health.
83 U.S. Education Department and U.S. Department of Health and Human Services. (2019, December 19). *Joint Guidance on the Application of HIPAA and FERPA Student Health Records*. https://studentprivacy.ed.gov/resources/joint-guidance-application-ferpa-and-hipaa-student-health-records; and U.S. Department of Education (2023, April). *Family Educational Rights and Privacy Act: Guidance for School Officials on Student Health Records*. https://studentprivacy.ed.gov/resources/family-educational-rights-and-privacy-act-guidance-school-officials-student-health.
84 U.S. Education Department and U.S. Department of Health and Human Services. (2019, December 19). *Joint Guidance on the Application of HIPAA and FERPA Student Health Records*. https://studentprivacy.ed.gov/resources/joint-guidance-application-ferpa-and-hipaa-student-health-records.
85 Individuals with Disabilities Education Improvement Act, 34 CFR § 300.623.
86 Individuals with Disabilities Education Improvement Act, 34 CFR §§ 300.618 through 300.621.
87 Individuals with Disabilities Education Improvement Act, 34 CFR § 300.624(a).
88 *Letter to Herbert*, 211 IDELR 229 (OSEP 1980).
89 Individuals with Disabilities Education Improvement Act, 34 CFR § 300.624(a).
90 *Letter to Longest*, 213 IDELR 173 (OSEP 1988).
91 Individuals with Disabilities Education Improvement Act, 34 CFR § 300.613(b)(3).
92 Family Educational Rights and Privacy Act of 1974, 20 U.S.C § 1232h(b) and Family Educational Rights and Privacy, 34 CFR § 98.4(a).

93 Family Educational Rights and Privacy Act of 1974, 20 U.S.C §§ 1232h(a) through (b); Family Educational Rights and Privacy, 34 CFR § 98.3.
94 Federal Trade Commission. (2020, July). *Complying with COPPA: Frequently Asked Questions.* https://www.ftc.gov/business-guidance/resources/complying-coppa-frequently-asked-questions.

List of Cases

B.F. v. Fulton County School District, 2008 WL 4224802 (N.D. Ga. 2008).
Brownsburg Community School Corporation, 59 IDELR 146 (Indiana State Educational Agency, CP-052-2012, 2012).
Clark County School Distr. v. Eighth Jud. Dist. Ct. in and for County of Clark 141 Nev. Adv. Op. 55 (2025).
Connecticut Department of Education Complaint No. 19-0486 (Schierberl, 2019).
Easton Area School District v. Miller, 232 A.3d 657 (Pa. 2020).
Gonzaga University v. John Doe, 536 U.S. 273 (2002).
Middleton-Cross Plains Area School District, 115 LRP 31928 (Wisconsin State Educational Agency, 15-029, 2015).
Owasso Independent School District No. I-011 v. Falvo, 534 U.S. 426 (2002).
S.A. v. Tulare County Office of Education, 2009 WL 3126322 (E.D. Cal 2009).
Tarasoff v. Regents of the University of California, 17 Cal. 3d 425 (Cal 1976).
T.F. v. Fox Chapel Area School District, 62 IDELR 74 (W.D. Pa. 2013), *aff'd on other Grounds*, 64 IDELR 61 (3d Cir. 2014).
W.A. v. Hendrick Hudson Central School District, 2016 WL 6915271 (S.D.N.Y. Nov. 23, 2016).

Laws Cited

Campus Sex Crimes Prevention Act, Pub. L. No. 106–386, § 1601, 114 Stat. 1537 (2000).
Child Nutrition Act of 1966, 42 U.S.C. § 1771 et seq.
Civil Action for Deprivation of Rights, 42 U.S.C. § 1983.
Elementary and Secondary Education Act of 1965, 20 U.S.C. § 6301 et seq.
Family Educational Rights and Privacy Act of 1974, 20 U.S.C. § 1232g.
Federal Trade Commissioner. Children's Online Protection Rule. 16 C.F.R. § 312.
Health Insurance Portability and Accountability Act of 1996, 45 CFR §§ 160; 164.
Individuals with Disabilities Education Improvement Act of 2004, 20 U.S.C. § 1400 et seq. (2004).
Protection of Pupil Rights Amendment Act, 20 U.S.C. § 1232h.
Rehabilitation Act of 1973, Pub. L. No. 93-112, 87 Stat. 355 (1973).
Richard B. Russell National School Lunch Act, 42 U.S.C. § 1751 et seq. (1946).
Uninterrupted Scholars Act of 2012.
U.S. Const. Amend. XIV.

2 Student First Amendment Rights

Anne M. McGinnis

"Students do not shed their constitutional rights at the schoolhouse gate." This is a quote from the 1969 landmark Supreme Court decision, *Tinker v. Des Moines*. We will analyze this case in detail later in this chapter. *Tinker* was the first Supreme Court decision to establish the current legal standard for the First Amendment rights of K-12 public school students. As also discussed below, there are some limitations on those First Amendment rights that would not apply to the general public in a public setting.

The First Amendment is brief, but carries significant weight: "Congress shall make no law respecting an establishment of religion, or prohibiting the free exercise thereof, or abridging the freedom of speech, or of the press; or the right of the people peaceably to assemble, and to petition the Government for a redress of grievances." In layperson's terms, the First Amendment protects the freedom of speech, religion, the press, and the right to peacefully congregate and make requests of the government. The First Amendment's ratification on December 5, 1791, was born out of the political climate of colonial America, including the belief that such rights were not provided under British rule.[1]

There have been many Supreme Court decisions that have examined freedom of speech in various contexts. The free speech rights afforded to the general public are more expansive than the free speech rights of public school students. For example, in *Cohen v. California* (1971), a 19-year-old protested the Vietnam War by wearing, "Fuck the Draft," on the back of his jacket in the Los Angeles County Courthouse. Cohen was sentenced to 30 days in jail for the words on his jacket, but the Supreme Court found this violated Cohen's First Amendment rights. The Court agreed that although the speech was provocative, it was not directed at anybody in particular and was unlikely to result in a physical altercation. As Justice Harlan wrote in the decision, "One man's vulgarity is another's lyric." The *Cohen* decision likely would have been different if Cohen wore the jacket in a public school setting, rather than a courthouse. *Cohen* was cited by another Supreme Court decision that examined the First Amendment rights of public school

DOI: 10.4324/9781003728993-3

students – *Bethel v. Fraser* (1986). That case noted that a student could have been disciplined for wearing the same jacket to school because schools can prohibit vulgar, lewd, and indecent language without infringing on a student's First Amendment rights.

Foundational Supreme Court Decisions

The First Amendment did not apply to public school students prior to the 1960s. Courts instead used a "reasonableness" test, applied in previous Supreme Court decisions such as *Meyer v. Nebraska* (1923) and *Bartels v. Iowa* (1923), to judge school policies and upheld the decisions of school officials unless students were able to prove such decisions were unreasonable. Accordingly, restrictions on student speech were typically upheld. Since 1969, there have been four landmark Supreme Court cases that have established the legal standard for student freedom of speech in public schools: *Tinker v. Des Moines Independent Community School District* (1969), *Bethel School District v. Fraser* (1986), *Hazelwood v. Kuhlmeier* (1988), and *Morse v. Frederick* (2007).

In *Tinker v. Des Moines Community School District*, a group of students wore black armbands to their public school in protest of the Vietnam War. The group of students included four siblings: John, Mary Beth, Hope, and Paul Tinker, and their friend, Christopher Eckhardt. The students ranged from ages eight to 16 and attended various schools within the Des Moines Independent Community School District. The case was initiated by John and Mary Beth Tinker and Christopher Eckhardt. The Tinkers' father was a Methodist Minister, and the family had a history of engaging in civil rights activism. Christopher's mother was part of the Women's International League for Peace and Freedom. We can assume the students were supported by their parents in their activism at school; a group of adults and students met at the Eckhardt home in December 1965 and planned to publicly protest the Vietnam War by wearing black armbands during the holiday season.

The principals of the Des Moines school were aware of the plan to wear black armbands to school and adopted a policy on December 14, 1965, providing that students would be asked to remove their armbands and would be suspended if they refused. Mary Beth and Christopher wore black armbands to school on December 16, 1965. John wore his on December 17, 1965. All three students were suspended until they returned without the armbands. The students returned when their scheduled protest period ended after New Year's Day.

The students' fathers first brought their complaint, on the students' behalf, in the United States District Court. The American Civil Liberties Union (ACLU) provided representation to the students. They alleged that the students' Constitutional rights were violated under Section 1983 – a civil rights statute that allows for the initiation of a lawsuit based on an alleged

Constitutional violation. The lawsuit requested an order prohibiting the school district from disciplining the students and nominal damages. The District Court dismissed the complaint, finding the school authorities' actions reasonably prevented a disturbance at school. The decision was appealed to the Eighth Circuit, whose panel was tied, ultimately upholding the lower court's decision.

The Supreme Court of the United States reversed in favor of the students, finding that a public school must provide a constitutionally valid reason for regulating the free speech of its students. The Supreme Court explicitly determined that the First Amendment applies to students in the public school setting, including a constitutional right to the freedom of expression. The school may only limit such expression when it "materially and substantially interferes with the requirements of appropriate discipline in the operation of the school" or "impinges on the rights of other students." Neither was present here. Accordingly, the Supreme Court determined the students were improperly disciplined for wearing armbands that expressed their political protest, as their conduct was a "silent, passive expression of opinion, unaccompanied by any disturbance or disorder."

The *Tinker* case changed the legal standard for students' First Amendment rights in public K-12 schools. It determined, for the first time, that students had the right to engage in a peaceful protest that did not cause a disruption to the school setting. Subsequent cases further refined the standard related to the First Amendment rights of students in public schools.

The Supreme Court next considered First Amendment rights for students in 1986 with *Bethel v. Fraser*. The case involved Matthew Fraser, a high school senior who attended Bethel High School in Washington State. In 1983, Matthew gave a speech in front of approximately 600 high school students to support another student who was running for student office. But as sometimes happens with teenagers, Matthew's speech was filled with sexual innuendo. The exact wording of the speech is helpful in understanding its graphic nature – it was not subtle (and apologies if it is offensive to the reader):

> *I know a man who is firm – he's firm in his pants, he's firm in his shirt, his character is firm – but most . . . of all, his belief in you, the students of Bethel, is firm. Jeff Kuhlman is a man who takes his point and pounds it in. If necessary, he'll take an issue and nail it to the wall. He doesn't attack things in spurts – he drives hard, pushing and pushing until finally – he succeeds. Jeff is a man who will go to the very end – even the climax, for each and every one of you. So vote for Jeff for A.S.B. vice-president – he'll never come between you and the best our high school can be.*[2]

One can imagine the outrage of school staff and administrators when listening to this speech. A school counselor reported the speech had a significant impact on the other students, including students who "hooted and yelled; some by gestures graphically simulated the sexual activities pointedly alluded to in [Matthew's] speech. Other students appeared to be bewildered and embarrassed."

Matthew admitted to the misconduct and that the sexual innuendo was deliberate. The school determined the speech violated its rule against obscene language that "materially and substantially interfere[d] with the educational process...including the use of obscene, profane language or gestures." He was suspended from school for three days and prohibited from speaking at graduation. Matthew first appealed the decision through the school district's internal appeal procedures. A hearing officer found Matthew's speech to be "indecent, lewd, and offensive to the modesty and decency of many of the students and faculty in attendance at the assembly." Matthew ultimately served two days of his three-day suspension.

Through his father and the support of the ACLU, Matthew initiated a federal lawsuit in the United States District Court for the Western District of Washington. He alleged his First Amendment rights were violated under Section 1983 and requested an injunction and monetary damages. The District Court found in Matthew's favor. Specifically, the District Court opined the school rule Matthew violated was "unconstitutionally vague and overbroad" and did not identify a prohibition against speaking at graduation as a potential consequence. The court also held that the discipline violated Matthew's First Amendment rights. Matthew was awarded $278 in damages, $12,750 in litigation costs and fees, and the school was ordered to allow Matthew to speak at graduation. On June 8, 1983, Matthew spoke at his high school graduation.

The school district appealed to the Court of Appeals for the Ninth Circuit. That court affirmed the District Court's decision, finding the speech did not disrupt the "educational process." Notably, the Court of Appeals found that permitting the school district to discipline students for such speech would result in providing the district with "'unbridled discretion' to determine what discourse is 'decent'" and that in so allowing, would "increase the risk of cementing white, middle-class standards for determining what is acceptable and proper speech and behavior in our public schools."

The Supreme Court reversed the Ninth Circuit's decision and upheld the school's authority to prohibit the use of language that was offensive and vulgar. The Court compared *Bethel* with *Tinker*, finding that Matthew Fraser's speech was not protected political speech. Rather, the First Amendment does not allow for student speech that is vulgar and lewd as such speech violates the "fundamental values of public school education."

The Supreme Court next considered the First Amendment rights of public school K-12 students in *Hazelwood v. Kuhlmeier* in 1988. The case involved high school students in a journalism class at Hazelwood East High School in St. Louis, Missouri, in 1983. The students wrote articles for the school newspaper, *Spectrum*, regarding other students' experiences with teen pregnancy and the impact of parental divorce.

The principal, Robert Reynolds, reviewed the articles the day before publication and determined the two articles regarding teen pregnancy and divorce would not be published due to inappropriate content. More specifically, Principal Reynolds believed the identity of the students in the article on teen pregnancy could be ascertained despite the use of pseudonyms. Principal Reynolds also believed the topics related to sex and birth control were inappropriate for the younger students. The article related to divorce was removed from publication because Principal Reynolds thought the parents who were the subject of the article should have been able to either respond or consent to the information shared. Principal Reynolds determined there was not enough time to revise the articles prior to publication. Accordingly, he removed two of the six proposed pages of the newspaper – including some material that was not related to student pregnancy or divorce – due to time constraints and the relative ease of removing full pages rather than individual articles.

Three students, including Cathy Kuhlmeier, commenced a lawsuit. The students claimed Principal Reynolds infringed on their First Amendment rights by withholding the articles from publication.

The District Court for the Eastern District of Missouri held that there was no First Amendment violation. The court borrowed from a decision from the *Eastern District of New York in Frasca v. Andrews* (1979), finding that school officials could restrict student speech when the activities are "an integral part of the school's educational function," provided the decision has "a substantial and reasonable basis." In *Hazelwood*, the paper was published as part of the school's journalism class, and so it was an integral part of the school's educational function. Principal Reynolds' concern for the privacy of other students was "legitimate and reasonable" – especially considering that the identity of the students could be easily ascertained. Principal Reynolds also acted within his authority when considering the mature topics in the articles that would be accessible to impressionable younger students. The topic related to the divorced parents was properly removed due to privacy considerations of the parties involved. Principal Reynolds' decision to remove two full pages – rather than just the articles at issue – was also found to be reasonable due to the short turnaround time for publication.

The Court of Appeals for the Eighth Circuit reversed the lower court's decision. That court found that the paper was "a part of the school adopted curriculum" within a public forum that was "intended to be and operated as a conduit for student viewpoint." Quoting *Tinker*, the Court of Appeals reasoned that as a public forum, school officials were prohibited from censoring the newspaper's contents unless "necessary to avoid material and substantial interference with school work or discipline...or the rights of others." There was no indication that the proposed articles would have caused a substantial disruption to the school.

The Supreme Court disagreed with the Court of Appeals and found in favor of the school district. Quoting *Bethel*, the Court found that public school students' First Amendment rights "are not automatically coextensive with the rights of adults in other settings." The Court disagreed that the newspaper was a public forum because the school district did not allow for the publishing or consumption of the paper for the general public. Rather, district policy defined the role of the paper as part of the school curriculum, and the paper was published through a journalism class at the school. The paper was also funded by the school. The Court identified a difference between tolerating student speech (as they ruled must be done in *Tinker*) and promoting student speech (which could be inferred had the articles been published in *Hazelwood*). Accordingly, student First Amendment rights are not infringed upon when the speech conflicts with a school's "legitimate pedagogical goals." Principal Reynolds removed the articles due to such legitimate pedagogical goals.

Our next Supreme Court decision was issued in 2007 in *Morse v. Frederick*. There, an 18-year-old student, Joseph Frederick, was late to school at Juneau-Douglas High School in Juneau, Alaska. That same day, the Olympic Torch Relay was passing through Juneau on its way to the 2002 Winter Olympics in Salt Lake City, Utah. Principal Deborah Morse allowed students and staff to observe the relay. Joseph joined his friends when he arrived to watch the event. Just as the torchbearers and news cameras passed by, Joseph and his friends held up a 14-foot banner that read: "BONG HiTS 4 JESUS." The banner was easily read by other students across the street. Principal Morse crossed the street and directed the students to take down the banner. All of the students complied, except for Joseph. Principal Morse subsequently suspended Joseph for ten days. Principal Morse said her rationale for the suspension was that the banner promoted illegal drug use in direct violation of school policy.

Joseph first appealed his suspension to the Superintendent, who upheld the suspension but limited it to the time served of eight days. The Superintendent found the school district had the authority to impose discipline because the actions took place during school hours at a school activity. Moreover, one could reasonably infer that "BONG HiTS 4 JESUS" was related to marijuana and promoted illegal drug use. Therefore, per the Superintendent, Joseph was suspended for promoting illegal drug use – and not due to the school "disagree[ing] with his message." Joseph's actions also "intrude[d] on the work of the schools" (a ruling from Fraser).

Joseph sued the school board and Principal Morse under Section 1983 – alleging they infringed on Joseph's First Amendment rights. The District Court issued a pre-trial ruling in favor of the defendants and found they were entitled to qualified immunity (a legal doctrine that protects government officials from personal liability in civil cases under certain circumstances) and did not infringe on Joseph's First Amendment rights. The District Court found that "Morse had the authority, if not the obligation, to stop such messages at a school-sanctioned activity."

On appeal, the Ninth Circuit reversed. Although the court agreed that Joseph's actions took place during a "school-authorized activity" and the banner promoted marijuana use, Joseph's First Amendment rights were violated because there was no evidence that his speech was likely to result in a substantial disruption to the school environment. The Ninth Circuit also found – unusually – that Principal Morse was not entitled to qualified immunity because she should have "understood that her actions were unconstitutional." This meant that, per the Ninth Circuit, Principal Morse could be held personally liable for her actions related to the banner.

The Supreme Court reversed the Ninth Circuit's decision. Joseph tried to argue this was not a school speech case as he was not in school at the time of the incident (he was late and did not yet "sign in" to school). The Supreme Court disagreed, finding the incident happened during school hours, at a school-sanctioned event, and school policy required students to comply with school rules at school events held off school grounds. Joseph was standing with other students and pointed the banner toward the school across the street. Therefore, the Supreme Court determined the proper analysis was the First Amendment rights afforded to public school students – rather than the First Amendment rights for the general public.

The Supreme Court observed that the message on the banner, while "cryptic," was "no doubt offensive to some, perhaps amusing to others." Joseph said the words were meaningless and only written to get the attention of the television cameras (he satisfied that objective). But the Supreme Court agreed with Principal Morse – finding that two reasonable interpretations of the banner could either be to promote the use of illegal drugs (by taking "bong hits") or to claim illegal drug use was worth celebrating ("bong hits [are a good thing]"). The Court also determined the message was not political – and so was not entitled to the same protections as the student speech/expression in *Tinker*. The Supreme Court ruled public schools may prohibit student expression that promotes illegal drug use when such expression is made at school events. The Court remanded to the Court of Appeals the question of whether Principal Morse was entitled to qualified immunity. But the parties reached a settlement prior to the lower court issuing a decision. Joseph was paid $45,000 to settle all remaining charges, and the school district hired a neutral constitutional expert to lead a forum on student speech at the Juneau-Douglas High School.

These Supreme Court decisions provide us with a foundation for analyzing public school students' First Amendment rights. From these decisions, we know the First Amendment protects student speech and conduct in narrow circumstances, such as a student expressing a political viewpoint that does not cause an actual or potential material and substantial disruption, and which is not vulgar, lewd, indecent, or which promotes illegal drugs. But students may be disciplined for speech or conduct that will "materially and substantially interfere with the requirements of appropriate discipline in the operation of the school" or "impinge upon the rights of others." Other cases throughout the country have further examined student First Amendment rights, as discussed below.

Other Student First Amendment Rights Decisions

All of the Supreme Court decisions above addressed student speech within the school setting (even *Morse v. Frederick*, despite the student's argument that his speech was not in the school setting). Schools have more authority to regulate student speech that occurs in the school setting as compared with student off-campus speech. However, such authority to regulate in-school speech has certain limitations.

The Second Circuit considered a student speech matter in the 2012 decision, *Cuff v. Valley Central School District*. The case involved a fifth-grade student who completed a class assignment that prompted students to write a "wish" on a picture of an astronaut. The student wrote that he wished to "blow up the school with the teachers in it." The student claimed he did not mean what he wrote on the picture; regardless, the school imposed a five-day out-of-school and one-day in-school suspension. The parents appealed to the school district's board of education, which upheld the suspension. The parents initiated a lawsuit, alleging the school violated the Student's First Amendment rights under Section 1983. The lower court granted summary judgment to the school district, finding that there was no dispute over the facts of the matter and the school was authorized to discipline the student for his drawing. The Second Circuit affirmed on appeal, ruling that there was no infringement of the student's First Amendment rights. The court applied the *Tinker* "substantial disruption" standard and determined school officials reasonably believed there could be a significant disruption based on the student's history of previous behaviors related to promoting violence and school personnel considering those incidents to be concerning. School officials also believed other students would engage in similar conduct if such threats were permitted. The court did not give weight to the student's claim that he did not intend to cause violence, based on previous Second Circuit decisions finding intent was irrelevant when related to student threats. Therefore, the student's suspension was upheld.

The First Amendment does not protect true threats of harm in schools. In *Lavine v. Blaine School District* (2001), a high school student from Washington State wrote a poem about a school shooter that was entitled "Last Words" and was about the killer's mindset. The student shared the poem with a teacher who believed it could be a true threat. The teacher shared the poem with the school psychologist who agreed it could be a true threat based on the student's history of suicidal ideation and other stressors in the student's life, including a physical altercation with his father and a recent breakup. The school imposed an emergency expulsion that was rescinded after 17 days. The court rejected the student's argument that the school violated his First Amendment rights, finding the school had a reasonable belief of a potential substantial disruption to the school setting when it imposed the emergency expulsion.

As demonstrated by *Tinker*, student political speech has particular protections. A recent decision out of Indiana, *E.D. v. Noblesville School District* (2025), explored such protections when a student wished to start a pro-life student club, Noblesville Students for Life, at her public high school. The school approved the student's request, and the student advertised the club at the school's activities fair, handed out pro-life materials, displayed pro-life signs, and wore a pro-life shirt. The student requested the administration's approval of other flyers to distribute that included images of signs with the words, "Defund Planned Parenthood" and "I am the Pro-Life Generation." Such flyers, if approved, would be initialed by school officials and placed in designated areas in the school. The administration denied approval for the flyers and encouraged the student to resubmit the flyers without the pictures for approval. The student's mother intervened and the administration then perceived the group to no longer be "student run" due to the mother's involvement and encouragement of the group. The school suspended the club for the remainder of the semester. The student reapplied, and the club was reinstated the following semester. The student initiated a lawsuit and posited that her First Amendment rights were violated. The court sided with the school, finding the message on the flyers could be perceived as the school's endorsement because they would be posted with other school-sponsored activities. Therefore, the school was within its authority to regulate the flyers in a greater manner than if the flyers had made it clear that the student was speaking only on her own behalf. The court also found the school had a legitimate educational purpose in the restriction due to the school's desire to "maintain neutrality on matters of political controversy." Finally, the court upheld the school's suspension of the club for the remainder of the semester because the school had a reasonable belief that the student's mother was leading the group and the student was insubordinate in attempting to reverse the school's initial decision to deny approval for the flyers.

In *Holloman v. Harland*, a 2004 case involving student political speech, Alabama high school student Michael Holloman was punished for raising his fist during the Pledge of Allegiance rather than reciting the Pledge with the rest of his class. A fellow student previously refused to say the Pledge of Allegiance, and the principal informed the student he had to apologize to his teacher and threatened to report that student's refusal to recite the

Pledge to his Air Force Academy recruiter and the Congressperson who recommended the student to the Academy. The principal also informed the students in Michael's class that they would be punished if they joined the other student's protest. Michael then raised his fist instead of putting his hand over his heart while the Pledge was recited the following day. The teacher reprimanded Michael in front of the class and said she was "disappointed" that Michael behaved "disrespectfully." Michael said he raised his fist "in protest of what happened" to the other student who refused to recite the Pledge. The principal imposed a three-day detention on Michael and said he would not receive his diploma until he served the detention. Michael was also required to apologize to the class. But there was not enough time left in the school year for Michael to serve the detention before graduation day. The principal instead offered a paddling as punishment, to which Michael agreed. Michael was paddled by the principal and permitted to attend his graduation.

The Eleventh Circuit examined whether Michael had First Amendment protections in refusing to recite the Pledge. Relying on *Tinker*, the court found Michael was entitled to such protections as his behavior did not cause a disruption. The court also relied on a 1943 Supreme Court decision, *West Virginia State Board of Education v. Barnette*, which held students could not be required to salute the American flag or recite the Pledge of Allegiance. Notably, the court found that neither the principal nor the teacher was entitled to qualified immunity, positing the law clearly established the right to express non-disruptive political beliefs in a school setting. Therefore, both the principal and the teacher could be held individually liable for the infringement of Michael's First Amendment rights.

Off-Campus/Social Media Speech

Student speech outside of school hours and/or that occurs off campus presents an increasingly frequent and unique challenge for schools. For example, students may make threats of harm to other students or the school community outside of school hours and off campus. Or students may violate the code of conduct with the language they use outside of school. Social media further complicates off-campus student speech and can cause significant harm to other students through cyberbullying. School administrators are left to determine whether they have the authority to enforce their codes of conduct for student speech that occurs outside of the confines of the school setting.

The general rule for student speech that occurs off campus and outside of school hours is that it is only actionable by the school if there is a nexus to the school, or the school can show it is reasonably foreseeable that the speech will reach the school. For example, in *Kowalski v. Berkeley County Schools* (2011), the Fourth Circuit determined a student may not be suspended for expression on the internet unless it would "materially and substantially disrupt the work and discipline of the school." This is consistent with the *Tinker* standard, which requires a school to show that the student speech either caused a material or substantial disruption to the school operations, or it is reasonably forecasted to cause such disruption.

Some off-campus student threats either do cause disruption or could be reasonably forecasted to cause such disruption. One such case, *McNeil v. Sherwood School District* (2019), involved a high school sophomore in Sherwood, Oregon who wrote a hit list at home of 23 students who "must die." The student's mother found the list and informed the student's therapist, who in turn informed the police (likely due to "*Tarasoff*" duty to warn obligations), who subsequently informed the school. The school notified the parents of the 23 named students in accordance with Oregon state law. The media reported on the story, and the school district issued a press release providing limited information on the matter. The school was contacted by parents, the media, and the public with concerns related to the list.

The school suspended the student for one year. Relevant factors in determining whether this was a credible threat included "the nature of the hit list, [the student's] access to firearms, and the close proximity of [the student's] home to the high school." The student sued and alleged the suspension infringed his First Amendment rights. The lower District Court upheld the suspension. The Ninth Circuit affirmed, ruling the student had no First Amendment protections for the hit list because there was a reasonable nexus between the student's speech and a disruption to the school setting. The court used the following test to reach its decision – stating that such "test is flexible and fact specific, but the relevant considerations will include: (1) the degree and likelihood of harm to the school caused or augured by the speech…(2) whether it was reasonably foreseeable that the speech would reach and impact the school…and (3) the relation between the content and context of the speech and the school."

McNeil provides a set of facts that arguably did cause a substantial disruption to the school – the families of 23 students learned their children were threatened, and those threats were determined to be potentially credible. The story was picked up by the media and the situation caused school administration to field concerns from numerous parents and community members. Other factors that could lead to a substantial disruption include taking significant administrator time to investigate, a police investigation, a lockdown, and/or school closures. One example came out of *Pennsylvania in A.N. v. Upper Perkiomen School District* (2017). There, the court found a substantial disruption to the school when a student posted a video online, outside of the school day, about school shootings, which led to a police investigation and the school's closure.

In contrast to the facts in *McNeil*, courts do not uphold restrictions on student off-campus speech when there is no nexus between the speech and the school setting. In *Layshock v. Hermitage School District* (2011), twelfth-grade student Justin Layshock created a fake Myspace profile of his principal that was mocking and demeaning to the principal. The school imposed a 10-day suspension, ordered the student to finish high school in an alternative education program, and forbade the student from graduating with his class. The student sued. The District Court found the suspension to be unconstitutional. On appeal, the Third Circuit agreed the school violated the student's First Amendment rights, finding: "we do not think the First Amendment can tolerate the School District stretching its authority into Justin's grandmother's home and reaching Justin while he is sitting at her computer after school in order to punish him for the expressive conduct that he engaged in there." Note, however, that other courts have reached different conclusions with similar facts.

In *Snyder v. Blue Mountain School District* (2011), the Third Circuit upheld the suspension of a student who created a fake Myspace profile of a middle school principal when the profile included sexually explicit, false, and defamatory language. That court held that, "The Constitution allows school officials the ability to regulate student speech where it reaches beyond mere criticism to significantly undermine a school official's authority in challenging his fitness to hold his position by means of baseless, lewd, vulgar, and offensive language."

The Supreme Court recently considered student First Amendment rights related to off-campus speech in the 2021 case, *Mahanoy Area School District v. B.L.* B.L. was a 14-year-old student at Mahanoy Area High School in Pennsylvania who tried out for the varsity cheerleading team. As part of the cheerleading requirements, B.L. agreed to "respect" the school and individuals who were part of the cheerleading team, refrain from "foul language and inappropriate gestures" related to being on the team, in addition to refraining from "any negative information regarding cheerleading, cheerleaders, or coaches…on the internet." B.L. did not make the varsity team but was accepted to the junior varsity team. She then posted two photos to her Snapchat – the first of which was a photo of B.L. and her friend holding up their middle fingers and the words, "fuck school fuck softball fuck cheer fuck everything." The second picture was related to B.L. not making the team and an upside-down smiley face emoji. The images could only be viewed for 24 hours by B.L.'s "friends" on Snapchat. But one of the friends, who was the daughter of one of the cheerleading coaches, showed the posts to the coaches. The photos also spread throughout the students at school, caused other students to be upset, and resulted in some chatter among the students in class.

The coaches determined the posts violated the cheerleading rules and suspended B.L. from the junior varsity cheerleading team. The principal, superintendent, and school board upheld the decision. B.L.'s parents sued in the Middle District of Pennsylvania, alleging the school infringed B.L.'s

First Amendment rights and the cheerleading rules were overly broad and unconstitutionally vague. The court granted an injunction to allow B.L. to be on the junior varsity cheerleading team while the court considered the merits of the case. The court then granted B.L.'s motion for summary judgment – meaning, the court decided in B.L.'s favor without a trial. The U.S. Court of Appeals for the Third Circuit affirmed. The school district appealed to the Supreme Court.

The Supreme Court decided in B.L.'s favor. Although there is not a total prohibition against schools regulating off-campus speech, the Supreme Court found that in this situation, the school did not have the authority to regulate B.L.'s off-campus speech. The Court applied the standards created by the foundational Supreme Court cases related to student speech which only allowed student speech to be regulated in three circumstances: "(1) indecent, lewd, or vulgar speech on school grounds [*Bethel*], (2) speech promoting illicit drug use during a class trip [*Morse*], and (3) speech that others may reasonably perceive as 'bear[ing] the imprimatur of the school,' such as that appearing in a school-sponsored newspaper [*Hazelwood*]." The Court also identified that *Tinker* allowed for speech to be regulated when it "materially disrupts classwork or involves substantial disorder or invasion on the rights of others."

The Court opined that off-campus speech, such as B.L.'s Snapchat posts made while she was off campus, is generally under the purview of the parent, and not the school. Moreover, allowing a school to regulate off-campus speech in the same manner as on-campus speech would result in students having highly regulated speech in all circumstances. The Court also posited that the school has an interest in allowing for student free speech off campus "because the free marketplace of ideas is a cornerstone of our representative democracy."

The Court ultimately found that it was B.L.'s parents who had an interest in addressing her speech, rather than the school. The Snapchat posts did not cause a substantial disruption at school or threaten the rights of others. Her speech was therefore protected by the First Amendment, and the school did not have the authority to discipline B.L. for the Snapchat posts.

Since *Mahanoy*, we may be seeing a shift in how courts examine the authority of a school district to discipline students for off-campus speech. The Second Circuit considered this issue in 2025 in *Leroy v. Livingston Manor Central School District*, where a New York high school student posted to social media a picture with his friend kneeling on his neck and the words, "Cops got another." This picture was not posted during school hours or on the school's campus. The student reported he intended the picture to be a joke, but he removed it after a few minutes upon realizing it could be considered racist and based on the murder of George Floyd by a police officer.

Another student took a screenshot of the picture before it was removed, and the photograph was posted on other social media accounts. This resulted in indignation from the community, a school investigation, a student protest, and class discussions. The student was suspended for the remainder of the year.

The student sued, and the school district argued the off-campus social media post caused a substantial disruption and, as a result, was not protected speech. The lower District Court sided with the school district. But the Second Circuit reversed after applying the *Mahanoy* standard and considering "(1) the nature of [the student's] speech;" (2) "where, when, and how he spoke," and (3) "the school's interests in regulating the speech." The court found that the post was not a true threat that would be excluded from First Amendment protections, despite other students reporting that the post caused them to feel unsafe. The court also found that the "where, when, and how" of the post was only shared with the student's private Snapchat friends, posted outside of school, and off campus. The post did not mention the school or a particular student at the school and was posted using the student's personal cell phone. The court determined the school's interests in regulating the speech were the same as in *Mahanoy*, and such interests were insufficient to justify the discipline imposed on the student. The court disagreed with the school district's argument that the student's actions created a substantial disruption that was sufficient to outweigh the student's First Amendment rights. Importantly, the court acknowledged that it was not creating a bright-line rule in determining whether a student's off-campus speech may be disciplined by their school district; rather, such issues should be considered on a case-by-case basis.

Would *Mahanoy* and *Leroy* have different outcomes if the nature of the social media postings were different? Neither post was threatening in nature. But what if a student posted to his Snapchat on Saturday night a picture of the student holding what appeared to be a firearm and the words, "Everybody get your cams out at school on Monday. I'm going viral." Would this be considered a threat that would warrant the school's interest in regulating the speech? What if the student was known to be in a significant mental health crisis and recently identified as high risk for engaging in violent behavior from threat assessments conducted by the school? Would that increase the ability of the school to discipline the student for the social media posting? Would there be a different outcome if it turned out the student was holding an airsoft rifle that merely looked like a firearm? Or what if the student later told the school he did not intend his words to be a threat? What if 15% of the student population did not go to school on Monday due to fears of potential violence because of the student's post, and school administration spent the entire day on Monday fielding calls from concerned parents, meeting with law enforcement, organizing mental health teams to support frightened students, and issuing a statement to the community? Would this be sufficient to consider the student's post to cause a substantial disruption to the school setting? These questions demonstrate that the facts and circumstances matter in analyzing whether a school has the authority to address student social media speech that is made off campus.

Student Freedom of Expression and Dress

Student dress codes are also subject to a First Amendment analysis. Schools routinely develop and enforce dress codes for students for various reasons, such as equating orderly dress with orderly learning, avoiding class distinctions through dress, etc. There was significant litigation related to student dress in the 1960s and 1970s.[3] But the Supreme Court has never accepted a case involving student dress or grooming, causing us to look to lower courts for legal standards related to dress codes.

Dress codes may not be vague or overly broad. For example, in *Newsom v. Albemarle County School Board* (2003), the Fourth Circuit found that a Virginia school district's dress code was overly restrictive as it prohibited "messages on clothing, jewelry, and personal belongings that relate to weapons." A sixth-grade student wore a t-shirt with three individuals holding firearms, the letters "NRA," and the phrase "SHOOTING SPORTS CAMP." The student agreed to turn the shirt inside out after a conversation with the assistant principal. The student subsequently filed a lawsuit, alleging his First Amendment rights were infringed upon by being instructed to turn his shirt inside out and that the dress code was overly broad. The court agreed and ruled that the dress code could not outright ban any reference to firearms, as that would include the wearing of lawful clothing depicting firearms, such as clothing related to military service.

A court is more likely to uphold a dress code's enforcement when it is viewpoint neutral. In *Palmer v. Waxahachie Independent School District* (2009), the Fifth Circuit upheld a code of conduct's ban of any printed messages on student clothing, with the exception of school-sponsored clothing. There, a high school sophomore wore a shirt with the words "San Diego." The assistant principal directed the student to change his shirt as the dress code prohibited any words on clothing. The student's parents then brought the student a "John Edwards for President '08" shirt to wear instead. The student was again not permitted to wear that shirt because it contained a printed message. The court rejected the student's claim that the school violated his First Amendment rights as the school allowed student speech by "other mediums during the school day" and the dress code did "not restrict student dress outside of school."

Federal law, such as Title IX (which prohibits sex-based discrimination) and the U.S. Constitution's Equal Protection Clause from the Fourteenth Amendment, is typically interpreted to require dress codes to be gender neutral. This means that although it is permissible to have a dress code enforcing skirt length, for example, the language in the code cannot be gender-specific by specifying that only female students have restrictions on skirt length. Rather, any student who wears a skirt must adhere to the length requirements regardless of the student's gender. This issue was considered in *Peltier v. Charter Day School* in 2021, where a North Carolina public charter school enacted a dress code requiring girls to wear skirts, skorts, or jumpers and allowing boys to wear pants or shorts. Several students and their parents filed a lawsuit, alleging the code was discriminatory and reinforced gender stereotypes. The Fourth Circuit agreed, finding the skirt requirement violated the Equal Protection Clause of the Constitution as it placed a burden on female students and impermissibly promoted gender stereotypes. The court also determined the requirement violated Title IX as the sex-based dress code was discriminatory on the basis of sex.

Consider this scenario. A high school student, Freya, believes strongly in the Black Lives Matter movement. She wears a Black Lives Matter patch on her backpack and has her backpack with her throughout the day, so the patch is highly visible to the school community. A group of students is offended by Freya's patch and has started wearing Blue Lives Matter patches on their backpacks. Freya finds this to be offensive. Are Freya's actions protected by the First Amendment? What about the other students?

A frequently cited decision on student First Amendment rights related to dress and political speech is the Second Circuit's 2006 case, *Guiles v. Marineau*. There, Zachary Guiles was a student at Williamstown Middle High School in Vermont. He wore a shirt to school in protest of then-President George W. Bush that included a picture of the President on the body of a chicken with images of drugs and alcohol. Zachary wore the shirt several times over a few weeks. A parent complaint resulted in a school employee asking Zachary to cover the parts of the shirt related to drugs and alcohol, turn the shirt inside out, or wear a different shirt. The school employee's request was pursuant to the school's dress code that prohibited clothing that was distracting or displayed drugs or alcohol. Zachary refused, was issued a discipline referral and sent home. Zachary returned to school with the same shirt, but with the drugs and alcohol covered by duct tape with the word "censored."

Zachary sued the school, asking for an order that would prevent the school from imposing the dress code policy against him, and that the discipline referral be expunged from his record. The District Court ruled in favor of the school officials, finding under *Bethel* that the shirt was "plainly offensive or inappropriate" and the school had the authority to enforce its dress code policy. But the District Court also ordered that the discipline referral be expunged. Both Zachary and the school officials appealed to the Second Circuit. The Second Circuit reversed, finding that the images on the shirt were permissible because they were not lewd, vulgar, or indecent, and did not disrupt the educational process. Rather, the images on the shirt constituted the student's political message.

In *B.H. v. Easton Area School District* (2013), the Third Circuit considered a student dress code violation when two students wore a breast cancer awareness bracelet with the words "I ♥ boobies! (Keep a Breast)". The school district suspended the students and banned them from wearing the bracelets. The court disagreed with the school district's argument that the bracelets were lewd, vulgar, or disruptive under *Bethel*. The bracelets did not cause a substantial disruption under *Tinker*. Rather, the bracelets were intended to address the social issue of breast cancer. Accordingly, the Third Circuit found in favor of the students and held that their First Amendment rights allowed them to wear the bracelets.

A recent decision from Massachusetts also considered student political speech (or, one could argue, discriminatory speech) in the context of dress in *L.M. v. Town of Middleborough*, Massachusetts (2024). The issue was related to a student's right to wear a shirt with the words, "There Are Only Two Genders," at his middle school. The student was told he could not wear that shirt and then returned to school one month later with the words "Only Two" covered by tape with the word "Censored" written on the tape. The student was disciplined because administration believed the words violated the dress code, which provided: "Clothing must not state, imply, or depict hate speech or imagery that target[s] groups based on race, ethnicity, gender, sexual orientation, gender identity, religious affiliation, or any other classification…" The student was previously permitted to wear other clothing that depicted his political beliefs, including "First Amendment Rights" and "Don't Tread on Me." The student's parents sued, claiming that the punishment violated the student's First Amendment rights. The lower District Court upheld the school's decision by applying the *Tinker* standard and finding the shirt "invade[d] the rights of others." The First Circuit affirmed, finding the shirt could "poison the educational atmosphere" as it was reasonable to believe the shirt would "negatively affect the psychology of young students with the demeaned gender identities." The student was therefore not afforded First Amendment protections for the shirt, and his suspension was upheld.

Other decisions related to student dress tell us that context matters. In *Dariano v. Morgan Hill Unified School District* (2014), a school principal prohibited students from wearing American flag shirts on Cinco de Mayo. The events took place on May 5, 2010, at Live Oak High School in the Morgan Hill Unified School District in Northern California. The school was planning a Cinco de Mayo celebration. According to school officials, this was similar to St. Patrick's Day and Oktoberfest celebrations that were also held at the school. But there was a history of gang-related and racial violence at the school – especially between Caucasian and Latino students. These issues resulted in an estimated 30 fights in six years, and a police officer stationed at the school every day. The previous violence included an altercation between Caucasian and Latino students on Cinco de Mayo the previous year. At that altercation, some students hung an American flag and chanted "USA" while both sides of students shouted profanities and threats at each other.

The following year, a group of Caucasian students wore American flag shirts to school on Cinco de Mayo. Some of those students were confronted by other students related to the shirts, including threats of a physical altercation later in the school day. School administration directed students to either turn their American flag shirts inside out or take them off. The students refused. The administrators explained that it was due to a safety concern and directed students with prominent American flags on their shirts to either turn their shirts inside out or go home for the day with excused absences. Some of the students were threatened the following day and did not go to school on May 7 because of those threats.

The students who were not permitted to wear American flag shirts sued the school and administrators, alleging their First Amendment rights were violated (among other allegations under federal and state law). The District Court found the students' First Amendment rights were not violated. The students appealed to the Ninth Circuit, which affirmed the lower court's decision. The Ninth Circuit determined the administrators' actions were reasonable to protect student safety due to the credible threats of violence. The Supreme Court denied the students' request for review. This case demonstrates that an action that would typically be seen as neutral or even political (and thus, typically protected) – wearing an American flag shirt – could be restricted when determined necessary to prevent reasonably forecasted violence.

Other decisions identify that the type of flag worn could make a difference. More specifically, decisions have consistently held that the wearing of a Confederate flag may be prohibited due to its controversial history. In *Hardwick v. Heyward* (2013), the Fourth Circuit upheld the authority of a South Carolina school to ban students from wearing clothing depicting controversial symbols, such as the Confederate flag, when it could be reasonably forecasted to cause a substantial disruption in the school environment. Similarly, a Texas school's dress code provision stating, "no tolerance for clothing or accessories that have inappropriate symbolism, especially that which discriminates against other students based on race, religion or sex" was upheld by the Fifth Circuit in *A.M. on behalf of McAllum v. Cash* (2009). Specifically, the court found the school district permissibly prohibited student displays of the Confederate flag at school.

Let us go back to Freya's situation. Wearing the Black Lives Matter patch is likely considered protected political speech. But similarly, the students wearing Blue Lives Matter patches are also protected under the First Amendment. It is irrelevant that Freya and the other students feel offended by each other's actions. Feeling offended is not a reason to limit another individual's First Amendment rights. But it is possible the wearing of the patches could be restricted if it were reasonably foreseeable that they would cause a substantial disruption to the school. For example, school administration could direct students not to have the patches at school if they learn that Freya is planning on forcibly removing the Blue Lives Matter patches from her classmates or that a group of students is planning on attacking Freya in the restroom because of the patch. Such actions could cause a significant disruption to the school setting and result in the political speech no longer being protected by the First Amendment. But regardless, educators are in a unique position to use these situations as learning experiences for students, including understanding and respecting divergent viewpoints.

Litigation related to student dress and First Amendment rights also applies to student hairstyles. In *Olff v. East Side Union High School District* (1972), the Ninth Circuit ruled that a school could not refuse to allow a male student to attend school due to having long hair, despite the student's hair length violating the school policy. Rather, a student's hair length is protected by the First Amendment. But other cases have reached different conclusions. For example, in *George v. Abbott* (2025), a high school student was disciplined for wearing long locs in violation of the school dress code. The student argued the discipline violated his Constitutional rights and a Texas law called the Crown Act, which prohibits discrimination on the basis of hair texture or protective styles. The case was ultimately dismissed in federal court after two years of litigation. The court ruled the school district had permissible interests for regulating hairstyles as they were "substantially related to career readiness" and based on a recent study indicating such requirements were linked to higher school ratings and lower disciplinary infractions and dropouts. The Supreme Court has not yet considered the permissibility of school districts to regulate student hair as part of a dress code, and therefore, no federal standard currently exists.

Student First Amendment Rights and Freedom of Religion

Student First Amendment rights also protect their freedom of religion under the Free Exercise Clause, which allows for an individual to freely practice their religion, and the Establishment Clause, which prohibits the government from establishing a religion and requires the separation of church and state. This can create unique issues within a public school setting as a public school is considered a government entity. The Supreme Court applied the First Amendment to invalidate a state law that required prayer in schools in the 1962 decision, *Engel v. Vitale*. New York State law mandated that schools lead a voluntary prayer and the Pledge of Allegiance each morning, but the Court ruled the prayer violated the Establishment Clause. This applied regardless of students having the discretion to determine whether to participate in the prayer and the prayer being nondenominational.

The historical test for whether a government entity violates the Establishment Clause was previously provided by the Supreme Court decision *Lemon v. Kutzman* (1971) – also called the "Lemon Test." Under Lemon, a government's actions were considered constitutional if they (1) did not have a religious purpose; (2) had a "principal or primary effect...that neither advances nor inhibits religion"; and (3) did "not foster 'an excessive government entanglement with religion.'" The Supreme Court applied the Lemon Test to prohibit prayer at school-sponsored activities, such as graduation ceremonies in *Lee v. Weisman* (1992). But Lemon has also been interpreted as allowing religious movies to be shown on public school property outside of school hours in *Lamb's Chapel v. Center Moriches Union Free School District* (1993). The Supreme Court appears to be moving away from the Lemon Test. In 2022, the Court considered the constitutionality of a football coach saying a prayer on the field after games in *Kennedy v. Bremerton School District* (2022). There, the Court upheld the coach's right to offer a post-game prayer on the field, finding the First Amendment may neither require nor prohibit an individual from exercising their religion. The coach's prayer was not related to his duties as an employee; rather, the prayer was a private action because it was after the game concluded. Through Kennedy, the Supreme Court adopted a test that seeks to identify "historical practices and understandings," rather than using the Lemon Test, to determine whether the Establishment Clause was violated. This shift in framework emphasizes what has traditionally been considered a permissible exercise of religion in a public setting.

Although a public school must adhere to the separation of church and state and cannot lead prayer in school, students are permitted to pray during non-instructional time. This was addressed in the Elementary and Secondary Education Act (ESEA), which included a provision that withheld federal funds if a public school district prohibited students from participating in "constitutionally protected school prayer" in a manner that violated Education Department guidelines. This resulted in the Federal Education Department issuing such guidelines on "Constitutionally Protected Prayer and Religious Expression in Public Elementary and Secondary Schools."[4] The guidance explicitly allows students to pray and read religious materials at school, provided doing so does not cause a material disruption to the learning environment.

Although students are permitted to pray in school, courts have consistently found that students may not lead others in organized prayer during school hours. A Mississippi District Court found in *Herdahl v. Pontotoc County School District* (1995) that the Establishment Clause was violated when a student club was permitted to share prayers and readings from the Bible over the loudspeaker during morning announcements, and student-led prayers were permitted in classrooms during school hours. The students were members of the "Aletheia Club," which was formerly known as the "Christ in Us Club." Most of the prayers ended with the phrase, "in Jesus Christ, Amen." The lawsuit was initiated by the mother of five students who attended the school district whose children were exempt from participating in the prayer and were escorted out of the classroom before the prayers began. The court found the students were in a prohibited "captive audience" situation as the prayers were broadcast throughout the school building. The prayer did not have a secular purpose and had the effect of the school district endorsing a particular religious practice, which therefore violated the First Amendment.

The Supreme Court considered the Constitutional right of students to engage in religious groups on campus in *Widmar v. Vincent* (1981). The Court held that a public university could not refuse to allow its student religious group to use campus facilities when non-religious groups were permitted to use such facilities. This decision directly led to the adoption of the Equal Access Act in 1984, which is a federal law that ensures public secondary schools provide equal opportunities for religious, political, or philosophical clubs and for other clubs when those schools receive federal funds and operate a limited open forum. A limited open forum is created when a school allows other noncurricular clubs to be established at school. The Equal Access Act was upheld in *Board of Education v. Mergens* (1990). A public high school prohibited students from forming a religious club, citing the Establishment Clause and requirement for separation of church and state, in addition to there being no faculty advisor for the club. The Supreme Court found the administration's actions to be unconstitutional because the school allowed for other noncurricular clubs, so the school was required to allow a religious noncurricular club. The club was permissible under the Establishment Clause because it was not required for students to participate, it was not taught in class, it was not otherwise related to the curriculum, and members did not receive credit for their participation.

A public school may also not require a student to participate in certain activities when those activities violate the student's religious beliefs. The Supreme Court considered this issue in 1943 in *West Virginia State Board of Education v. Barnette*. The public school district required its students to salute the flag and say the Pledge of Allegiance. But a family argued this violated the Establishment Clause due to their Jehovah's Witness faith. The Supreme Court agreed, finding public school students could not be compelled to salute the flag, and the school's requirement to do so violated the First Amendment.

Another case in California examined whether including a yoga program in the physical education curriculum infringed on a student's religious rights and therefore violated the Establishment Clause in the 2014 decision, *Sedlock v. Baird*. Parents initiated a lawsuit and claimed their children's participation in the mandatory yoga program was against their religion and violated the Establishment Clause. The state court disagreed and applied the Lemon Test to determine the yoga program was secular, did not advance or inhibit religion, and did "not excessively entangle the school district in religion." Therefore, the yoga program did not violate the students' First Amendment rights.

It is possible the decision in *Sedlock* would be different if considered today since the Supreme Court of the United States' 2025 decision, *Mahmoud v. Taylor*. There, the Supreme Court considered the constitutionality of a Maryland school district's use of LGBTQ+ books as part of its curriculum. Parents of various religious backgrounds, including Muslim, Roman Catholic, and Ukrainian Orthodox, sued and asserted they should have the right to opt their children out of participating in "LGBTQ+-inclusive" curriculum when such curriculum violated their religious beliefs and rights as parents. The Supreme Court agreed, finding a public school could not interfere with a parent's right to direct their child's religious upbringing. Accordingly, requiring the LGBTQ+-expansive books as part of the curriculum – without a parental opt-out option – violated the Free Exercise Clause of the First Amendment. It is too early to know the impact of *Mahmoud* as of the writing of this book; however, absent other legal developments, most public schools are narrowly interpreting the decision to apply only to the rights of parents to opt their children out of reading required books in the curriculum that may interfere with a student's religion.

Conclusion

There are several considerations when determining whether student speech or expression should be limited in a public school setting. First, it is important to consider student intent. Students may not be disciplined for speech or conduct with the purpose of expressing a political viewpoint or opinion and when there is no concern for a material and substantial disruption. But a student may be disciplined for speech or conduct that demeans or threatens certain individuals or groups; for conduct that may promote illegal drug use; school-sponsored speech; and when the speech is vulgar, lewd, or indecent. A key question is whether the student speech/expression demeans certain individuals or groups or disrupts the educational environment. But in the absence of one of the exceptions, school officials may not prohibit or discipline students for expressing personal, political, or religious views or opinions at school.

There are some suggested best practices for educators in upholding student First Amendment rights. It is useful to be aware of relevant state laws and the school code of conduct to understand the limits of enforcing student freedom of expression. School officials should also be aware of the current status of relevant cases within their jurisdiction, as cases like

Mahanoy may indicate student First Amendment rights are broader than previously understood. But even if student expression is protected by the First Amendment, it can still have a significant impact when directed at individuals or otherwise impacts the safety or well-being of the school community. Accordingly, schools may want to consider implementing a curriculum to support students in making good choices related to their speech and other forms of expression, including social media. Similarly, using conflict resolution methods – rather than discipline – may be more defensible in addressing student expression directed toward other students or school officials that does not rise to creating, or potentially creating, a substantial disruption to the school setting.

Notes

1 Ronald Reagan Presidential Library and Museum. (n.d.). *Constitutional Amendments – Amendment 1 – "The Freedom of Speech."* https://www.reaganlibrary.gov/constitutional-amendments-amendment-1-freedom-speech.
2 "Text of speech made by student for nomination." (1986, March 2). *Los Angeles Times*. https://www.latimes.com/archives/la-xpm-1986-03-02-mn-1388-story.html.
3 Ahrens, D. M., & Siegel, A. M. (2019). Of dress and Redress: Student Dress Restrictions in Constitutional Law and Culture. *Harvard Civil Rights-Civil Liberties Law Review*, 54(49), 49–106. https://journals.law.harvard.edu/crcl/wp-content/uploads/sites/80/2019/03/AhrensSiegel.pdf
4 United States Department of Education. (n.d.). *Guidance on Constitutionally Protected Prayer and Religious Expression in Public Elementary and Secondary Schools*. https://www.ed.gov/laws-and-policy/laws-preschool-grade-12-education/preschool-grade-12-policy-documents/guidance-on-constitutionally-protected-prayer-and-religious-expression-in-public-elementary-and-secondary-schools.

List of Cases

A.M. ex rel. McAllum v. Cash, 585 F.3d 214, 223 (5th Cir. 2009).
A.N. v. Upper Perkiomen School District, 228 F. Supp. 3d 391 (E.D. Pa. 2017).
Bartels v. Iowa, 262 U.S. 404 (1923).
Bethel v. Fraser, 478 U.S. 675 (1986).
B.H. v. Easton Area School District, 725 F.3D 293 (3d Cir. 2013).
Board of Education of Westside Community School v. Mergens, 496 U.S 226 (1990).
Cohen v. California, 403 U.S. 15 (1971).
Cuff ex rel. B.C. v. Valley Central School District, 677 F.3d 109 (2d Cir. 2012).
Dariano v. Morgan Hill Unified School District, 745 F.3d 354 (9th Cir. 2014).
E.D. v. Noblesville School District, No. 24-1608 (7th Cir. 2025).
Engel v. Vitale, 370 U.S. 421 (1962).
Frasca v. Andrews, 463 F.Supp. 1043 (E.D.N.Y. 1979).
George v. Abbott, 2025 WL 1685239 (S.D. Tex. 2025).
Guiles v. Marineau, 461 F.3d 320 (2d Cir. 2006).
Hardwick ex rel. Hardwick v. Heyward, 711 F.3d 426, 436 (4th Cir 2013).
Hazelwood School District v. Kuhlmeier, 484 U.S. 260 (1988).

Herdahl v. Pontotoc County School District, 887 F. Supp. 902 (S.D. Miss. 1995).
Holloman ex rel. Holloman v. Harland, 370 F.3d 1252 (11th Cir. 2004).
J.S. ex rel. Snyder v. Blue Mountain School District, 650 F.3d 915 (3d. Cir. 2011).
Kennedy v. Bremerton School District, 597 U.S. (2022).
Kowalski v. Berkeley County Schools, 652 F.3d 565 (4th Cir. 2011).
Lamb's Chapel v. Center Moriches Union Free School District, 508 U.S. 384 (1993).
Lavine v. Blaine School District, 257 F.3d 981 (9th Cir. 2001).
Layshock v. Hermitage School District, 650 F.3d 205 (3d Cir. 2011).
Lee v. Weisman, 505 U.S. 577 (1992).
Lemon v. Kutzman, 403 U.S. 602 (1971).
Leroy v. Livingston Manor Central School District, 158 F.4th 414 (2025).
L.M. v. Town of Middleborough, Massachusetts, No. 23-1535 (1st Cir. 2024).
Mahanoy Area School District v. B.L., 594 U.S. ___ (2021).
Mahmoud v. Taylor, 606 U.S. ___ (2025).
McNeil v. Sherwood School District (9th Cir. 2019).
Meyer v. Nebraska, 262 U.S. 390 (1923).
Morse v. Frederick, 551 U.S. 393 (2007).
Newsom v. Albemarle County School Board, 354 F.3d 249 (4th Cir. 2003).
Olff v. East Side Union High School District, 404 U.S. 1042 (1972).
Palmer v. Waxahachie Independent School District, 579 F.4d 502 (5th Cir. 2009).
Peltier v. Charter Day School, 9 F.4th 251 (4th Cir. 2021).
Sedlock v. Baird, 235 Cal. App. 4th 874 (Cal. App. 2015).
Tinker v. Des Moines Independent Community School District, 393 U.S. 503 (1969).
West Virginia State Board of Education v. Barnette, 319 U.S. 624 (1943).
Widmar v. Vincent, 454 U.S. 263 (1981).

Laws Cited

Civil Action for Deprivation of Rights, 42 U.S.C. § 1983.
Creating a Respectful and Open World for Natural Hair Act, 88(2) Tex. Sess. Law ch. 567 (2023).
Elementary and Secondary Education Act of 1965, 20 U.S.C. § 6301 et seq.
Equal Access Act of 1984; 20 U.S.C. § 4071.
Title IX of the Education Amendments of 1972, 34 C.F.R. § 106.
U.S. Const. Amends. I and XIV.

3 Educator Liability

Shirley A. Woika

Imagine that you are a teacher in your second year of practice. A student in your fourth-grade classroom trips over the carpet in the back of your classroom and falls hard, knocking out his front tooth. The child is sent to the nurse's office, and parents are called. The mother arrives at the school to pick up her child and is very upset. She tells the nurse to expect to hear from her attorney. The nurse informs the principal of the mother's statement, and the principal stops by your classroom at the end of the day. She informs you that this parent has a history of complaints with the school and asks you to ensure that you are thorough and complete in filing the required Accident/Injury on School Grounds form.

From what you can recall of your limited knowledge of school law, you are very concerned. You remember from your mandated reporter training that the loss of a permanent tooth is considered a permanent loss. You are fearful that this child has suffered a permanent loss for which you will be held responsible. Thoughts flood your mind. Will I be held personally responsible, or will the district shoulder some of the blame? Could I lose my job and end up unemployable because of this injury? Will the school district defend me? Should I get a lawyer? Did I do anything wrong?

Scenarios like this are common in schools. By the end of this chapter, you will understand the issues involved and your potential liability risk.

Legal Literacy in Schools

In 2007, David Schimmel and Matthew Militello[1] reported the results of a legal literacy survey conducted with more than 1,300 teachers in K-12 schools across seventeen states. The legal scenarios presented in the survey pertained to issues that had been clearly resolved by the courts for more than a decade. For example, one item asked if teachers could be found liable for a student injury caused by a teacher while breaking up a fight. Another asked whether teachers could be held liable for any student injury that occurs when students are left unsupervised.

DOI: 10.4324/9781003728993-4

Overall, the findings indicated that teachers had not taken a course in school law and were either uninformed or misinformed about their rights as educators and those of students. Educators were left feeling fearful and anxious about legal issues in schools. If they make a single error, they fear they will ruin their professional careers, lose their jobs, be sued for an innocent error, and lose their homes if found liable for an injury.

Liability

The term liability is used by people all the time, but what is the legal definition of liability? Liability refers to the legal responsibility for actions or failures to act that result in harm, injury, or financial loss to another. *Civil liability* focuses on compensation for injured parties, whereas *criminal liability* focuses on punishing unlawful conduct. The standard of proof required to show liability differs in civil and criminal cases. Civil cases require proof by a *preponderance of the evidence*. This standard of proof indicates that the defendant is more likely than not responsible for the injury. Criminal cases require proof *beyond a reasonable doubt*, a much higher standard. Individuals may face both a civil lawsuit filed by the injured party and a criminal prosecution by the state or federal government arising from the same incident.

Tort law is a branch of civil law that focuses on wrongful injuries. The legal term tort is defined as a wrong that is committed by one person against another person or another person's property that results in harm. It is a breach of a duty owed, but not a breach of contract. Although laws vary by state, there are legal remedies for tort claims, including monetary compensation when the injury results from unreasonable conduct. A tort is not a criminal matter, although a specific action could be both a tort and a crime. A tort is a civil matter in which the injured persons sue the wrongdoers to make up for their losses. A civil matter is between individuals, whereas a criminal matter involves charges brought by the government, which represents the public against the accused. Monetary damages in civil suits are typically sought for physical injury, property damage, emotional distress, and loss of income.

There are three main types of torts: intentional interference, strict liability, and negligence. As the name implies, intentional torts are committed with intent. An example of intentional interference would be assault and battery. An example from the school setting could involve the use of corporal punishment, such as paddling a student. The tortfeasor, or person who commits the tort, is deliberately trying to harm the injured person. Other examples of intentional interference include false imprisonment or defamation.

Strict liability applies when an activity is inherently dangerous. Animal attacks and defective products are examples in which strict liability may be involved. In such cases, liability is considered *strict* or *absolute*, even when negligence or direct fault cannot be proven, and there was no intent to harm. Suppose a school custodian unknowingly combines toilet bowl cleaner and Clorox when cleaning. The resulting chlorine gas can cause asphyxiation and chemical burns. If students are injured, strict liability would apply.

Negligence and strict liability differ. In strict liability cases, the dangerousness of the activity or the product is central to the claim, rather than the school's fault or intent. The person harmed by negligence must prove that the school failed to exercise reasonable care.

Consider an example in the school setting. Participating in a contact sport like football or lacrosse is inherently dangerous. Districts mitigate risk by informing parents of the risks, providing safety equipment such as pads and helmets, instructing players in safe practices, and requiring a physical examination before participation. When a student is injured while playing football, the district would cite its practices to demonstrate that the risks were shared with participants, precautions were taken, and the student and family accepted those risks.

Negligence

Most liability cases in schools involve allegations of negligence. There are four key elements considered when determining negligence. There is no single legal case credited with establishing these four factors; rather, these elements emerged over hundreds of years of common law. Some cases are considered influential in identifying these factors. One such case was *Palsgraf v. Long Island Railroad Company* in 1928.

The Palsgraf case is seminal. A seminal case is a decision typically from a high court that establishes a new principle that informs legal interpretation in subsequent cases. In this case, Helen Palsgraf was waiting for a train on a platform on Long Island. When the train stopped, two men ran to catch it as it was leaving the platform. One man jumped aboard the train but lost his balance. A guard on the car reached out to pull him in, and another guard on the platform pushed the man from behind. The man was carrying a package and dropped it on the rails while boarding. The package contained fireworks. It exploded. The explosion's force knocked over some scales at the other end of the platform where Helen was waiting. She was struck and injured. This case established the concept of foreseeability as a limitation on the duty of care. In other words, a defendant only owes a duty to an injured party if the danger was reasonably foreseeable based on the defendant's actions. Liability is not imposed for remote consequences or for those that were not foreseeable.

The four elements used to determine negligence in legal cases are listed and detailed below:

1. Duty of care

This element focuses on the legal obligation to adhere to a standard of reasonable care and to avoid carelessness that could foreseeably harm others.

A driver has a duty to obey the speed limit, comply with traffic laws, and remain attentive while driving to ensure the safety of others. Therefore, we expect that fellow drivers will not speed or text while driving.

Managers in a workplace have a duty of care to the workers. They need to provide and maintain a safe physical workspace. They need to ensure that industry standards and safety regulations are in place and adhered to. They need to provide job descriptions and train their employees. Regular breaks and reasonable working hours are expected. Protecting employees from discrimination, bullying, and harassment may constitute a duty of care. Risk assessments in the workplace may also be necessary.

In the educational setting, teachers have a duty to their students to take reasonable steps to protect them from foreseeable harm. Students and parents expect schools to be safe environments with adequate supervision. Schools are expected to respond to issues like bullying and to address unsafe conditions. When schools cancel classes due to a snowstorm, they anticipate the risk of unsafe driving conditions and aim to keep students safe.

The duty of care element in schools is comprised of several factors. Safety refers to the physical environment of the school. Equipment should function properly, and the building should be in good repair. Precautions should be taken to prevent accidents. Supervision is another factor related to the duty of care. Adequate and appropriate supervision during school hours and school-related activities is expected. If 200 children are on the playground for lunch recess, there should be adequate supervision. Duty of care also extends to protecting students from foreseeable harm. This could include abuse, discrimination, bullying, and harassment. Schools should also mitigate risks of potential dangers. Unsafe equipment, slippery floors, icy sidewalks, and chemicals in science laboratories can harm students, and schools must take steps to ensure student safety. Emotional well-being and mental health must also be considered. Here, the duty of care would require schools to respond to reports of harm.

Some populations may warrant additional caution. Very young children require more supervision than older children. Students with special needs may require greater supervision than their typically developing peers.

Some activities are inherently more dangerous than others and require special precautions. For example, injuries are more likely to occur during physical education classes or sports practice than in the general classroom. There is a greater risk of injury in classes such as chemistry and industrial arts than in others. Special precautions in these instances may include wearing knee pads in volleyball class and protective eyewear when conducting experiments in chemistry class or when using the circular saw in industrial arts class.

The duty of care of schools and school personnel can extend beyond the school building. Districts have a duty of care to make sure school transportation is safe, and they must take reasonable steps to ensure that students are safe at after-school events. Field trips present significant challenges for supervision and safety. For example, it is unlikely that the school nurse will be present to assist with medical issues that may arise, and the school has limited control over environments beyond the school setting.

2. Breach of Duty

This element focuses on whether the duty to act responsibly and consistently with an established standard of care was breached. To determine whether a breach of duty occurred, the harmed individual must identify the duty that existed and demonstrate that it was not met.

Establishing breach of duty may take many forms. For example, if a driver is speeding and texting while driving, an individual harmed by these actions would have to show that a driver's duty to others includes driving safely, following traffic rules, and remaining attentive while behind the wheel. The injured person would then argue that speeding is unsafe and a failure to follow traffic rules, and texting is a distraction to a driver. Engaging in these behaviors breached the duty of care expected of licensed drivers.

Landlords have a duty to maintain their properties to ensure they are safe for tenants. Lights and outlets should work. Doors and windows should open and close. There should be running water and other utilities. Toilets should flush. There should be no cockroaches, mice, or other pests. If a renter reports a roach infestation and that the kitchen sink will not drain, the landlord has a duty to make repairs. If landlords do not take such steps or do not adequately address these problems, they have breached their duty.

In a school setting, breach of duty may take many forms. Schools have a duty to provide a safe learning environment and warn students of any unsafe conditions. Schools must provide adequate supervision and proper instruction.

A parent could fall and slip on an icy sidewalk in front of the school, sustaining a hip fracture. The parent might argue that the school has an obligation to keep sidewalks clear and that it breached that duty.

A student could break an arm on the playground during lunch by falling off the monkey bars. Parents might claim that the equipment is outdated and no longer safe, or that playground supervision was inadequate, given the student-to-supervisor ratio. Maybe the supervision ratio was adequate, but all the supervisors were talking in a group at one edge of the playground. What if the playground supervisor was on her cell phone texting her boyfriend when she should have been supervising students? These are some of the factors that the parents of the injured student would explore to determine whether a breach of duty occurred.

3. Causal Link

This factor focuses on determining the connection between negligence and injury. The causal link may be referred to by other terms such as legal cause, proximate cause, or causal nexus. For negligence to result in liability for a sustained injury, negligence must be shown to be the cause of the harm. The term proximate cause may be used when there is some doubt about the causal relationship. If negligence is not a main factor that resulted in the injury, there is no liability.

Several additional legal terms are relevant when discussing the causal link between negligence and injury. Negligence must be a *substantial* cause of the injury. A substantial factor is one that a reasonable person would consider as having contributed to the harm. It is not merely a remote or trivial factor.

A *reasonable person* is another legal term. A reasonable person is a hypothetical construct of ideal human behavior. In legalese, reasonable means ordinary. The actions of a person are reasonable if consistent with the care and caution that a reasonable person would use in the same or similar situation. A reasonably prudent person is someone who uses common sense and good judgment in specific circumstances. A reasonable person stops at stop signs and follows traffic laws. Reasonable people do not attack a store clerk if their lottery ticket does not win, and reasonable people follow orders from a police officer.

The reasonable person standard varies with several factors. Reasonable behavior differs between children and adults, so courts have considered factors such as an individual's age, sex, and disability when assessing reasonableness; however, the rules for applying the reasonable person standard vary across states. For example, courts differ in their approach to holding individuals with mental health issues responsible for their behavior. Some states may use the standard of a reasonably prudent person, while other states may compare the person to the reasonable actions of a person with the same mental illness. The same is true for how intellectual disabilities are considered across states, with some states holding to the reasonably prudent person standard and others comparing the person to other individuals with an intellectual disability.

The reasonable person standard may also be defined by an individual's specialized training or unique skills and knowledge. For example, the courts might consider what a reasonable medical doctor with extensive training and experience would do in a given situation. This would obviously entail a much higher duty of care than that expected of an ordinary person.

The reasonably prudent person standard may be applied more stringently to teachers. Teachers are required to have specialized training and a college degree to be certified. They present themselves as having special skills and expertise related to the educational process. Therefore, the reasonable behavior of a teacher would be held to a higher standard than that of the average person without this training and expertise. In a negligence case, a teacher could be held to the standard of a reasonably prudent teacher, which would reflect a higher standard of care than that of a reasonably prudent person.

Consider the following example to determine if there is a connection between the teacher's action and the resulting harm. The teacher is unwell and leaves her class unattended for three minutes while she uses the restroom. During her absence, a tree branch falls through a classroom window. Four students are injured. Even if the teacher were negligent in leaving her class unattended, the tree branch would have fallen whether she was in the room or not. There is no causal nexus. Parents might argue that the school should have known that the tree was rotting and should have taken precautions to keep their children safe, but the teacher's negligence did not cause the injury. Therefore, the teacher would not be held liable for the students' injury.

When determining if a causal relationship exists between negligence and injury, negligence must be substantial enough that a reasonable person would conclude that the act or failure to act resulted in the injury.

4. Injury

An actual injury must have occurred in a negligence case. The injured persons must show that they suffered harm or an actual loss as a result of a defendant's action. This loss may include physical injury, pain and suffering, property damage, or financial loss, such as lost wages or medical expenses.

Suppose a school district operates a half-day kindergarten program and runs a separate bus at lunchtime to drop off afternoon students at the school and then pick up and deliver morning students to their homes. One day in mid-September, a bus driver finishes his morning run and parks his bus along the highway by his house until his lunchtime bus run. When he boards the bus at noon, he finds a kindergarten student on board. She apparently fell asleep on the morning ride to school, and he did not notice her when he exited the bus. The bus driver panics because he knows he is required to walk the length of the bus before exiting to prevent this, but he neglected to do so. This child also happens to have a mild intellectual disability. She is pleased to see the bus driver and does not appear upset. She is not injured.

For a parent to prevail in a negligence claim, all four factors must be met. The bus driver had a duty to the child, and he neglected that duty by failing to complete a bus check before exiting the bus. He left a five-year-old child with an intellectual disability unsupervised on a bus parked along a highway for about three hours. Many terrible things could have happened to this child. She could have left the bus and gotten lost or hit by a car. If it had been warmer, she could have experienced heat exhaustion or dehydration. She could have become distraught and suffered some emotional trauma, but she did not appear to be harmed. Absent actual harm, the parents would not prevail in a negligence claim against the district. The element of injury is important. It is not about what could have happened or the danger that existed. An actual injury must have occurred.

Although laws vary from state to state, there are some general legal principles that apply across states. Educators have a duty to their students to exercise reasonable care, and they may be found negligent if they fail to do so. If negligence causes a student to be injured, educators can be found liable.

School District Immunity

School district immunity is another legal concept that warrants some discussion. Public schools are funded by the government; therefore, it has been argued that governmental immunity applies to them. This type of immunity is also referred to as sovereign immunity. It was established to exempt the government from liability, and it dates back to the concept of "the King can do no wrong." Immunity from liability is generally granted to schools, as government agencies, for performing required duties, unless they are otherwise limited by state statutes. In general, the government is immune from liability unless a law or the courts specifically repeal that immunity. In other words, the government cannot be sued unless it consents.

Several principles are used to justify immunity. If the state legislature has not removed or limited immunity, then school districts are immune. Immunity must be ended by legislation rather than by the courts. Payment of damage claims with public funds is considered an illegal expenditure because the general public derives no benefit. Additionally, it has been argued that ending immunity would result in an increase in cases and impose a financial burden on schools.

Criticism of school district immunity dates back to a 1959 case in Illinois. In *Molitar v. Kaneland Community Unit District No. 302*, a student was injured in a school bus accident and sued the school district. The bus left the road, hit a culvert, exploded, and burned. Thomas Molitar was injured in the accident. He sustained permanent and severe burns and injuries, and his father filed suit arguing that the injuries were the result of the bus driver's negligence. He sought $56,000 in damages.

The school moved to dismiss the complaint on the grounds that the school district is immune from tort liability. The trial court agreed with the district, and the father appealed to the Supreme Court of Illinois, claiming that dismissal violated his constitutional rights. The case was transferred to the Second District Appellate Court, which affirmed the trial court's decision. The case then went before the Supreme Court of Illinois. The court was asked if school district immunity should hold when a pupil is injured on a school bus owned and operated by a school district. Under an Illinois statute, a student injured by an insured school district bus may recover the amount of the insurance, whereas under another doctrine, a person injured by an uninsured school district bus may not recover any damages. Ultimately, the courts found that school district immunity could not be justified on either the sovereign immunity argument or the public funds argument.

In other words, the Supreme Court of Illinois determined that the sovereign immunity argument could not be justified. The court felt that school districts should be held accountable for the actions of their employees, like any other employer. School district immunity had also been justified in the past based on the premise that taxpayer funds given to an individual through a lawsuit do not help the general public. In this case, the district had insurance for its buses, so the insurance company would pay the damages rather than the taxpayers.

Liability follows negligence, and individuals and corporations are responsible for their employees' negligence. The doctrine of governmental immunity runs contrary to this basic principle. The court determined that "the rule of school district tort immunity is unjust, unsupported by any valid reason, and has no rightful place in modern-day society." The Molitar decision was reversed and remanded to the circuit court, with instructions to set aside the order dismissing the complaint and to proceed as outlined in the decision. Thus, the courts determined that immunity did not apply.

Despite this case, Illinois restored school district immunity through legislation by enacting the Tort Immunity Act in 1965. The 1959 court decision in *Molitor v. Kaneland Community District* sparked this legislation. The Act provided legal protection to public schools and granted immunity from liability for most injuries, except in cases of willful and wanton neglect. It also limited the time to file a complaint to one year rather than the typical two years allowed in other personal injury cases.

In the 1997 Illinois case of *Henrich v. Libertyville High School*, a district was immune from liability for negligent or improper supervision by teachers.

This case involved a 17-year-old student, Joshua Henrich, who was required to play and participate in a game of water basketball during a physical education class in the school's pool area. The student's medical history was significant. He underwent spinal fusion surgery on his lower back and had a physician's letter on file restricting participation in contact sports. The student was severely and permanently injured during the game. The student and his mother filed suit against the district. They argued that the district should have restricted the student from the activity because it involved physical contact with other players. Further, the parent claimed that the district permitted another student, known to be a particularly rough player, to participate in the game, and that a noncertified or inadequately trained substitute teacher failed to provide adequate supervision. Joshua and his mother argued that these acts constituted willful and wanton misconduct and caused the injuries. The district moved to dismiss the case on immunity grounds and argued that the student's legal team failed to demonstrate that the conduct was willful and wanton. The Immunity Act clearly stated that a school district is not liable for injuries caused by improper supervision of an activity on public property. Thus, the decision was upheld on appeal, and the district was immune to liability for injuries resulting from negligent and improper supervision.

Strict sovereign immunity still exists in some states and precludes legal action against public schools. While it provides some protection for schools in these states, it does not protect teachers or other school personnel as individuals.

In many states, school district immunity has been diminished or repealed over time, either through case law or statutory changes. Some states have set specific dollar limits for damages. This usually corresponds to the limit of insurance coverage that the school district has purchased.

Some states differentiate between governmental and proprietary functions. Governmental functions include actions a district takes as a policymaker, such as selecting a curriculum or enforcing school rules, whereas proprietary functions fall outside of governmental functions. Renting out the school gym or auditorium to a community group constitutes a proprietary function of a school district. In such states, immunity typically applies to governmental functions but not to proprietary functions.

Several states have abolished immunity for school districts, but they have adopted save-harmless provisions to protect teachers and other school personnel from liability up to a specific damage amount. These save-harmless or hold-harmless clauses are viewed as insurance policies against personal liability for school staff, provided they are acting within the scope of their employment.

A case that highlights issues of school district immunity is *L.F.V. v. South Philadelphia High School* (2025). In this case, a female student was sexually assaulted by two male students behind the bleachers during a physical education class. All three students were minors. While the parents did not argue that the district was liable for the sexual abuse itself, they argued that the school district was liable for negligent supervision that enabled the sexual abuse to occur. In response, the district argued that immunity applied because the perpetrators of the abuse were not district employees.

The Court based its decision on two prior cases that did not involve schools. One was related to a police chase wherein a fleeing subject caused injury in a car crash. In this case, the Pennsylvania Supreme Court held that the police shared liability for the injuries, even though they did not directly cause them. The other case involved injuries resulting from a head-on collision with a drunk driver. A signage error had been incorrectly placed and directed drivers to turn into the injured party's lane. These two cases established that a public agency may be found liable if its own negligence significantly contributed to the injury. In these cases, this was true even when the harm was caused by a third party's criminal act that was not an employee of the governmental agency.

In applying this principle to the question of the district's role in sexual abuse, the Commonwealth of Pennsylvania rejected that district's argument of immunity. This means that even in a state like Pennsylvania, which recognizes governmental immunity, there are limits to that immunity. The ruling in *L.F.V. v. South Philadelphia High School* shows that schools may be held liable for sexual abuse, even if committed by a third party, if their own neglect was a significant contributing factor.

In Pennsylvania, the Political Subdivision Tort Claims Act (PSTCA) protects local government agencies from liability. It was enacted to avoid the financial burden that civil lawsuits impose on essential public services, such as education, by diverting public funds to settlements. The Pennsylvania legislature also wanted to address the accountability of governmental agencies, so some exceptions to governmental immunity were added specifically to claims involving sexual abuse. In a narrow view of these restrictions, a school would be liable for abuse only if a teacher or other school personnel personally perpetrated the abuse. A broader view would find a school liable for abuse if its own negligence enables the abuse to occur, even if the abuser is not an employee of the district.

Student Injury Cases

Let us examine some student injury cases while considering the four elements required in negligence cases. Some of the cases presented are recent cases, while some are more dated. The older cases are generally regarded as seminal cases. As noted earlier, a seminal case is one that introduces or clarifies a legal principle and is viewed as influential because of the impact on legal reasoning moving forward. These cases are often cited in decisions that follow. Such a case is viewed as a benchmark or a reference point for understanding a specific legal issue.

The first case, *Yanes v. City of New York*, was heard by the Supreme Court of New York in 2020. The facts of the case show that a teacher at Beacon High School gave a class demonstration known as the Rainbow Experiment in front of her tenth-grade chemistry students. The demonstration shows how various nitrates burn with flames of different colors. The teacher wore safety glasses, but her students did not. Students were not provided with any safety instructions prior to the demonstration. The teacher set up four different nitrates in dishes, added methanol to each as an accelerant, and ignited the nitrates. When the flames died down, the teacher attempted to reignite them by pouring methanol from a gallon jug into the dishes. The nozzle of the jug faced away from her and towards the student. A fireball erupted from the jug of methanol and engulfed sixteen-year-old Alonzo Yanes, who was two to three feet away from the demonstration. There were no fire blankets or chemical showers in the classroom, so Alonzo rolled on the floor and yelled for help until another teacher retrieved a fire blanket from the next classroom. His teacher reportedly stood and stared in shock as Alonzo screamed for about a minute.

Alonzo was in excruciating pain and was taken to the hospital by ambulance. He was in critical condition with second- and third-degree burns to 31% of his body and injuries to his trachea, lungs, and an eye. His ears were destroyed and could only be fixed with prostheses. His parents reported that Alonzo was unrecognizable upon seeing him. His doctor gave him a 43% chance of surviving. Altogether, Alonzo underwent approximately 120 painful medical procedures. He was hospitalized for two months and spent another three months in inpatient care at a children's hospital. He never returned to his "normal" life. There is no cure for some of his injuries. For example, nerves do not regenerate, and the loss of sweat glands is irreversible. Additionally, Alonzo is stared at in public. His friends were stunned by his appearance and stopped hanging out with him.

Procedures outlined in the Department of Education's Science Safety Manual were not followed. No safety instructions were given prior to the experiment. The teacher admitted that she should not have brought the gallon jug of methanol to the demonstration table. Because methanol was used, the classroom should have had a fume hood, a chemical shower, and a fire blanket. The principal testified that she delegated safety to the vice principal and that it was his responsibility to make sure teachers followed the safety procedures. Neither the principal nor the vice principal was aware of the safety manual prior to the accident. Additionally, this demonstration had previously resulted in serious burns to other high school chemistry students. As a result, the United States Chemical Safety Board issued a warning specific to this demonstration.

The jury awarded Alonzo $59 million for past and future pain and suffering. In further legal action, the award was reduced to $29 million. This was the highest pain and suffering award approved by the New York appellate courts to date.

As is often the case, the suit was filed against the New York City Department of Education, the Board of Education of the City of New York, and the chemistry teacher. This is because the Department and Board of Education have much deeper pockets than an individual teacher. Part of the defense could have focused on whether the teacher's actions should make the entire Department of Education liable for the injury.

Consider the four elements of negligence. Students are owed a duty for a safe classroom environment. As noted previously, a chemistry class does present a greater risk than other classes. That is why safety procedures are in place, and safety equipment is available. Based on a warning from the United States Chemical Safety Board, this demonstration should not have been presented. The nitrates used in the demonstration dictated the availability of a vent hood, a chemical shower, and a fire blanket. These were not available in the classroom. Although the teacher chose to wear eye protection, this protection was not extended to students. Thus, it seems clear that there were multiple failures specific to the standard of care expected in a chemistry class. Additionally, the teacher's actions and inactions directly caused the student's injury. Clearly, the student experienced catastrophic and life-threatening injuries from which he will never fully recover. Negligence was clear, and the student prevailed in the suit.

Consider another negligence case that is not as clear-cut. In the case of *Orson D. Munn III et al., v. The Hotchkiss School*, a claim of negligence was brought against the Hotchkiss School, a private boarding school in Connecticut. The school sponsored a month-long trip to China in June and July of 2007. Cara Munn was 15 years old at the time and participated in the educational trip with other students and faculty from the school. One adventure involved hiking to the top of Mount Panshan. Most students and chaperones opted to ride a cable car down the mountain, but Cara and two or three other students were permitted to walk down the mountain independently. The students were dressed in shorts and tee shirts or tank tops. The group left the paved pathway and became lost in the forest before eventually finding their way and rejoining the rest of the group. Cara sustained numerous insect bites during this excursion and developed an itchy welt. Ten days later, she began to exhibit signs of tick-borne encephalitis. Her condition deteriorated quickly, and she became partially paralyzed and semicomatose. She was taken to a local hospital, then transferred to Beijing, and finally airlifted to New York.

Cara experienced significant injuries as a result of the tick-borne encephalitis. She is partially paralyzed and has lost the ability to speak as well as some cognitive functioning. She has limited hand dexterity and cannot type.

She has lost control of some of the muscles in her face and drools, and she has difficulty eating, swallowing, and displaying socially appropriate facial expressions.

Cara's family filed a negligence action in federal court to recover damages due to the injuries she incurred. What do you think happened in the courts? Can a school in Connecticut be held liable for a tick bite in China? Was this foreseeable? Does the fact that she was unsupervised on the descent matter, or could she have been bitten by a tick even if she had been supervised on the descent?

The first element in negligence cases focuses on the school's duty to protect students. This was a central question in this case. The facts of the case showed that the director of the school's international programs had viewed information from the United States Centers for Disease Control and Prevention. The website included a warning that tick-borne encephalitis was present in the area of China where the students would be visiting. Furthermore, the site included instructions for travelers related to the prevention of the disease by taking precautions to protect against insect bites. These precautions included wearing long sleeves and long pants outdoors and using insect repellent containing the chemical compound DEET. Cara's family claimed the school was negligent for failing to warn students and their parents about the risks of insect-borne diseases and failing to provide protective clothing and insect repellent.

Interestingly, students and parents were provided with written medical advice via email, which also included a link to the Centers for Disease Control and Prevention (CDC) website. The link was incorrect and directed users to a page on Central America rather than China. Additionally, the packing list provided to students included bug spray, lotion, or wipes; however, they were listed as miscellaneous items along with a travel umbrella and a musical instrument. As presented, the miscellaneous items appeared to be optional.

The initial jury decision in 2013 regarding this Connecticut case was in favor of the parents. The jury awarded $41.75 million to the student; however, the award was decreased to $41.5 million. The school appealed to the Second Circuit Court of Appeals. The Court of Appeals determined that the evidence presented supported the jury's verdict. It agreed that the student's illness was foreseeable and noted that schools have a duty to exercise reasonable care to protect students from foreseeable harm. The Court saw no reason to create an exception for foreseeable insect-borne disease. Two legal questions were then forwarded to the Connecticut Supreme Court for guidance. These questions focused on whether Connecticut's public policy supported imposing a duty to warn or protect against the risk of insect-borne diseases on a private school when planning a school trip, and whether the award of more than $41 million was excessive.

In August of 2017, the Supreme Court of Connecticut found that public policy did impose an affirmative duty on a school to warn and protect students against the risk of insect-borne diseases when organizing international travel. An affirmative duty is a legal obligation requiring that a positive action be taken to protect another person from harm. It goes beyond the passive duty to not cause harm. An affirmative duty only exists in certain circumstances, such as when there is a special relationship. A teacher has a special relationship with students, given that they act in place of the parent.

In reaching its decision regarding imposition of the duty to warn or protect, the Supreme Court considered many factors. It concluded that insect-borne diseases pose a serious risk and that school personnel had access to information about the risk at the travel destination. The protective measures were easy to implement and low-cost. It was reasonable for students to expect the school to share warnings and to provide information to minimize risk. While the school argued that such a legal obligation would result in a chilling effect on school travel, the Court did not agree. Rather, minimizing risk with minimal measures might even encourage travel. The school also argued that increased litigation would result from the creation of a new cause of action. Here again, the Court disagreed. Instead, the Court noted that the decision would clarify the already existing duty of schools to take reasonable steps to keep students in their custody safe. Finally, there was no indication that the jury was "prejudiced, incompetent, or otherwise compromised, but only that its verdict was improperly large."

As a side note, the issue of permission forms, releases, or waivers was raised in this case. School trip waivers are designed to inform parents of the inherent risks associated with a given activity, thereby shielding the school from liability in the event of an accident or injury. For example, parents of children who participate in a ski club recognize that injuries may occur while skiing and waive their right to sue by signing the waiver. In Munn, the school used a waiver to shield itself from liability; however, the district court excluded the waiver, finding it ambiguous and inconsistent with Connecticut's public policy. Although waivers serve a purpose, there are situations, such as a lack of supervision or negligence, that would not be bound by such a waiver.

Here is another case involving a student injury.

A fifth-grade teacher kept three students in her classroom for recess as a punishment for misbehavior at breakfast. As recess ended, the teacher instructed these students to take their seats and stepped outside of the classroom to supervise the return of her remaining thirty students. As a student returned to the classroom, his left eye was struck by a pencil that was launched from the hand of one of the detained classmates when he tripped. While in the hallway, the teacher talked with another teacher. The injured student interrupted their conversation to get the teacher's attention.

Parents filed a negligence claim on the basis that students were not properly supervised. The teacher left three students with discipline problems unattended. While she was supposed to be supervising other students in the hallway, she became engaged in conversation with another teacher and neglected her supervisory duties.

In the trial court, the case was heard by a judge rather than a jury. What do you think happened? Take a minute to consider the duty owed, a possible breach of duty, whether the breach caused the injury, and whether the injury actually occurred.

The parents were awarded damages of $15,000. The district subsequently appealed to the Superior Court of Pennsylvania, arguing that it was not liable for any injury because the event was not reasonably foreseeable. Teachers cannot be expected to anticipate or protect against unexpected acts that occur daily in schools, regardless of whether supervision was adequate. In other words, a teacher is not automatically liable for an injury that occurs in her absence merely because she was not present. Proper supervision depends on many circumstances. Further, if the injury results from the unanticipated actions of a third party, the teacher would not be held liable. If the event was an accident that could have occurred regardless of the teacher's presence, the teacher would not be liable for any injury sustained by the student. It has generally been concluded that a teacher's momentary absence from a classroom is not negligence.

In the appeals decision for *Simonetti v. School District of Philadelphia* (1982), the judgment was reversed. The appeals decision was in favor of the school district. One of the judges offered a dissenting opinion, opining that the teacher could have positioned herself to supervise both the three detained students in the classroom and the remainder of the classroom. The judge also found that the teacher was distracted by a conversation with a colleague when she should have been supervising her students. The judge affirmed the finding of negligence in his dissenting opinion; however, the appeals panel reversed that decision.

This case demonstrates that there are valid and compelling arguments on both sides. That is precisely why these issues end up in court. A decision made at one level can be overturned on appeal when the judges reviewing the case are knowledgeable about the legal issues involved. Although the appeals panel reversed the decision in this case, one judge dissented. These matters are often not black-and-white. There are many shades of gray. In this case, the district was ultimately not found liable for an unanticipated injury caused by another student during a momentary lapse in teacher supervision.

In *Godoy v. Central Islip Union Free School District* (2012), a New York State case, parents filed suit against a district and its physical education (PE) teacher. During a floor hockey game in PE class, the teacher joined the game, and a student's right hand was injured when it made contact with the teacher's hockey stick as he attempted to block the teacher's shot. The parents argued that the teacher was negligent in supervision because he was playing the game instead of supervising it. The parents also claimed that the students did not have any protective equipment. No evidence was provided to support the negligence claim or that the injury could have been anticipated and prevented. The school district prevailed, and the complaint was dismissed. This case shows that failing to provide evidence for each of the four elements of negligence will likely result in dismissal.

Suicide Risk Assessment Cases

Let us examine a common situation that routinely arises in schools. A few students show up at their middle school counselor's office and report that a girl named Nicole said that she was going to kill herself. Nicole is not on the counselor's caseload; therefore, the counselor informs Nicole's counselor of this. Both counselors decide to speak with Nicole and share their concerns based on the reports from other students. During the counselors' conversation with Nicole, she says that she never made any such statements, and she denies any suicidal thoughts or plans. The counselors jointly determine that no further action is warranted. They followed up on a report but have found nothing to substantiate the claim that Nicole is suicidal. From their perspective, they had a duty to check in with the student based on information they received, and they fulfilled that duty.

Assuming Nicole goes on her merry way, and all is well, there is nothing more to the story. Everything worked out fine.

But what if that is not what happens? What if Nicole actually dies in a murder-suicide pact with a student from another school, less than a week later, at a public park off school grounds during a school holiday? In fact, this is exactly what occurred in *Eisel v. Board of Education of Montgomery County*, a 1991 case from the Maryland Court of Appeals.

In this case, Nicole Eisel's father filed a case against the Board of Education claiming that the school's failure to act resulted in Nicole's death. To determine whether the school is liable, let us consider the four factors.

1. Did a duty exist?

   The school board, principal, superintendent, and both counselors were named in the initial complaint. The circuit court found the claims of negligence against the superintendent and principal insufficient. The duty of a school counselor to intervene in order to prevent a student's suicide was supported. The specific question posed in this case focused on whether the counselors' duty included an obligation to notify the parent of suicidal statements reported to the counselors when the student denied making the statements.

   Mr. Eisel's legal team argued that counselors had a duty to notify parents of any child who expressed suicidal ideation. The school district's own policy stated this obligation when a student expressed suicidal thoughts. Mr. Eisel further argued that the counselors' failure to notify him of Nicole's suicidal statements resulted in negligence because it prevented him from exercising custody and control over his daughter. Finally, he argued that the relationship a counselor has with a student is a therapeutic relationship, which places a special duty to act when a suicide is foreseeable.

In contrast, the attorneys for the school district argued that there was no duty to intervene or notify the parents regarding Nicole's alleged suicidal statements and that confidentiality between a counselor and a student precludes imposing a duty to notify parents. It was further argued that the causal link between the counselors' inaction and Nicole's suicide was broken because suicide is a deliberate and intentional action. The school also argued that the case should be dismissed because the parent failed to state a claim, as supported by a summary judgment finding an absence of duty.

The court noted that there was no case precedent regarding the duty of school counselors to intervene in cases of threatened student suicide; however, the court also noted that a school board policy required parent notification. The court found that Nicole's suicide was foreseeable because fellow students had reported suicidal statements to the counselors. The Maryland Youth Suicide Prevention School Programs Act was a public policy requiring schools to intervene to prevent youth suicide, so the court rejected the district's argument that suicide was a superseding cause that removed the counselors from liability. The confidentiality argument was rejected because the district's own policy required parent notification of suicidal ideation.

Once established that a duty was owed and that duty included parental notification, the remaining questions were easier to answer.

2. Was that duty breached?

   Yes, the duty was breached. School counselors, by their own board policy, should have notified the parent.

3. Did breach of duty cause injury?

   The parent argued that the breach of the duty resulted in Nicole's death. Had he been informed of her suicidal statements, her father argued that he could have exercised custody and control over his daughter to keep her safe.

4. Did actual injury occur?

   Yes, Nicole died.

   How was the case decided?

   Initially, the circuit court ruled in favor of the school on summary judgment on the premise that there was no duty. In further action, the court ultimately determined that even a remote possibility of suicide is enough to establish a duty to act because the risk of inaction is death, a severe and irreversible consequence for the student and family. The burden on the counselors was slight; they simply needed to communicate their concerns to a parent via a phone call. Had they done this, they would have fulfilled their duty.

A seminal case often cited with regard to the suicide of school-age students is the 1998 case of *Armijo Chavez v. Wagon Mound Public Schools from New Mexico*. This case concerns a sixteen-year-old student, Philadelfio (Phil) Armijo, and was brought forward by his mother, Juanita D. Chavez, and his father, Atanacio Armijo.

Phil had attended school in Wagon Mound for seven years. He was identified as a special education student with a learning disability as well as emotional problems, including depression and impulsivity. On December 1, 1994, Phil harassed a younger student and was verbally reprimanded by the school principal. In response, Phil threatened to harm the teacher who reported him, the teacher's son, and the teacher's car. Viewing him as at-risk for violence, the principal suspended Phil from school and directed the school counselor to drive him home. The principal also contacted the police to inform them of the suspension and directed them to stop Phil if they saw him attempting to return to school.

The parent/student handbook stated: "If a student is placed on out-of-school suspension, but his/her parents will not be home, that student will be placed instead on in-school suspension." Neither the principal nor the counselor contacted Phil's parents, Juanita Chavez and Atanacio Armijo, to inform them of the suspension. When the counselor took Phil home, Phil exited the vehicle and ran around the back of the house as the counselor drove away. When Phil's parents arrived home later that day, Phil was discovered in his bedroom. He had used a rifle to inflict a gunshot wound to his chest, and he was deceased.

After hearing about Phil's death, his teacher aide reported that Phil had been depressed and nervous for the past few months. She noted that she had talked about his misbehavior before he was removed from school, and he had said that maybe he would be better off dead. Parents filed a complaint against the school, the counselor, the principal, and the aide in their individual capacities. They alleged that Phil's rights under the Individuals with Disabilities Education Act (IDEA) had been violated, which resulted in his death, and that school officials were not trained to deal with potentially violent and suicidal students. Further, they filed suit against the individuals involved for allegedly violating Phil's substantive due process rights.

The court found that Phil was a member of a definable group. He was a special education student who had expressed suicidal thoughts. It was determined that the principal and counselor put Phil at substantial risk of harm by taking him home when he was distraught, without parental notification or supervision, where he had access to firearms.

These actions were viewed as potentially reckless and could be construed as conscious-shocking. These actions increased the risk of harm to the student.

The case was permitted to move forward. The Court held that a reasonable jury could find that the school's actions of taking the student home in the middle of the school day, without his parents at home, and where he had access to firearms, despite knowing that he might be suicidal, increased his risk of harm. However, specific claims against the teacher aide were dismissed because she was not involved in the decision to send the student home without parental notification. There was no evidence that the teacher aide had caused or created the danger.

In 2002, a similar case from the Seventh Circuit also used the state-created danger argument in a suicide case. In *Martin v. Shawano-Gresham School District* in Wisconsin, a middle school student was reported to have cigarettes in school. When her locker was searched, she indeed had a pack of cigarettes. The student then told the assistant principal that another student, a thirteen-year-old seventh grader named Timijane, was also in possession of a cigarette. She told the assistant principal that Timijane had a cigarette hidden in a sock in her locker. Timijane was pulled out of class and questioned. Although she denied having any cigarettes, a cigarette was found in a sock in her locker. She cried and said that she was holding it for someone else; nonetheless, she was still in possession of tobacco on school grounds. She was reprimanded and suspended for three days. At the end of the school day, she took the bus home.

Her mother arrived home around 4:00. She had first stopped at the baseball field because Timijane had softball practice that afternoon, but Timijane was not there. When she arrived home, Mrs. Martin listened to a voice message from the assistant principal regarding the suspension. She then went to the school and caught the assistant principal in the parking lot. When she asked where Timijane was, she was told that she had taken the bus home. Mrs. Martin returned home where she found Timijane in the basement. She had died as a result of hanging herself. After her death, a book entitled *After a Suicide* was found in Timijane's locker; however, the assistant principal had not noticed the title of the book when he was searching for cigarettes.

The parents sued multiple school district personnel, the school, and the district. The court found that the school did not create or increase the risk of harm. The state-created danger was not supported. Regardless of her suspension, Timijane had been dismissed at the end of the school day as she would have been on any other school day. There was also no foreseeable risk of suicide. While Timijane had cried in front of her teacher after being suspended, she did not do or say anything that suggested she was suicidal.

Applied Practice

Cases that highlighted specific issues, such as school district immunity and the elements of negligence, were presented in the previous section. The remaining case examples may raise more than one legal issue or introduce additional considerations. Identify the key issues in each.

Sample Case #1

Jessica Gonzalez was a first-grade student in the Ysleta Independent School District in Texas. She was sexually molested by her teacher, Andres Mares. The district had a policy in place since 1984 that required any suspicion of child abuse or neglect to be reported to the Texas Department of Human Resources and/or to a law enforcement agency. From 1983 to 1987, every complaint of abuse led to the removal of the teacher from any contact with school children. Andres Mares was the exception to this pattern of removals.

In November 1981, Mr. Mares was a Spanish teacher at Ascarate Elementary when a parent reported inappropriate contact with the parent's young daughter. He frequently allowed female students to sit on his lap during class. The principal wrote an informal memorandum and orally reprimanded Mr. Mares. A month later, the same parent reported that Mr. Mares placed his hand around her daughter's waist. The child and Mr. Mares both acknowledged the incident. The teacher was disciplined by the principal, who issued a second oral reprimand that directed Mr. Mares to enter a general improvement plan. This appeared to work, as there were no further allegations for the next few years.

In January 1985, a parent of a fifth-grade girl requested that her daughter be removed from Mr. Mares' Spanish class. When asked why, she reluctantly stated that the teacher had placed his hand on her daughter's waist and stuck his tongue in her ear. The principal consulted with the assistant superintendent as well as the Director of Employee Relations. The teacher reported that he did place his hand on the girl's waist, but he denied any further improper conduct. The female student reported that Mr. Mares walked up to her from behind when she was drawing at the board and put his arm around her waist and his tongue in her ear. The principal believed that the student was telling the truth, and the administrators considered the incident to be actionable sexual abuse. Despite this, none of the district administrators contacted the Department of Human Resources. Instead, they decided to note the incident on Mr. Mares' classroom performance evaluation. All three administrators testified that they reached this conclusion because the parent clearly stated that she did not wish to proceed further with the matter.

Mr. Mares was formally evaluated on February 15, 1985, with a score one point below *exceeds expectations*. Mr. Mares felt the evaluation was unfair and challenged it. His score was subsequently raised in April.

When Mr. Mares was elected President of the Ascarate Elementary School PTA, the parents of the girl were stunned. They disagreed with the district administrators and reported that they had been cooperative with the district's investigation of their complaints of sexual assault on their daughter, and they did not request that the district halt the process. They believed that a recorded hearing would occur and that Mr. Mares would be directed to seek counseling and to avoid one-on-one student contact. They were also under the impression that he would be transferred to another school where he could be closely monitored to ensure compliance with the agreement. When the parents learned that he was the PTA president, they realized that the steps they thought were to be taken had not occurred.

At the same time, the student's father was elected to the YISD Board of Trustees. Once in his position, he approached the principal to determine if the reprimand promised to his wife was in the teacher's file. When it was clear that the matter had been dropped, the parent called an emergency meeting of the Board of Trustees in May, where he presented documents detailing the alleged abuse of his daughter. The deputy superintendent was asked to personally investigate the incident and report to the Board. Ultimately, the deputy superintendent recommended that the school officials involved should be reprimanded for failure to follow through, but he recommended against holding a hearing on the matter. Because the teacher denied the abuse and there were no corroborating witnesses, the deputy superintendent felt that there was not enough evidence to hold the hearing solely on the basis of the testimony of a little girl. Recommended teacher discipline included a written reprimand, a directive to seek counseling, and a transfer to another elementary school within the district. While the parent objected, the board chose to follow the recommended action plan.

Mr. Mares' first year at Glen Cove Elementary was uneventful; however, he was accused of molesting Jessica Gonzalez on March 9, 1987. According to court documents, Mr. Mares followed Jessica to the drinking fountain and placed his hand inside her underwear to touch her genitals when she leaned over to get a drink. When Jessica told her mother about the incident that afternoon, Mrs. Gonzalez immediately went to the school with a friend to speak to the principal. She also contacted the police. The principal reported the allegations to the Texas Department of Human Resources in accordance with district policy and notified the administration. Mr. Mares was immediately suspended without pay while awaiting a hearing before the Board of Trustees. The Board opted to continue the suspension without pay pending the outcome of the criminal investigation.

The trial was held in Texas state court, and Mr. Mares was convicted on charges of indecency with a child. In August of 1987, he was subsequently fired by the Board due to his felony conviction.

In March of 1989, the Gonzalezes filed a suit in the U.S. District Court for the Western District of Texas. They claimed that the district's policies regarding sexual abuse resulted in harm to their daughter. While the district conceded that Jessica's right to personal security had been violated, it argued that the district's responsibility was at issue. The case went before a jury. The jury ultimately awarded the Gonzalez family $500,000.

The district appealed to the Fifth Circuit. A main point of contention concerned the standards used to determine negligence. The district argued that it could be found liable for injuries only if it acted with deliberate indifference to students' constitutional rights. The district's reprimanding and reassigning the teacher was inconsistent with the concept of deliberate indifference. Although, in retrospect, the district's action was inadequate, it was not deliberately indifferent. The jury's July 1993 verdict was reversed, and the appeal was decided in favor of the school district.

This case brought into play the standard of ***deliberate indifference*** for governmental agencies with limited immunity. This is a higher standard of fault than that imposed by the four elements of negligence. Of course, school district immunity varies by state, but this standard is often cited as a basis for limiting such immunity.

Sample Case #2

Douglas Chanthabouly made a suicide attempt in January of 2005. At that time, Douglas was hearing voices and claimed to get into fights with people he did not know; however, his medical records reported that he had never assaulted others. His thoughts were illogical. Judgment was poor. He was subsequently diagnosed with paranoid schizophrenia and briefly hospitalized. Douglas then participated in outpatient mental health services for 11 months. He was prescribed antipsychotic medication to control his auditory hallucinations. In January of 2006, his case manager reported that he was stable on medication.

Douglas reportedly still occasionally heard voices, but they were not commanding him to harm himself. He was able to distinguish between reality and his hallucinations. While both Douglas and his mother reported that he was lonely and had difficulty socializing with peers, he did not get into fights or arguments with others. His discipline record showed a suspension for defying authority rather than for a fight. Staff reported they did not observe any violent behavior and noted that he was cooperative and polite. No teachers approached the counselor with concerns related to Douglas. The school resource officer noted that Douglas sometimes spoke and laughed to himself, but he did not observe Douglas engaging in fights or being bullied.

In 2005, Douglas' mother requested an evaluation for special education. Douglas was found eligible for services as a student with an emotional/behavioral disability. He received writing instruction for an hour per day in a special education classroom. A sample paragraph that Douglas wrote follows:

> *I nevered try dirt. I know a sludge face named Sam. He loves dirt. He eats dirt and he's going to live in dirt. He says he's going to live there forever. I think sludge faces are weird.*

On January 3, 2007, students at Henry Foss High School returned to school after the holiday break. Before the first bell rang at 7:30 a.m. that day, Douglas pulled out a handgun in the hallway of his school and shot fellow student Samnang (Sam) Kok in the face from a distance of about one foot. A second or two later, he stood over Sam's body and fired two additional shots before exiting the building. Sam died as a result of the injuries sustained in the shooting. Douglas was arrested about two hours later, a few blocks from the school.

In his criminal trial, Douglas was charged with first-degree murder, alleging premeditated intent. His defense team acknowledged that he was the shooter; however, they claimed he was mentally ill. Douglas was assessed via a forensic evaluation at Western State Hospital, and the trial court determined that he was competent to stand trial. Following the trial, Douglas was found guilty of a lesser charge of second-degree murder. He was sentenced to 23 years in prison and will be placed under community supervision for the rest of his life upon his release.

Sam Kok's family filed suit against the Tacoma School District (*Kok v. Tacoma School District No. 10*). If you were preparing the case for the family, what would your arguments be? What are the primary considerations?

Start with the elements of negligence. Do schools have a duty to keep students safe on school premises? Was the duty violated? Did the violation cause the injury? Was there an actual injury?

The family claimed that the environment was not safe because the district placed a student with a severe mental illness in the school setting. They argued that the district knew or should have known that Douglas was mentally ill and, therefore, potentially extremely dangerous.

In response, the district moved for a summary judgment. A summary judgment is a decision by a judge in a civil lawsuit that offers a resolution without a complete trial. A motion for summary judgment is filed based on the argument that there are no material facts in dispute and the undisputed facts have a prescribed outcome as a matter of law. The district's argument focused on its position that Douglas' actions were not foreseeable. Because schools are held liable only for foreseeable injuries, the district sought dismissal of the case. Summary judgment was granted to the district and the claim was dismissed; however, the Douglas estate filed a motion for reconsideration and argued that there were disputed facts related to foreseeability. The estate then discovered that the judge's spouse had represented the district in other matters and felt the judge should be recused. Both motions were denied, and the family appealed to the Supreme Court. The Supreme

Court declined to review the case directly and transferred the case to the Court of Appeals of Washington, Division 2.

Regarding foreseeability, the appeals panel noted that this is generally a question for a jury; however, "because reasonable minds would not differ in concluding that Chanthabouly's acts were not foreseeable by the District," the trial court's summary judgment to dismiss the claim was affirmed. The appeals panel noted that the obligation to exercise reasonable care of students in its custody extends only to foreseeable risks of harm. While a district is required to protect students from harm by a third party, it is not liable simply because a student is harmed. The parents argued that the school created a danger by allowing a student with schizophrenia in the general school environment. The decision noted that a diagnosis of schizophrenia alone is not an indication of danger, and the student's behavior at school did not suggest any aggressive behavior. Additionally, the district had obligations under the Americans with Disabilities Act (ADA) and the IDEA to educate the student in the least restrictive environment. Medical providers concurred that there was no risk of harming others. His psychiatrist noted he had a prior suicide attempt, but he did not believe the student was a threat to others. The family presented a deposition from a doctor who opined that the student should not have been in the general school population; however, this individual had not worked in the public school system and had limited knowledge of the district's responsibilities.

Sample Case #3

Mr. Moniz was a physical education teacher and head football coach at Portsmouth High School. On December 14, 2017, he began to receive prank phone calls and texts from an anonymous number at his home. The calls were critical of his coaching abilities but were not threatening. He notified administrators and the school resource officer and was advised to contact the police. A preliminary investigation led the assigned detective to the name Nathan and later confirmed that the calls came from the residence of sophomore Nathan Bruno. On February 1, 2018, Nathan's father was informed of the situation when a detective notified him that the police had traced the Internet Protocol (IP) address associated with the harassment to the Bruno home. The following day, Mr. Bruno took his son to the police department where Nathan admitted his involvement. He reported that other students were also involved, but he would not identify these individuals. Following the meeting, Mr. Bruno took his son's phone. Mr. Bruno reached out to Mr. Moniz, who agreed to accept an apology from Nathan.

Although not on the football team himself, Nathan reported that his two accomplices were on the team; however, he would not identify them by name. When Mr. Moniz heard this on February 6, he emailed Mr. Bruno stating that he would not accept Nathan's apology unless he identified the other students involved. The principal and athletic director pulled Nathan from class to question him about the two football players involved in the prank calls to the coach. Nathan refused to share their names. When Nathan returned to class, a friend noted that Nathan seemed very upset.

Later that day at lunch, Nathan sat with his usual friend group, which included a group of football players. The coach stared down the players, prompting them to leave the table for fear of retaliation for socializing with Nathan. The coach later testified that he was not in the cafeteria, but others disputed his account. At the end of the day, a football meeting was held at which Mr. Moniz threatened to step down as coach if the players involved in the prank calls did not identify themselves. After the school staff left the meeting, upperclassmen on the team spoke to the sophomores and tried to have those involved identify themselves. Two other students then admitted their involvement in the case, but Mr. Moniz felt that there were others involved based on information from the detective.

When Nathan got home from school, his father told him the coach refused to accept his apology unless he identified the other students. Nathan refused. Three football players then arrived at the Bruno residence to inform Nathan about the coach's threat to quit over the incident unless the others were identified. They reported that two boys had identified themselves to Mr. Moniz as the two players involved, and Nathan confirmed that they were the two others who joined him in the prank calls during a gaming party at his house. Mr. Bruno spoke with Mr. Moniz by phone around 5 p.m., but Mr. Moniz continued to share his doubts that the students who self-identified were the students involved.

Nathan asked his father if he could skip physical education the following day to avoid interaction with Mr. Moniz. Mr. Bruno agreed that Nathan could skip class. Around 8 p.m., Mr. Bruno went to bed. Nathan later reheated some pizza, watched some television in the living room, and went to bed.

Around 5:00 a.m. on February 7, 2018, Mr. Bruno saw an email Mr. Muniz had sent the night before at 7:58 p.m. in which he agreed to meet with Nathan after all. Mr. Bruno responded to the email at 5:18 a.m. and agreed that Nathan would meet with Mr. Muniz at a Dunkin' Donuts after school that day to apologize. Mr. Bruno left for work at 6:00 a.m. but asked his brother to stop by to make sure Nathan got up for school. When Nathan's uncle arrived, he discovered that Nathan had hung himself. The autopsy revealed that there were no drugs in his system, and foul play was ruled out. No suicide note was left.

In 2019, Mr. Bruno filed wrongful death actions. Three questions were posed to the jury for each defendant. These questions focused on whether the standard of care owed to Nathan was breached and, if so, whether the breach was the proximate cause of the mental state or state of insanity of Nathan Bruno. Additionally, the jury was asked if they found that Nathan's "mental state or state of insanity prevented him from realizing the nature of his condition or made it impossible for Nathan to resist a suicidal impulse."

The court found that the coach, the principal, the assistant principal, and the detective involved breached the standard of care owed to Nathan; however, only the breaches by the coach and the detective were causally connected to Nathan's mental state. The jury placed liability on Coach Moniz and awarded one million dollars to Nathan's estate and 2.2 million dollars to his father for the loss of his son. A third category of damages permitted under the Rhode Island Wrongful Death Act is pecuniary damages. These damages are for lost future earnings. No damages were awarded under this category. With an award of $3.2 million, interest of $2,596,471.23 was added, for a total judgment of $5,796,471.23.

Additional motions were filed after the trial. The school requested a new trial, arguing that foreseeability was not demonstrated. As a matter of law, foreseeability was not an additional requirement under the uncontrollable impulse exception. Additionally, the district argued that a number of adverse childhood events (ACEs) made Nathan more susceptible to childhood suicide. These included divorce of parents, a mother with substance abuse and addiction, father's prior substance use during the first 18 months of Nathan's life, changes in custody, domestic altercations between parents, limited contact with his mother, and other events. Evidence of this type was excluded from the trial to avoid prejudice. The district's request for a new trial was denied. The district, finding the jury award excessive, also wanted a limit on recoverable damages pursuant to a cap set forth in statute. The statute indicates that damages recovered in "any tort action against any city or town or any fire district, ... shall not exceed the sum of one hundred thousand dollars." Because the civil suit against Mr. Moniz was filed against him in his official capacity as well as in his personal capacity, the statutory cap did not apply.

Mr. Bruno filed another post-trial motion in June of 2025. Because Mr. Moniz was found liable for his son's death, Mr. Bruno's legal team successfully argued that he was entitled to pecuniary damages. He was awarded an additional $1,525,893 on top of the previous award for the estimated income Nathan would have earned had he not died.

Threat Assessment

Threat assessments are similar to suicide assessments, and many of the same factors are considered when determining an appropriate course of action. Threat assessments are dealt with separately in Chapter 4.

Note

1 Schimmel, D., & Militello, M. (2007). Legal Literacy for Teachers: A Neglected Responsibility. *Harvard Educational Review*, 77(3), 257–284.

List of Cases

Armijo by and through Chavez v. Wagon Mound Public Schools, 159 F.3d 1253 (10th Cir. 1998).
Bruno v. Mills C. A., NC-2019-0433 (R.I. Super. Ct. June 20, 2025).
Eisel v. Board of Education of Montgomery County, 597 A.2d 447 (Md. 1991).
Godoy v. Cent. Islip Union Free School Dist., 1667384, 2012 WL 6868846 (N.Y. Sup. Ct. Sept. 6, 2012).
Gonzales v. Ysleta Indep. Sch. Dist., 996 F.2d 745 (5th Cir. 1993).
Henrich v. Libertyville High School Dist. 128, 289 Ill. App. 3d 809, 683 N.E.2d 135 (2d Dist. 1997).
Kok v. Tacoma Sch. Dist. No. 10, Entity Under the Laws of State, 179 Wash.App. 10, 317 P.3d 481 (Wash. App. 2014).
L.F.V., a Minor v. S. Philadelphia High Sch., No. 243 EAL 2025 (Pa. Dec. 2, 2025).
Martin v. Shawano-Gresham School Dist., 295 F.3d 701 (7th Cir. 2002).
Molitar v. Kaneland Community Unit Dist., 163 N.E.2d 89 (Ill.1959).
Munn v. Hotchkiss Sch., 326 Conn. 540, 165 A.3d 1167 (2017).
Palsgraf v. Long Island R. Co., 248 N.Y. 339, 162 N.E. 99 (N.Y. 1928).
Simonetti v. School Dist. of Philadelphia, 308 Pa. Super. 555, 454 A.2d 1038 (1982).
Yanes v. City of New York, 2020 NY Slip Op 32607(U), INDEX NO. 161066/2014 (N.Y. Sup. Ct. August 10, 2020).

Laws Cited

Americans with Disabilities Act of 1990, 42 U.S.C. § 12101 et seq. (1990).
Individuals with Disabilities Education Act, 20 U.S.C. § 1400 (2004).
Individuals with Disabilities Education Improvement Act of 2004, 20 U.S.C. § 1400 et seq. (2004).
Maryland Youth Suicide Prevention School Programs Act, Maryland Code, Education § 7-503 (Effective April 8, 2008).
Pennsylvania Political Subdivision Tort Claims Act, *Pennsylvania Consolidated Statutes, Title 42, § 8541-8564* (42 Pa.C.S. §§ 8541-8564). (Enacted October 5, 1980, P.L. 693, No. 142).
Rhode Island Wrongful Death Act. Rhode Island General Laws § 10-7-2 (January 2024).
Tort Immunity Act, Illinois General Assembly. (1965). *Illinois Public Act 76–952* (codified as 745 ILCS 10/1-101 et seq.).

4 Threat Assessment

Shirley A. Woika

The First Amendment of the United States Constitution protects five basic freedoms, including freedom of speech. It states that "Congress shall make no law ... abridging the freedom of speech." Therefore, citizens have the right to share their thoughts and opinions freely without censorship or backlash from the government. They can say what they want. This right to free speech goes beyond spoken or written words. For example, other forms of protected speech may include symbols, protests, performances, or clothing.

While the right to free speech is broad, it is not unlimited. Some types of speech that are less protected or not protected include obscenity, defamation, fraudulent or misleading commercial speech, child sexual abuse material, true threats, and speech that incites violence or lawlessness. The focus of this section is true threats.

What Is a Threat?

The concept of a true threat suggests that some speech may appear threatening but may nonetheless be protected. A Supreme Court case that helped distinguish between threats and true threats was *Watts v. United States* (1969). This case involved Robert Watts, an 18-year-old who had been drafted into the military and participated in an anti-war political rally in Washington, D.C. to protest the draft. As part of his speech, he said, "If they ever make me carry a rifle, the first man I want to get in my sights is L.B.J." Lyndon B. Johnson, or LBJ, was president of the United States at the time. Robert was charged with a felony under a federal statute that makes it a crime to *willfully and knowingly* threaten the president. As the case proceeded to the United States Supreme Court, the decision was reversed. The Court determined that the statement was merely *political hyperbole* and did not present a true threat to the president.

A *true threat* is viewed as a serious expression of the intent to cause bodily harm to another. The term was defined in the United States Supreme Court case of *Virginia v. Black* in 2003. True threats are "statements where the speaker means to communicate a serious expression of an intent to

DOI: 10.4324/9781003728993-5

commit an act of unlawful violence to a particular individual or group of individuals."

A true threat does not include jokes or hyperbole. Hyperbole is the deliberate and obvious exaggeration of speech to emphasize a point or for effect, and it is not intended to be taken literally. No real danger is implied. For example, playing with a baby and saying, "You are so cute that I could just gobble you up" would not be viewed as a true threat to the baby. Thus, the context in which speech occurs is important in determining if the speech is protected free speech or a true threat.

If speech is determined to be a true threat, then it is not protected by the First Amendment. There are specific criteria that speech must meet to be viewed as a true threat. These criteria include reckless disregard for the speech, knowledge that it would be perceived as a threat, and using it regardless. The speech has to convey a serious expression of intent, not just a joke or political hyperbole. The speech has to contain a clear threat of unlawful violence and be directed at a specific person or group of people. The speaker's intent must be to place the victim in fear of bodily harm or death. If speech is a true threat, it is not protected and can be prosecuted as a crime.

In *Counterman v. Colorado*, decided in June 2023, the United States Supreme Court further clarified the definition of a true threat. This case focused on distinguishing between true threats of violence that can be punished as crimes and free speech that is protected by the First Amendment. The case originated in Colorado when Billy Counterman began to send Facebook messages to a female singer and songwriter named Coles Whalen. These messages began in 2010 and continued for six years. There were thousands of messages.

Billy wrote messages like "You're not being good for human relations. Die. Don't need you." and "Staying in cyber life is going to kill you." Coles tried to block Billy several times, but he would just create new accounts and continue to send her messages. Billy was arrested in 2016, and he was prosecuted for stalking Coles. Upon conviction, he was sentenced to 54 months in prison. The state of Colorado did not present any evidence that Billy had physically stalked Coles. Because the threat involved only speech, it opened the case to a review of First Amendment free speech protections. The Colorado Court of Appeals agreed with his conviction in 2021, using the standard that a person could "reasonably perceive" that the threats were serious. The Colorado Supreme Court denied review of the case.

Billy then petitioned the Supreme Court for a writ of certiorari on January 13, 2023. A writ of certiorari is a court process used to request a judicial review of a lower court decision. In this case, the Biden administration decided to submit an amicus brief, noting that threats of violence, especially against public officials like members of Congress and judges, had increased. Recall that an amicus brief, or friend of the court brief, is submitted by an individual or organization that is not involved in the case and offers information, expertise, or insight that may be relevant to the issues of the case. It is at the court's discretion to consider the amicus brief or not. Amicus briefs are most typically submitted when cases have broad public interest and concern civil rights.

Oral arguments were heard by the U.S. Supreme Court on April 19, 2023. One of the justices, Neil Gorsuch, noted,

> We live in a world in which people are sensitive, and maybe increasingly sensitive. As a professor, you might have issued a trigger warning from time to time when you had to discuss a bit of history that's difficult or a case that's difficult. What do we do in a world in which reasonable people may deem things harmful, hurtful, threatening? And we're going to hold people liable willy-nilly for that?

The court's opinion was delivered on June 27, 2023, in a 7–2 decision. The Supreme Court found that the Court of Appeals erred when it interpreted the "true threat" standard as a burden on the government to prove that a reasonable person would understand his statements as threats. The Court opined that for speech to be considered a "true threat," the government must instead prove that the speaker was reckless in his comments rather than that the speaker intended to harm with his comments. Justice Elena Kagan wrote on behalf of the Court, "The State must show that the defendant consciously disregarded a substantial risk that his communications would be viewed as threatening violence. The State need not prove any more demanding form of subjective intent to threaten another." The reckless standard was clarified as involving "insufficient concerns with risk, rather than awareness of impending harm."

The Supreme Court then vacated the decision of the Colorado Court of Appeals and sent the case back to the lower court for reconsideration. Billy could still be convicted of stalking under the new standard established by the Supreme Court.

In summary, this decision found that a person's subjective intent to threaten another person must be established based on recklessness, at a minimum, to file criminal charges. This standard of recklessness provided further clarification of a prior Supreme Court decision (*Elonis v. U.S.*), which required proof that the person intended to issue a threat and knew the communication would be viewed as threatening to move forward with a criminal conviction for a true threat.

In *Elonis v. United States* (2015), Anthony Elonis posted violent rap lyrics on Facebook that appeared to threaten his ex-wife, co-workers, an FBI agent, the local police, and a class of kindergarten students. He argued that he was a rap singer, that his comments constituted his art form, and that they were a therapeutic release for his personal difficulties at that time. He noted that he had posted the disclaimer, "This is not a threat," for several of his comments. Lower courts used the ***reasonable person standard*** and found Elonis criminally responsible for the threats because a reasonable person would find the posts threatening. The Supreme Court reversed the decision, arguing that criminal liability demands more than negligence; it requires an intent to threaten on the part of the speaker.

There has been debate surrounding the *Counterman v. Colorado* decision, with some opponents arguing that the Supreme Court has held that stalking is protected by the First Amendment and has effectively turned stalkers into defenders of free speech. On the other side of the aisle, there are those who are relieved to see that the Supreme Court will not criminalize inadvertent threatening speech, arguing that it would be challenging to speak with others at all if one could be sent to prison for failing to accurately predict how spoken words would be received by the listener.

Let us consider a case involving a threat in a school setting. The 1996 case of *Lovell v. Poway Unified School District* is a great example. In this case, a 15-year-old high school student in California, Sarah Lovell, was seeking to have her schedule changed. She had been back and forth between the assistant principal and the school counselor. Although the assistant principal ultimately approved the course changes, the school counselor found that the classes were already overloaded when she attempted to implement them in the system. The counselor told Sarah that she might not be able to make the changes to Sarah's schedule after all. Sarah was very frustrated at this point. She said, "If you don't give me this schedule change, I'm going to shoot you." Sarah immediately regretted this, and she apologized to the counselor. Sarah claimed that she did not say those exact words, but she was suspended from school. A record of the incident became a part of her permanent school record.

Sarah's parents sued the school. They requested that the documentation be removed from their daughter's school file. The Ninth Circuit Court of Appeals agreed with the school and found that Sarah made a ***true threat***. The Ninth Circuit judges a threat from the speaker's perspective and determines if a reasonable person making such statements would predict that the listener would view the statement as a serious threat of harm. Because a true threat is not protected by the First Amendment, the principal was justified in suspending the student and in maintaining documentation of the incident in her file. From this perspective, Sarah should have known that making such a statement would be perceived as threatening.

Interestingly, a different outcome would likely have occurred in other states. At that time, appeals courts were divided on how to determine whether a true threat had been made. Some courts used the objective *reasonable listener standard* implemented in *Lovell v. Poway Unified School District.* Others used the subjective *speaker's intent standard.* This standard required proof that the speaker intended the communication to be a threat. It focused on the speaker's intent for the statement to be threatening, even if the speaker did not intend to carry out the threat.

When Does Free Speech Become a Threat?

There are exceptions to free speech. Free speech does not protect "fighting words," obscenities, or defamation. Speech in school can also be limited if it promotes illegal activities like drug use. When considering student speech, free speech does not extend to speech that causes a substantial disruption or interferes with school activities. Speech can be considered a threat when it is *a true threat.*

The Pennsylvania Supreme Court case of *J.S. v. Manheim Township School District* clarifies when student communication constitutes a threat. This case was decided in November 2021 and involved the fine line between student freedom of speech and schools' duty to provide a safe school environment. In this case, J.S. was accused of making terroristic threats to another student on social media. These communications did not occur at school or during the school day, but the school determined that they caused a substantial disruption to the school. J.S. was subsequently expelled.

So, what happened? J.S. and another student exchanged messages on Snapchat over a 10-day period from their respective private cell phones in their homes. They joked that another student looked like a school shooter. One student posted one of the Snaps to his story, and 20 to 40 other students viewed it for approximately five minutes while it was available. J.S. learned that the other student posted it on his profile and asked him to remove the posting. The other student complied and removed the Snap. Another student reported the communication to his parent, who was a school district employee. The parent notified the high school principal, who told the assistant superintendent and the police. Police showed up at J.S.'s house, where he and his parents were interviewed. Police determined there was no threat, and the superintendent sent an email to parents and teachers regarding the incident, stating that the school and campus were safe. Following a school investigation, J.S. was suspended for three days for violating the district's terroristic threat policy. Upon receipt of additional communications, the suspension was increased to 10 days for violating the district's cyberbullying policy.

A school district hearing was held on May 3, 2018, and the three-member committee of school board members recommended permanent expulsion. The school board supported the recommendation. J.S. appealed to the Lancaster County Court of Common Pleas on the basis that he was not granted due process because he was not given the opportunity to confront another student who testified at the hearing. He also argued that the decision was not supported by substantial evidence. The Court agreed with J.S. because the Department of Education specifically grants the right to cross-examine witnesses in an expulsion hearing. In this case, none of the communications occurred during the school day, on school grounds, or with a school device. The Court felt that the district's response was limited to making a police report. The Court also addressed the issue of substantial disruption and felt it did not apply, given the disturbing content and references to a school shooter. However, it was also determined that there was no true threat.

The district appealed, arguing in part that even if J.S. did not make a true threat, the punishment was justified based on Tinker because it caused a disruption due to "wide concern for student safety and a heightened police presence at the school." The PA Supreme Court ultimately agreed with the Lancaster County Court of Common Pleas. It was decided that the speech was protected and did not cause substantial disruption; therefore, the expulsion was improper.

Based on court decisions, freedom of speech becomes a criminal threat when the speaker's intent is to threaten or when the listener perceives a statement as a threat. Keep in mind that whether a form of communication constitutes a threat depends, in part, on the applicable standard in the relevant jurisdiction.

Confidentiality and Threat Assessments

Confidentiality is an important concept in schools. Schools must ensure compliance with regulations and guidelines governing the sharing of students' personally identifiable information (PII).

Confidentiality of educational records is set forth in Section 444 of the General Education Provision Act (GEPA) in Part 99 of the Code of Federal Regulations (34 CFR). These regulations are commonly referred to as the Family Educational Rights and Privacy Act (FERPA). Typically, written consent is required before records can be disclosed, and the written disclosure must specify the records to be disclosed, the purpose of the disclosure, and the intended recipient.

There are a few exceptions to the requirement of written consent before disclosing personally identifiable information. Section 99.36 of FERPA sets forth the conditions governing disclosure of information in the event of a health and safety emergency.

a) *An educational agency or institution may disclose personally identifiable information from an education record to appropriate parties, including parents of an eligible student, in connection with an emergency if knowledge of the information is necessary to protect the health or safety of the student or other individuals.*

(b) *Nothing in this Act or this part shall prevent an educational agency or institution from –*
   (1) *Including in the education records of a student appropriate information concerning disciplinary action taken against the student for conduct that posed a significant risk to the safety or well-being of that student, other students, or other members of the school community;*
   (2) *Disclosing appropriate information maintained under paragraph (b)(1) of this section to teachers and school officials within the agency or institution who the agency or institution has determined have legitimate educational interests in the behavior of the student; or*
   (3) *Disclosing appropriate information maintained under paragraph (b)(1) of this section to teachers and school officials in other schools who have been determined to have legitimate educational interests in the behavior of the student.*

(c) *In making a determination under paragraph (a) of this section, an educational agency or institution may take into account the totality of the circumstances pertaining to a threat to the health or safety of a student or other individuals. If the educational agency or institution determines that there is an articulable and significant threat to the health or safety of a student or other individuals, it may disclose information from education records to any person whose knowledge of the information is necessary to protect the health or safety of the student or other individuals. If, based on the information available at the time of the determination, there is a rational basis for the determination, the Department will not substitute its judgment for that of the educational agency or institution in evaluating the circumstances and making its determination.*

A memo addressing FERPA in safety emergencies, such as a school shooting, was issued in June of 2011 by the Family Policy Compliance Office (FPCO).[1] Information from a student's educational record may be disclosed without a release when the health and safety of others is threatened, as determined by the educational institution. The threat must be *articulable* and *significant.*

As an example, suppose that a school psychologist is completing an assessment, and the student provides her with the names of students he wishes were dead. Should this information be shared? If so, with whom?

The first step is to determine whether the health and safety exception applies under FERPA. This decision is made by the school entity. If the school determines that the health and safety exception is met, then the information should be shared with law enforcement to protect the public. It may also be prudent to notify school district personnel, such as the School Resource Officer and the administration, so that additional protections can be implemented to help ensure safety at school.

In summary, FERPA permits educational agencies to disclose personally identifiable information about students if agency representatives can identify an ***articulable and significant threat*** to the health or safety of others, and the disclosure is necessary to protect them. FERPA is not intended to impede school safety.

While FERPA protects student information, it also allows schools to share student records as part of a threat assessment to prevent violence. Personal observations of students by faculty and staff may be disclosed to threat assessment teams. In certain circumstances involving safety concerns, information may also be shared with law enforcement and mental health professionals. There must be a balance between confidentiality and safety.

State-Created Danger

Picture this scenario. John Smith, a first-grade student at a local elementary school, is presenting some significant behavioral challenges in his classroom. For several months, his behavior has been escalating. He has been involved in multiple incidents in which he attacked other students. He has beaten students up and stabbed them with pencils. The school district has a policy of expelling students possessing dangerous weapons on school grounds. The superintendent concedes that a pencil could qualify as a dangerous weapon. Should the pencil be regarded as a weapon? Should the student be expelled? Stop and think about it. What would happen in your local district?

One morning at about 9:45, John's teacher, Mrs. Judd, lines her first graders up in the hallway and heads off to computer class. She leaves John and four other students in the general classroom rather than taking them to computer class. This is done as a punishment for failing to complete their work.

Mrs. Judd does not know that John decided to bring a gun into school that day, and it is sitting in his desk at that very moment. He is unsupervised in a first-grade classroom with four other students and a loaded gun. And she has no clue.

John takes the gun out of his desk. He then puts a magazine of bullets into the gun. He threatens a student who enters the classroom, but he does not shoot the student. John then raises his gun and shoots a female classmate who is seated at her desk. At the moment of the shooting, Mrs. Judd is about 27 feet down the hall from her classroom. Unfortunately, the shot is fatal, and the little girl dies.

The devastated parent, Veronica McQueen, files suit against the district, alleging that her daughter's substantive due process rights were violated.

The claim against the teacher is based on the theory of state-created danger. She also files claims against the superintendent for supervisory liability and against the school district for municipal liability. While the state is usually not responsible for injuries caused by a third party, a state-created danger is an exception to this rule. Does the parent have a case under the state-created danger claim?

To answer that question, let us consider what must be shown to prove a state-created danger. First, the parent must prove that the school's actions (or inaction) created or increased the risk of harm to her child. The school had to do something that made the student more likely to be harmed than she would have been had the school not taken that step. This action could be a specific action by a district employee. It could also take the form of a school district policy, or it could occur if the district failed to take the required action to prevent harm. To hold the school liable for the student's harm, the parent must show that the school's actions or inactions created a danger that would not otherwise have existed.

Schools have a legal obligation to take positive action to prevent harm to students. This is beyond the general duty to not cause harm through its own actions. This duty exists when there is a special relationship. A student-teacher relationship is an example of a special relationship that prompts the affirmative duty to prevent harm. Within such a special relationship, failure to act is tantamount to taking an action that causes harm.

A state-created danger could exist if the school knew that John was aggressive and failed to take reasonable steps to prevent harm to others. In *McQueen v. Beecher Community Schools*, the parent argued that the school knew that John had a history of aggression. The school, therefore, had an affirmative duty to take reasonable steps to protect other students from harm. The school is more likely to be held liable when a specific action created the danger. Would deliberately leaving students unsupervised in a classroom with a student who was known to be aggressive toward other students be considered a voluntary act that created a new danger? Were the students left unsupervised in the presence of a known threat?

The parent would also have to show that the danger was foreseeable. The school cannot be held liable if it is unaware of the danger. If the district has knowledge of a student's aggressive or violent behavior, the potential for harm may be foreseeable. If the student has a history of violent or threatening behavior, the likelihood of triggering a foreseeability finding is higher than when there is no disciplinary record or when disciplinary referrals are limited to minor offenses, such as arriving late to school.

Further, it would have to be shown that the school's action or inaction was the direct cause of the harm. To do this, a causal nexus between the action or inaction and the harm must be established. Failure to adequately supervise a student with known problem behaviors was alleged to be the cause of the student's injury.

The term *conscience-shocking* is also used in state-created danger cases. Acts or failures to act are often viewed as stemming from negligence rather than as conscience-shocking in state-created danger claims. It is challenging to prove that a school consciously disregarded a known danger. The term conscience-shocking suggests that the action or inaction is so reckless that it goes beyond negligence. It shocks the conscience. For example, leaving a suicidal patient alone with a loaded handgun or allowing a child to be taken out of school early with an adult the child does not know, who is not listed on the student's emergency information as a trusted adult, would be viewed as conscience-shocking. School officials would have to be aware that their actions placed a student at serious risk of harm, yet they disregarded that risk.

Ultimately, the state-created danger claim was rejected by the courts in *McQueen v. Beecher Community Schools*. It was argued that the danger was not foreseeable. No one knew that John brought a gun to school that day. The district successfully argued that the danger existed whether the teacher was in the classroom or not.

Remember, schools have an affirmative duty to take action to protect students from known harm. For a state-created danger to prevail, the school must have taken, or failed to take, an action that resulted in harm to a student, and the harm must have been foreseeable. There must be a causal connection between the action or inaction and the harm. The school had to disregard known risks and engage in conscience-shocking conduct that goes beyond negligence to be held liable for injury.

There are cases in which the state-created danger claims have been successfully argued. In the chapter on negligence, threat assessment specific to suicide was discussed. The case of *Armijo v. Wagon Mound Public Schools* was cited. This was the case that involved a counselor driving a student home during the school day to an empty house when he was suspended. This was against school policy, and the counselor knew that the student had a history of past suicidal threats and psychological problems. Despite this, the student was left unsupervised at home with access to firearms. When the student subsequently died by suicide, the parents prevailed in their lawsuit against the school district.

Another example of a case that was permitted to proceed through the courts involving a state-created danger was the case of *Taylor v. Altoona Area School District*. Dr. Shirley Woika, one of this book's authors, actually opined on this case as an expert for the family.

In this case, Mrs. Taylor registered her son Devin for kindergarten, noting on the registration form that he had severe asthma. The physician confirmed a diagnosis of severe asthma on the private physician's report. The school nurse generated a standard 504 plan for asthmatics and sent it home for the parent's signature. The plan specified that the student was to use his inhaler as needed, and if his symptoms persisted, he was to use his nebulizer. In case of an emergency, procedures included calling 911, notifying the parent, and starting CPR.

Mrs. Taylor could not afford duplicate inhalers and nebulizers for school, so they would be sent back and forth to school with Devin. At times, they would be forgotten in one setting or the other, and Devin would be without his medication. Devin was a walker and experienced some difficulties with the walk home, especially during the winter months. After an asthma attack on the way home from school, he was life-flighted to a specialty hospital where he remained for the next five days. When Devin returned to school, the school neither reconvened a team meeting nor initiated any revisions to the service plan. Despite his medical issues, Devin had a successful kindergarten experience and made good academic progress.

At the start of first grade, the nurse sent home a nearly identical service agreement, which the parent signed. Devin's symptoms seemed to increase in severity and were harder to control. In that year, he had seven ER visits and two hospitalizations. In September of the following school year, Devin experienced a significant asthma attack. He used his inhaler and put his head down on his desk. At some point, the teacher and aide noticed that he was unresponsive and called the office for assistance. The other students were removed from the room. The building administrator ran to the room and was unable to revive the student. She tried to call 911 but could not successfully get an outside line on the classroom phone, and someone was sent to the office to make the call. When EMTs arrived seven minutes later, Devin was still seated at his desk, and the principal was attempting mouth-to-mouth resuscitation. The first-on-scene EMT reported that no resuscitation efforts using standard protocol were attempted prior to his arrival. Devin was taken by ambulance and ultimately transferred by life flight to a specialty hospital, where he died several days later. Based on the fact that school personnel did not administer medications or CPR as specified in his service plan, a state-created danger claim was permitted to proceed.

To buffer themselves from state-created danger claims, schools should ensure that their policies are clear and that employees are trained to implement them. The case examples cited in which parents prevailed against schools involved the failure of school personnel to follow their own policies. It was concluded that failing to follow established policies resulted in conscience-shocking action or inaction. Therefore, schools should make sure that policies are regularly updated and reviewed with all employees.

Consider the case of *Doe v. Covington County School District*. In 2007–2008, Jane Doe attended an elementary school in Covington County, Mississippi. Between September 2007 and January 2008, the school permitted Tommy Keyes to sign Jane out of school and return her later in the day. He was neither a relative nor listed on the checkout form completed by her parents. He listed himself as her father on the first five occasions that he signed her out and as her mother on the sixth. He did this without her parents' knowledge or consent. While in his custody, Jane was sexually molested. Jane, her father, and her paternal grandmother sued the school district, as well as individual employees, in their official capacities (superintendent, school board, and school board president). The Does claimed that Jane's due process and equal protection claims had been violated.

The Does claimed that the district policy of allowing students to be released without verifying identification or determining whether the individuals were listed on the permission to check-out form created a danger to students and that the policy's implementation constituted deliberate indifference to student rights and safety. They argued that this policy was the direct and proximate cause of the harm to Jane. The Does did not allege that any school employees knowingly permitted Jane to leave the school premises with an unauthorized adult.

The district responded by arguing that Jane did not have a constitutional right to be protected from harm caused by a private actor who was not an employee of the school district. The court dismissed the federal claims by the Does because the Fifth Circuit has repeatedly denied the state-created danger theory.

In its Fifth Circuit Appeals decision, it was concluded:

> *We reaffirm, then, decades of binding precedent: a public school does not have a DeShaney special relationship with its students requiring the school to ensure the students' safety from private actors. Public schools do not take students into custody and hold them there against their will in the same way that a state takes prisoners, involuntarily committed mental health patients, and foster children into its custody. See DeShaney, 489 U.S. at 199–200; Griffith, 899 F.2d at 1439. Without a special relationship, a public school has no constitutional duty to ensure that its students are safe from private violence. That is not to say that schools have absolutely no duty to ensure that students are safe during the school day. Schools may have such a duty by virtue of a state's tort or other laws. However, "[s]ection 1983 imposes liability for violations of rights protected by the Constitution, not for violations of duties of care arising out of tort law."*

Let us examine a more recent state-created danger case from the Fifth Circuit. In *Fisher v. Moore* (2023), a mother sued the Fort Bend Independent School District in Texas. Court documents show that M.F. was a student at James Bowie Middle School (JBMS). Jodi Moore was her teacher. M.F. was a student with mental and physical disabilities. In the fall of 2019, she was 13 years old but had the intellectual ability of a four- or five-year-old child. She was serviced through an Individualized Education Plan (IEP). Her IEP stated that "escorting her during transitions within the school building will be required" for her safety.

R.R. was another student at the same school with a history of significant behavioral problems. He had been violent toward other adults and students within the school. Some documented incidents included hitting students in the head with rocks, poking a student's eye, hitting other students with a belt, threatening to burn a teacher to death, biting, kicking, and spitting. R.R. frequently made obscene remarks to female students and was viewed as a more serious threat to females. He also reportedly stated to staff that he wanted to be a rapist when he grew up. He entered the girls' restroom on several occasions and groped a female classmate. He also dropped his pants to expose his genitals and then urinated on a wall. He was also a student with special needs who was to be escorted and supervised at all times for the safety of others.

On September 4, 2019, both students were permitted to leave their respective classrooms without supervision. When school staff saw them exiting the boys' bathroom together, they learned that R.R. forced M.F. to perform oral sex on him. M.F. indicated that she was sexually assaulted. The security camera showed that they were in the restroom together at the time of the assault. The school was aware of the incident.

Two months later, on November 13, 2019, the teachers allowed M.F. to enter the hall of the school unsupervised. Unknowingly, R.R. was also allowed to leave his classroom without supervision. When M.F. entered a stall in the girls' bathroom, R.R. followed her in and climbed under the stall she was using. He sexually assaulted her for the second time.

The Texas Education Agency investigated the incident and found that the district had violated both students' IEPs. In March, M.F.'s mother, Denise Fisher, filed suit on her daughter's behalf against the district and individual school officials, including both teachers, the superintendent, the principal, and the manager of the district's special-needs program. She claimed that the school had "created or increased the danger to M.F." and "acted with deliberate indifference" in violation of the Due Process Clause of the Fourteenth Amendment and filed a claim under Title IX.

The school district made a motion to dismiss the claims, arguing that it was entitled to qualified immunity. While the Fourteenth Amendment provides that the State cannot deprive any person of life, liberty, or property without due process of law, it does not require the government to protect its citizens from acts by private actors. There is one exception: "when [a] 'special relationship' between the individual and the state imposes upon the state a constitutional duty to protect the individual from known threats of harm by private actors." In the decision, it was noted that other circuits have added a second exception, the state-created danger exception, to the general rule; however, "the Fifth Circuit has never recognized the[e] 'state-created-danger' exception." Therefore, M.F. failed to demonstrate a clearly established due process right on the facts.

The Court concluded:

> *The facts giving rise to this lawsuit are unquestionably horrific. And Title IX may well provide M.F. a remedy. But § 1983 does not, as the Supreme Court's qualified-immunity doctrine "protects government officials 'from liability for civil damages insofar as their conduct does not violate clearly established statutory or constitutional rights of which a reasonable person would have known.'" Our precedent has repeatedly declined to adopt the state-created danger doctrine. And a right never established cannot be one clearly established. As we recently put it, "A claim that we have expressly not recognized is the antithesis of a clearly established one."*
>
> *Controlling precedent requires us to REVERSE the district court and REMAND with instructions to enter judgment in Appellants' favor on M.F.'s § 1983 claim.*

Thus, the Fifth Circuit court has refused to adopt the state-created danger theory. This court has jurisdiction over the United States District Courts in Louisiana, Mississippi, and Texas. The Fifth Circuit also included Alabama, Georgia, and Florida until 1981, when these states were shifted to the Eleventh Circuit. Circuit courts review decisions regarding errors in law. They do not re-try cases. It is important to remember that differences exist across jurisdictions and in court decisions.

Legal Strategies Employed in Threat Assessment Cases

When a threat assessment is conducted on a student, several legal arguments are typically raised by the student's parents who object to the threat assessment being completed. They center on two main arguments that focus on a violation of constitutional rights and/or a violation of the protections for individuals with disabilities.

One line of argument focuses on several constitutional rights. These include First Amendment, Fifth Amendment, and Fourteenth Amendment challenges. As a reminder, the First Amendment focuses on freedom of speech. The Fifth Amendment includes several due process rights. For example, an individual can *plead the Fifth* to avoid self-incriminating testimony. In the context of objecting to a threat assessment, the due process rights of the students involved are challenged. The Fourteenth Amendment grants equal protection under the law to all of its citizens, including due process rights.

Under the First Amendment, free speech is protected, while a true threat is not protected speech. Therefore, parents may argue that their student was threatened, while the school will argue that the speech was not a true threat and did not necessitate punitive measures or a threat assessment. In cases where a threat assessment is completed, a parent may argue that the school overreacted to protected, non-violent speech by treating it as a true threat.

In schools, the precedent established in *Tinker v. Des Moines* in 1969 still holds today. Student speech must cause a substantial disruption to the school to restrict it. Therefore, the context surrounding the speech must be considered in the school setting.

Finally, the 2023 Supreme Court decision in *Counterman v. Colorado*, discussed earlier in this chapter, is relevant. For a student's speech to be deemed a threat, the school has to demonstrate that the student acted knowingly and recklessly.

Arguments specific to the Fifth and Fourteenth Amendments focus on violations of due process. When a threat assessment is completed, parents may argue that they were not notified that an assessment was underway and that no formal procedures were established for such assessments. This argument focuses on demonstrating that due process rights were violated due to the absence of established procedures.

Other due process arguments focus on the consequences of a threat assessment. For example, a student could be suspended, placed in another setting, or referred to law enforcement without the protections of formal due process afforded in disciplinary hearings. Finally, a threat assessment report may become part of a student's record. Such a report could have consequences for the students and impact their future opportunities. Students with such a document in their files could argue that their records have been tainted in the absence of an established, formalized appeal process.

Fourth Amendment challenges are also sometimes raised in threat assessment cases. The Fourth Amendment governs searches and seizures. Outside of schools, *probable cause* is the legal standard that dictates whether a search is warranted. In schools, the lower standard of *reasonable suspicion* applies. Although schools may conduct nontargeted or suspicionless searches by having students pass through metal detectors or by having drug-sniffing dogs sniff lockers, they must have a reason to suspect that a student has illegal drugs or a weapon to conduct a targeted search. Further, the scope of the search must be limited. For example, if school personnel are searching for a rifle, it would be appropriate to check a locker, but there would be no reason to search a pocket on a backpack. Arguments focus on the search not being justified with respect to its inception or scope.

Another Fourth Amendment argument focuses on the overreach of the school. This argument comes into play when a student challenges off-campus communications by arguing that the higher standard of *probable cause* must be met; therefore, the search was unlawful at its inception.

Another area of legal argument in threat assessment cases concerns disability rights challenges under the IDEA or Section 504 of the Rehabilitation Act. These arguments are typically raised when the student who made the threat is a student with a disability. Special education advocates argue that removal from school following a threat assessment process circumvents the manifestation determination process established for students with disabilities. It is also argued that the behaviors of students with emotional or behavioral problems, as well as those with autism, are misinterpreted with legal consequences for the students with disabilities.

When harm is caused to a student, the victim's family may sue the school. Typical defenses used by schools include governmental immunity, negligence, and standard of care.

Governmental immunity was previously addressed in the chapter on negligence. It is important to note that immunity varies across states, and there has been a trend toward limiting immunity. While legal protection may make it more difficult to hold schools accountable, immunity is not absolute. Note that immunity does not apply to private schools.

Negligence claims were the focus of Chapter 3. In threat assessment cases, the main arguments focus on showing that the school failed to fulfill its duty of care requirement to keep the student safe. As noted, foreseeability is an important consideration in negligence cases. The school can be held responsible only if it could have reasonably foreseen the harmful act and then taken appropriate steps to prevent it. In its defense, the school will try to show that the act was not foreseeable, or if it was, that it took reasonable steps to protect students and prevent harm. Schools will argue that they completed a threat assessment based on an established process in these efforts.

A parent may file a claim of gross negligence against a school if a student is harmed in a violent incident at school. To prevail on such a claim, the parent must show that the school was grossly negligent and showed a *wanton and willful disregard* for student safety. This has proven difficult to establish in school shootings or other student harm cases. The school must show that it took some action in response to a given situation to defeat this claim.

The standard-of-care defense is often used in threat assessment cases. The school argues that it met the established standard of care by following a process consistent with best practices, as outlined in school district policies, and by appropriately documenting it. School personnel will offer up their documentation, including the findings of the threat assessment team, to prove that they took appropriate actions based on the information in their possession at the time.

When legal attempts to hold districts responsible have failed using these arguments, the legal teams representing victims have become creative in finding ways to work around immunity and other defenses. They have filed suits against gun makers, individuals or retailers who have sold the weapon used, the parents of the shooter, other family members of the shooter, law enforcement agencies, video game companies, and social media platforms.

The shooting at Sandy Hook Elementary School on December 14, 2012, resulted in the deaths of 20 first-grade students and six educators before the gunman took his own life. Prior to the school shooting, 20-year-old Adam Lanza shot and killed his mother with a .22-caliber rifle in their home. He then destroyed the hard drive of his computer and left the house with an AR-15, a civilian version of the M16 semiautomatic assault rifle used in the military. He also loaded two semiautomatic pistols and a shotgun and several hundred rounds of ammunition into his mother's car before driving to school.

Once at school, he shot through the locked security door around 9:30 in the morning. When approached by principal Dawn Hochsprung and school psychologist Mary Sherlack, he shot both. Hearing the shots, the school went into lockdown. The gunman fired 154 rounds in under five minutes, and he killed 26 people before taking his own life. The main weapon used by the shooter throughout the attack was the AR-15. Each of the weapons used was legally purchased by the shooter's mother.

The legal actions that followed the shooting set a precedent for future cases. The families of nine of the victims sued the gun maker Remington in 2015. The suit alleged that the company should never have sold such a dangerous weapon, the Bushmaster XM15-E2S rifle, to the public. Additionally, the legal team argued that the company targeted young, at-risk males in its advertising and product placement in violent video games. For example, one of the advertisements depicted the rifle against a plain background with the statement: "Consider Your Man Card Reissued."

Remington argued that there was no connection between its marketing and the shooting. In the Sandy Hook case, the gun was actually purchased by the shooter's mother for herself rather than by or for the shooter. Remington also claimed that the suit should have been dismissed because broad immunity is granted to the gun industry. The Supreme Court of Connecticut ruled that Remington could be sued under state law for the manner in which the rifle was marketed. Remington appealed the decision to the United States Supreme Court, but the Court declined to hear the case.

Due to ongoing legal issues, Remington filed for bankruptcy in 2020. Its assets were sold. This civil suit was viewed as a landmark victory because it successfully challenged the Protection of Lawful Commerce in Arms Act, which had previously shielded the manufacturers of guns from liability by shifting the focus to marketing. The bankrupt company's insurers agreed to pay a $73 million settlement in 2022.

One parent stated that nothing will bring her son back, but it was her hope that the settlement would force gun companies, insurance carriers, and banking industries to make their products safer than they have ever been and ultimately stop future school shootings and save lives.

Sample Threat Assessment Cases

Let us examine a case involving a student threat that ended up in the courts. This is the case of *Cleveland v. Taft Union* from the California courts. Bryan Oliver moved from Tennessee to California with his mother and brothers when he was in eighth grade. As a high school student, he reported that he was being bullied in physical education class. When he reported it to the teacher, he said that the teacher told him to "man up." Bryan's mother reported this to the assistant principal, Rona Angelo, who reportedly responded with "boys will be boys." Bryan's mother then saw the superintendent, Mark Richardson. She reported that he was dismissive of her concerns but stated that he would look into them.

In March of 2011, Bryan was involved in a fight with other boys in physical education class and was suspended for three days because of his involvement.

On Saturday, February 25, 2012, Bryan threatened to shoot students and bomb the school's auditorium in a conversation with four other students while on a bus ride back to his school following a field trip to Universal Studios with students in an accelerated reading program. The librarian and two library media technicians served as chaperones. They overheard Bryan's threats and found them quite disturbing. On Monday, February 27, 2012, they subsequently filed incident reports with the assistant principal due to concern for the safety of students, staff, and Bryan. Other students on the bus also made reports about the incident.

Reports were filed with the assistant principal. Later that day, Bryan was suspended for five days for threatening physical harm to another person. His mother was called and informed of the situation. Assistant principal Rona Angelo also served as the leader of the School Threat Assessment Team (STAT). She initiated a threat assessment. In addition to the assistant principal, other STAT members included the school psychologist and the superintendent.

The school psychologist had completed over 150 threat assessments and identified his role as reviewing any available mental health information and meeting with the student to determine his intent and if he understood why others may have felt threatened by his actions. He would sometimes involve the school resource officer based on factors such as whether an assault or a weapon was involved, whether there was a plan, or if a hit list existed.

The school psychologist consulted with the school counselor, who reported no concerns with Bryan. He interviewed Bryan on February 28,

2012, about the bus incident. Bryan reported that the students were discussing how to respond to bullies, and he responded to a hypothetical question about a hit list. Bryan also shared a dream he had back in Tennessee about locking up bullies in a gym and shooting them. He said it was just a dream and that he would never do anything like that.

On February 29, 2012, Bryan drew stick figures with machine guns and smaller figures on the ground with red blood marks on their heads. Another student grabbed the drawing, and she gave it to the teacher, who reported it to the assistant principal. The student was frightened and disturbed by the drawing and reported that she felt her life was threatened. Assistant principal Angelo told the student not to worry because Bryan was getting help from the school counselor.

On the same date, two male students made incident reports. One said he heard that Bryan had a hit list and some of the students' friends were on it. The assistant principal informed a Black student that his name was on the list and asked why it might be there. The other incident report focused on Bryan saying that he was going to kill two students, including the Black student named on the hit list. A parent of a student met with Angelo to share concerns and was reassured. Angelo said she had handled the situation and that cops would take care of it. The school resource officer searched Bryan's home because of the concerns. No guns or a hit list were found. Bryan's mother confirmed that there were no firearms in the home.

A threat assessment was subsequently completed by the STAT. The threat assessment included interviews with the student, his mother, his school counselor, and the bus chaperones. A threat assessment report was generated by the school psychologist, and the assistant principal and superintendent discussed the situation with the school psychologist and the school resource officer. Bryan had not broken any laws, nor had he made a direct threat. Based on the psychological assessment, they decided that Bryan could return to school rather than initiate his expulsion. The risk level was categorized as four on a scale of one to five. The first category is for "high violence potential; qualifies for immediate arrest or hospitalization." Level four indicated "insufficient evidence of violence potential, sufficient evidence for the unintentional infliction of emotional distress upon others." The recommendation, based on the threat assessment, was that Bryan return to school, but he was to attend weekly meetings with the school counselor or school psychologist for a month. Both the school psychologist and the assistant principal signed the threat assessment report.

Bryan completed the suspension, and he and his mother both signed an attendance/behavior/academic contract for the remainder of the school year. The contract included a statement that random searches would be conducted with Bryan.

On March 1, 2012, the superintendent emailed faculty and staff about the bus incident, noting that a threat assessment had been completed, the student's home was checked for weapons, and that there was no truth to the rumors about a hit list.

On March 7, 2012, Bryan's mother attended an IEP meeting with district staff. Based on current assessment results, Bryan was dismissed from special education services at that time. His mother viewed this positively.

Over the course of the following month, Bryan did check in with the school psychologist, but on some occasions, check-ins consisted of the school psychologist waving to him and asking him how he was doing. Bryan's mother consented to a search of Bryan's bedroom a month after the incident, and there were no weapons.

Over the following year, many complaints were shared by parents and students. Parents and students reported escalating behaviors and safety concerns. Bryan reportedly continued to make threats, made drawings of school shootings, and posted a story about a psychopath who had his revenge against those who had bullied him. He used a pencil to make stabbing gestures in class, and he was rumored to have a hit list. He warned classmates not to come to school. More complaints were made to the assistant principal, but a threat assessment was completed in February. There was no cause for alarm. There was no further review by the threat assessment team and no further contact with Bryan's family.

A female student reported that Bryan showed her a hit list on a piece of paper at some point in the school year after the bus incident but before the end of the school year. It was comprised of two names, Bowe Cleveland and another student. She informed the assistant principal of the list, but she was assured that steps had already been taken regarding the matter.

On November 8, 2012, the librarian, who had been a chaperone on the field trip, overheard Bryan tell a female student that something drastic would happen if he did not get out of geometry. The librarian called security and shared the incident. The next day, she completed an incident report, noting that the statements had frightened her. She also informed the assistant principal.

On December 14, 2012, Bryan left his regular classroom during seventh period to take a test. When he returned, his backpack had been hidden under the teacher's desk, and some of his books were missing. Bryan made an incident report. A note dated December 17, 2012, was added stating that the books had been found.

Coincidentally, December 14, 2012, is also the date that the Sandy Hook school shooting occurred, which resulted in the deaths of 28 people, including 20 children, 6 staff members, the shooter, and the shooter's mother.

Later that December, Bryan's older brother obtained a 12-gauge shotgun for skeet shooting. He stored the gun on a shelf in their shared bedroom, with the ammunition and clay skeets being kept in the garage.

Later that month, the assistant principal called a female student to her office. The student had posted about Bryan on social media. The student shared that she was afraid of Bryan and feared that he would bring a gun to school. She said that Bryan had brought a knife to school freshman year and pulled it on another student. Bryan also said he watched movies about serial killers and thought about Bowe Cleveland, and he had approached her to tell her that she should punch and kick Bowe Cleveland. She also expressed concerns about a hit list. The student reported that the assistant principal told her that the hit list had been investigated and that everything had been addressed.

On January 9, 2013, Bryan warned a female classmate three times not to go to school the following day because something bad was going to happen. He gave the same warning to his friends. Just before her mom picked her up after school, Bryan told her that he was going to kill Bowe Cleveland. She did not believe that he was actually going to do it.

The following day, on January 10, 2013, Bryan arrived at his first-period science class with his brother's shotgun. He shot Bowe Cleveland in the chest. He shot at another student but missed. Two female campus supervisors were in the attendance office when a loud noise was reported in the science building. They jumped in a golf cart and drove to the science building, where they found Bryan in a classroom with a shotgun. One of the supervisors talked him into putting the gun down and took him into a nearby room. When asked what happened, Bryan said that he had been picked on every day of his life. He woke up that day and decided he could not take it anymore, and he just snapped. Bryan admitted that he shot Bowe and named another student he had also planned to shoot.

Police arrived on the scene and removed Bryan. Bryan was charged through the criminal court system with two counts of attempted murder with enhancements. He pleaded no contest and was sentenced to 27 years and four months in prison.

Bowe Cleveland survived but was severely wounded. In April 2013, a civil suit was filed against the district, the superintendent, the principal, and the assistant principal. The personal injury complaint was filed for negligence, premises liability, and negligent infliction of emotional distress. While Chapter 3 addressed negligence, *premises liability* is a new term. *Premises liability* holds property owners responsible for injuries that occur on their property due to dangerous conditions. It requires property owners to keep their properties safe and to warn people of dangers. The shooter himself, Bryan Oliver, was *not* listed as a defendant in the suit.

In California, schools have some state immunity for injuries that result from the acts or omissions of their employees. The district made a motion before the trial to preclude evidence, opinion, or argument regarding the adequacy of the threat assessment. They asserted immunity because public entities or employees acting within the scope of their employment are not liable for failing to conduct a physical or mental examination or for failing to make an adequate physical or mental examination. More specifically, California Government Code § 855.6 states that a public entity nor its employees are

> *liable for injury caused by the failure to make a physical or mental examination, or to make an adequate physical or mental examination, or any person for the purpose of determining whether such person has a mental condition that would constitute a hazard to the health or safety of himself or others.*

Bowe's legal team argued that the district immunity only applied to the physical and mental examination. It did not cover acts and omissions of the threat assessment team. For example, failure to share information does not constitute a physical or mental examination and is not subject to district immunity.

The motion was partially granted. The trial court ruled that liability could not be based on criticism of the school psychologist's examination, predictions, or warnings. The trial court also determined that the district could have taken a range of steps not covered by immunity. These acts or omissions were treated as administrative errors rather than as part of the mental examination. The jury therefore determined that there were acts not covered by immunity that could breach the district's duty of care.

In addition to the immunity defense, the district also filed for apportionment of fault against Bryan as well as his mother and brother. The district proposed that Bryan was 100% responsible for the shooting, but an alternate view was also proposed in which Bryan was 85% responsible, with his mother and brother bearing 10% and 5%, respectively, for Bowe's injuries.

While there were no state or federal regulations regarding how to conduct a threat assessment in 2012, the school psychologist relied upon guidance from Dewey Cornell and Peter Sheras titled *Guidelines for Responding to Student Threats of Violence*.[2]

Expert testimony was relied upon in rendering a decision in this case. The school district relied on Dr. Kris Mohanie, a clinical police and forensic psychologist, as its expert, while Bowe's team relied on Dr. John Reid Meloy, a forensic psychologist. Dr. Meloy opined that the district's threat assessment did not meet the standard of care and outlined his reasons as follows:

1. The threat assessment was not carried out by the team collectively.
2. The school resource officer (i.e., the law enforcement officer assigned to the school) should have been a core member of the team.

3. The threat assessment team failed to communicate among themselves about Bryan.
4. The threat assessment team failed to adequately communicate with Bryan's parents.
5. The threat assessment team failed to recommend counseling to Bryan's parents as an intervention technique.
6. The threat assessment team did not continue to collectively monitor Bryan and reassess the safety plan.

It was Dr. Meloy's opinion that "if the threat assessment team had operated within the standard of care, it was more likely than not that the shooting would have been prevented."

The jury was instructed to consider if negligence occurred, if harm occurred, and if the negligence was the substantial factor that caused the harm. The jury found that negligence had occurred and caused the harm. They assigned 27% of the responsibility to the assistant principal, 19% to the school psychologist, 4% to the superintendent, 3% to the principal, and 1% to a campus supervisor. The jury assigned 27% to Bryan, 10% to his mother, and 9% to his brother. In total, district personnel were assigned 54% responsibility for Bowe's injuries, while Bryan and his family were assigned 46% of the responsibility. Damages were $1.4 million for past noneconomic damages and $2.4 million in future noneconomic damages. That is a total of $3.8 million in damages. Based on the district's responsibility, the judgment against the district was 54% of the total damages, or $2,052,000.00.

The California Court of Appeals for the Fifth District agreed with the trial court in a decision dated March 25, 2022. The school district was not immune. The court found that employees of the school district were 54% responsible for the $3.8 million in total damages for Bowe Cleveland. Thus, the district was found to be more responsible for the injuries than the shooter.

The appellate court opined:

> The multiple failures of District employees to handle information with ordinary care combined (i.e., concurred) to cause the assessment team's failure to adequately address the threat that Bryan posed, resulting in plaintiff's injuries. This is not a case of an unknown assailant where the trier of fact had to guess how the unidentified assailant might have been stopped. Here, the causal chain was identified by Meloy, who testified that if the threat assessment team had operated within the standard of care, it was more likely than not that the shooting would have been prevented.

In *Cleveland v. Taft*, the shooting incident occurred in January 2013. Later that same year, the Arapahoe High School shooting took place. On

December 13, 2013, Karl Pierson entered Arapahoe High School through an unsecured door at 12:33 PM. He was armed with a shotgun, a knife, Molotov cocktails, and ammunition. He was spotted by a custodian who notified administration by two-way radio. Shots were fired shortly after. Subsequently, the school resource officer notified the sheriff's office and headed toward the shots.

The first person Karl saw was Claire Davis, a 17-year-old student. He shot her, and she died eight days later. Karl then headed for the library with the intention of killing Tracy Murphy, the school librarian and the coach of the debate team. Mr. Murphy had removed Karl from a leadership position on the debate team, and he felt very threatened by Karl. He had even considered changing jobs out of fear for his safety. Tracy knew Karl was coming for him, and he had planned for this contingency. Although he was shot at, he was able to exit the library through a door that led out of the building. Karl ignited the cocktails and started a fire. He died from a self-inflicted gunshot wound in the library.

A threat assessment had been completed; however, the school psychologist reported a low level of risk. Claire Davis's parents gave up their right to sue the school if the school agreed to have external evaluators come in and review what went wrong. The parents stated the following:

> *The angry young man that murdered our daughter was a student in crisis who desperately needed guidance in a different direction from the one he pursued. The lesson to learn is not that our schools should be less tolerant and more punitive, rather that our schools are now, as never before, in a unique position to identify and secure help for troubled students.*[3]

The external review exposed failures with the threat assessment process. In all, a total of 38 concerning behaviors were reviewed after the fact. Many of these incidents had not been reported, and the dots had not been connected. This incident ultimately led to the enactment of the Colorado Claire Davis Act, which took effect on July 1, 2017. It imposed a limited waiver of sovereign immunity for schools if they fail to exercise *reasonable care* to protect all students, faculty, and staff from *reasonably foreseeable* acts of violence that occur at school or at school events.

While *Cleveland v. Taft Union* applies only to the Fifth Circuit, and the Claire Davis Act applies only to Colorado, there are lessons for all. It would be prudent for threat assessment teams to evaluate their written policies and procedures, as well as their practices, to determine how well they meet the expectations of practice as outlined by Dr. Meloy in his expert testimony. Is the threat assessment conducted by a team working collectively? Is the school resource officer a member of the core team? Is there good communication among team members, including parents? Are appropriate recommendations being made, and are they effectively implemented? When new information is shared, is the situation reassessed? Is there a "once and done" mentality? Is the safety plan reassessed?

Notes

1 Goodrum, S., & Woodward, W. (2016). *Report on the Arapahoe High School Shooting: Lessons Learning on Information Sharing, Threat Assessment, and Systems Integrity.* Center for the Study and Prevention of Violence, University of Colorado Boulder.
2 Cornell, D., Sheras, P., Kaplan, S., McConville, D., Douglass, J., Elkon, A., McKnight, L., Branson, C., & Cole, J. (2004). Guidelines for Student Threat Assessment: Field-test Findings. *School Psychology Review*, 33, 527–546.
3 U.S. Department of Education, Family Policy Compliance Office. (2011, June). *Addressing Emergencies on Campus* [Guidance document]. Washington, DC.

List of Cases

Armijo by and through Chavez v. Wagon Mound Public Schools, 159 F.3d 1253 (10th Cir. 1998).
Cleveland v. Taft Union High Sch. Dist., 76 Cal.App.5th 776 (Cal. App. 2022).
Counterman v. Colorado, 600 U.S. 66 (2023).
Doe v. Covington County Sch. Dist., 675 F.3d 849 (5th Cir. 2012).
Elonis v. United States, 575 U.S. 723 (2015).
Fisher v. Moore, 62 F.4th 912 (5th Cir. 2023).
J.S. v. Manheim Twp. Sch. Dist., 2 MAP 2021 (Pa. Nov. 17, 2021).
Lovell v. Poway Unified School Dist., 90 F.3d 367 (9th Cir. 1996).
McQueen v. Beecher Cmty. Sch., 433 F.3d 460 (6th Cir. 2006).
Soto v. Remington Arms Co., LLC, No. JHD-CV-15-6055535-S, 2022 WL 453556 (Conn. Super. Ct. February 15, 2022).
Taylor v. Altoona Area School Dist., 513 F.Supp.2d 540 (W.D. Pa. 2007).
Tinker v. Des Moines Indep. Community Sch. Dist., 393 U.S. 503 (1969).
Virginia v. Black, 538 U.S. 343 (2003).
Watts v. United States, 394 U.S. 705 (1969).

Laws Cited

California Government Code § 855.6 as Cal. Gov. Code § 855.6 (updated January 1, 1963).
Claire Davis Act, Colorado Revised Statutes, § 24-10-106.3 (2015).
Family Educational Rights and Privacy Act of 1974, 20 U.S.C. § 1232g.
Protection of Lawful Commerce in Arms Act, Pub. L. No. 109–92, 119 Stat. 2095 (2005).
U.S. Const. amend. I.

5 Common Issues that Lead to Due Process and How to Avoid Them

Shirley A. Woika

What Is Due Process?

Due process is a fundamental Constitutional right, guaranteed by the Fifth and Fourteenth Amendments, that protects citizens and non-citizens from arbitrary decisions by the government. Due process focuses on making sure that legal matters are handled in an equitable and fair way. It gives people the opportunity to defend their rights and ensures a fair hearing. The most relevant provision for due process rights in the realm of special education is based on the first section of the Fourteenth Amendment, which reads:

> *All persons born or naturalized in the United States, and subject to the jurisdiction thereof, are citizens of the United States and of the State wherein they reside. No State shall make or enforce any law which shall abridge the privileges or immunities of citizens of the United States; nor shall any State deprive any person of life, liberty, or property, without due process of law; nor deny to any person within its jurisdiction the equal protection of the laws.*

Public education is not a fundamental constitutional right guaranteed by the federal government, but it is considered a property interest or entitlement for K-12 students reserved for the states. States mandate school attendance, and they establish school systems. This creates a property interest. States have considerable discretion in how they educate students, but each state must provide a public education and cannot exclude students without due process.

Due process procedures outline the legal steps that must be taken to make sure that individual rights are protected. Special education due process systems are organized differently. States have a one-tier or a two-tier system. In a one-tier system, the state's educational agency (SEA) is responsible for conducting due process hearings. If the decision is appealed, the appeal goes directly to the federal or state court system. If a two-tier system is in place, the school district conducts due process hearings. If the

DOI: 10.4324/9781003728993-6

decision is appealed, it proceeds to a state-level review hearing before it can be appealed in a court. Timelines for issuing decisions and rights of appeal vary across systems.

Dispute Resolution

There are multiple options for resolving disagreements in special education before requesting a due process hearing. Some options are informal while others are more formal.

Mediation

Mediation is a voluntary dispute resolution process that must be made available for IDEA conflicts. Information about the mediation process is outlined in section 300.506 of the IDEA. It reads:

a) *General. Each public agency must ensure that procedures are established and implemented to allow parties to disputes involving any matter under this part, including matters arising prior to the filing of a due process complaint, to resolve disputes through a mediation process.*
(b) *Requirements. The procedures must meet the following requirements:*
  (1) *The procedures must ensure that the mediation process –*
(i) *Is voluntary on the part of the parties;*
(ii) *Is not used to deny or delay a parent's right to a hearing on the parent's due process complaint, or to deny any other rights afforded under Part B of the Act; and*
(iii) *Is conducted by a qualified and impartial mediator who is trained in effective mediation techniques.*

If the parties do not agree to use the mediation process, a disinterested party explains the benefits of mediation and encourages the parties to use it. However, mediation is ultimately a voluntary process in which both parties need to agree to engage in mediation. States are to maintain a list of qualified mediators who are knowledgeable about special education and related services. The parents do not have to pay for mediation services.

Parents may decide to bring an attorney to a mediation session. The inclusion of attorneys in the mediation process is not specified in the IDEA. Their participation varies from state to state. For example, Pennsylvania only allows a district to have an attorney present if the parents opt to bring an attorney. In New York, the school district is entitled to legal representation at mediation and may choose to include an attorney even if the parents do not have legal representation.

States vary with respect to pendency. Pendency is also known as the "stay-put" provision. The IDEA specifies that from the date a due process hearing is filed until a final decision is reached, students will remain in their current educational placement unless parents and the school both agree to a change. Some states extend the "stay-put" provision to include mediation as well.

If mediation is successful and the dispute is resolved, both parties sign a legally binding agreement outlining the resolution. Any discussion that occurred during the mediation process is viewed as confidential and cannot be used as evidence in any future due process or civil proceedings.

The mediator must be impartial, so there should be no conflict of personal or professional interests. The individual serving as the mediator cannot be an employee of the local or state educational agency involved in the student's education or care. Being paid by the agency only for mediation services does not constitute employment by the agency.

Resolution Meeting

When the IDEA was amended in 2004, a resolution meeting was required within 15 days of receiving notification that a parent had filed a due process complaint. This must happen before the school initiates the due process hearing. While mediation is a voluntary process, a resolution meeting is required.

Information about the resolution meeting is clearly stated in the IDEA at §300.510(a). This section reads:

a) *Resolution meeting. (1) Within 15 days of receiving notice of the parent's due process complaint, and prior to the initiation of a due process hearing under §300.511, the LEA must convene a meeting with the parent and the relevant member or members of the IEP Team who have specific knowledge of the facts identified in the due process complaint that –*
   - (i) *Includes a representative of the public agency who has decision-making authority on behalf of that agency; and*
   - (ii) *May not include an attorney of the LEA unless the parent is accompanied by an attorney.*

(2) *The purpose of the meeting is for the parent of the child to discuss the due process complaint, and the facts that form the basis of the due process complaint, so that the LEA has the opportunity to resolve the dispute that is the basis for the due process complaint.*

(3) *The meeting described in paragraph (a)(1) and (2) of this section need not be held if –*
   - (i) *The parent and the LEA agree in writing to waive the meeting; or*
   - (ii) *The parent and the LEA agree to use the Mediation process described in §300.506.*

(4) *The parent and the LEA determine the relevant members of the IEP Team to attend the meeting.*

This section clarifies that the purpose of the resolution meeting is to resolve the issue without moving to a hearing. A local education agency representative (LEA rep) authorized to make decisions on behalf of the school and a parent must be included in the resolution meeting, and they determine which other members of the IEP Team should be included. The school cannot have an attorney present at the meeting unless the parent brings an attorney as well. The meeting must be held unless both parties agree to waive it or to use the mediation process to resolve the conflict.

If the issue is not resolved to the parent's satisfaction within 30 days of the parent filing the due process complaint, the hearing can proceed. Unless both parties have agreed to forgo the resolution meeting, a parent's failure to participate in the resolution meeting will delay the hearing until the meeting is held. If the school makes reasonable attempts to involve the parent in the resolution meeting and the parent refuses to participate, the school may request that a hearing officer dismiss the complaint after the 30-day resolution period has expired. Similarly, if the school refuses to schedule or fails to participate in the resolution meeting, the parent may request a hearing officer to begin the due process hearing timeline.

Note that these requirements apply when the school receives notice that a parent has requested a due process hearing. Therefore, when the school is the party that files the due process complaint, a resolution meeting need not be convened.

If an agreement is reached at the resolution meeting, a written settlement agreement is prepared and signed by both parties. The agreement is enforceable. Either party has the right to void the agreement within three business days of its execution.

Other Dispute Resolution Procedures

Another dispute resolution process available in most states is IEP Facilitation. While not required by the IDEA, it is another conflict resolution process that parents and schools can use. IEP facilitation is an optional early resolution process that involves an impartial facilitator, but both parties must agree to participate. The facilitator's goal is to help the IEP team communicate and problem-solve to arrive at an IEP that is agreeable to both parties. The process is less formal than mediation or due process, and it may be appropriate when parents and schools are struggling to agree on issues related to a student's IEP. It may also be appropriate if it is anticipated that the IEP meeting itself will be complicated or controversial. The process could be requested by either the parents or the school, or it could be recommended by a state education agency. The focus is on developing an acceptable IEP, so any issues beyond the IEP will likely not be addressed.

Finally, filing a complaint with the state is another option to resolve a conflict. A written state complaint is a document alleging that a school district is not in compliance with the IDEA and requesting an investigation into the matter. Any person or organization may file a written complaint with the state when there is a concern that impacts a specific child or a broader issue that affects students system-wide. This is the only dispute resolution procedure available to a complainant who is not related to the student. The decision of the complaint investigation may include corrective actions that are child-specific or system-wide. Once filed, a decision must be issued within 60 calendar days.

To file a complaint, facts supporting the claim must be provided in the complaint. The school district must be provided with a copy of the complaint. Mediation may be accessed within this process, but it is not required. The IDEA does not require states to have an appeal process for decisions rendered; however, some states have made some options available.

The Due Process Hearing

The IDEA requires that a due process complaint be filed within two years of the date at which the party knew or should have known of the problem.

In special education due process hearings, an impartial hearing officer (IHO) or an administrative law judge (ALJ) renders a decision in the case. The IHO or ALJ oversees the timeline for the hearing, conducts the hearing, and writes the decision based on the evidence and testimony presented throughout the hearing. The IHO or ALJ may also dismiss the due process complaint if the issues are resolved before the hearing.

Unless an extension is granted, a final decision must be provided in writing within 45 calendar days from the end of the resolution period. While the fee for the hearing officer or administrative law judge is provided at public expense, the school and parents must pay their own expenses. These expenses may include attorneys' fees and fees paid to witnesses. The IDEA includes a fee-shifting provision in which reasonable attorneys' fees may be awarded to the parent (paid for by the school district) if they are a prevailing party or to the school district if the action was frivolous, unreasonable, or without foundation, or if the hearing was initiated for an improper purpose (such as to harass, cause unnecessary delay, or needlessly increase the cost of litigation). While parents are not required to have an attorney and can represent themselves (or appear in court "pro se"), it takes significant preparation to present a case effectively. Evidence, witness lists, and other documents must be prepared and submitted. If the decision is appealed, a judge (rather than a hearing officer or administrative law judge) makes the decision.

A special type of due process hearing request, the expedited hearing request, is also available in certain circumstances. The expedited hearing request is available only in situations related to a student's discipline-related decision that impacts the student's placement or to the determination of whether the problematic behavior was related to the student's disability.

Case Law

A recent United States Supreme Court case has provided some clarification regarding administrative procedures for resolving special education cases. In *Perez v. Sturgis Public Schools* (2023), a unanimous decision was issued and held that 1) the administrative exhaustion requirement in the Individuals with Disabilities Education Act (IDEA) applies only to suits brought under another federal law that seek relief also available under IDEA, and 2) the petitioner was not required to exhaust administrative procedures under IDEA before seeking relief in the form of compensatory damages under the Americans with Disabilities Act (ADA).

This case involved a deaf student, Miguel Luna Perez, who attended public schools in Michigan from the age of 9 to 20. When he was not permitted to graduate, Mr. Perez filed an administrative complaint with the Michigan Department of Education claiming a denial of FAPE because the sign language interpreters provided were unqualified and the district misrepresented his educational progress. The administrative court dismissed his claims under the ADA and Rehabilitation Act, and the parties settled the IDEA claims through the administrative court, with the school agreeing to pay for Mr. Perez to attend the Michigan School for the Deaf, sign language instruction, and attorneys' fees.

Mr. Perez then filed a case in federal court seeking monetary damages that were not available to him under the IDEA. The Western District of Michigan dismissed the case, stating that Mr. Perez could not bring an ADA claim for monetary damages until he exhausted administrative remedies under the IDEA. Mr. Perez appealed the decision to the United States Court of Appeals for the Sixth Circuit. He argued that he had received everything available to him under the IDEA claim through the settlement, and that his ADA claim had been dismissed. Thus, he had exhausted his administrative remedies. The Sixth Circuit upheld the district's decision to dismiss the case. Mr. Perez then filed a Petition for a Writ of Certiorari.

A Writ of Certiorari is the main way that parties ask the Supreme Court to hear a case of national importance or with conflicting decisions. The Supreme Court accepts cases at its discretion. There is no right to have cases heard by the Supreme Court. While about 7,000 requests are made, only about 100–150 cases are reviewed annually.[1]

The Supreme Court agreed to hear the case and review the decision from the Sixth Circuit. The case was heard in January of 2023 with a unanimous decision (9–0) for Mr. Perez handed down in March of 2023. The decision means that Mr. Perez's ADA claim for money damages can move forward.

The *Perez v. Sturgis Public Schools* decision shows that there are circumstances in which administrative remedies do not have to be exhausted before seeking relief in the court system.

Why Due Process?

There are several reasons why schools may find themselves in a due process hearing. Issues can be related to Child Find. Schools have an obligation to identify, locate, and evaluate students who may qualify for and need special education services. Violating procedural requirements for multidisciplinary (MDT) or Individualized Education Program (IEP) teams may lead to due process. Failing to support students' behavioral and mental health needs can also result in challenges to schools. Additionally, English learners pose unique challenges for schools in assessment and programming, which may lead to due process hearings. Relevant regulations and cases resolved through the due process system will be presented next to demonstrate how regulations are applied to actual cases.

Child Find

There are multiple sources of law regarding child find. These include federal and state statutes, federal and state administrative law such as regulations and guidance documents, and federal and state case law.

Under the IDEA, public schools are obligated to identify, locate, and evaluate all students with disabilities who may need special education and/or related services. The child find obligation arises when there is a *reasonable suspicion* that a student may qualify as a student with a disability. Once the reasonable suspicion standard is triggered, a school entity must request parental permission to evaluate the child within a reasonable period of time.[2]

Indicators such as grades, progress monitoring data, or information about a student's outside diagnosis could trigger the reasonable suspicion standard. Case law suggests that the child find duty does not require a formal evaluation of every struggling student. Instead, a student must have a disability that requires special education services. Child find, however, is violated when the school overlooks clear signs of disability, and a district can be found negligent when it fails to order an evaluation or when there is no rational justification for not conducting one.

In *A.P. v. Woodstock Board of Education* (2008), a fourth-grade student received support in his general education classroom and made satisfactory academic progress. When he was later found eligible for special education services, his parents argued that the Child Study Team's pre-referral process impeded their rights to a special education evaluation. They claimed the district did not uphold its child find obligation. The due process hearing officer ruled in favor of the school on all issues. Upon appeal, the ruling was upheld. While local education agencies are required to identify and evaluate students with disabilities to determine their eligibility for special education and related services, they are not held liable for failing to identify every child with a disability. Connecticut schools are required to implement procedures and programs to support students in the general education setting before referring a student for evaluation. Further, the parents could have requested an evaluation at any point in the process, but they did not.

Failing to meet child find requirements could result in denial of a free appropriate public education (FAPE) if the child qualifies for special education services. The failure to evaluate and classify may entitle the student to compensatory education or tuition reimbursement for a unilateral placement in a nonpublic school.

Child find violations have been found based on a lack of academic progress. In *Avaras v. Clarkstown Central School District* (2018), a struggling first grader was provided with 16 months of Response to Intervention (RTI) services beginning in kindergarten. With Tier 1 and Tier 2 interventions in place for the last seven months of kindergarten, minimal progress was noted. The district then provided Tier 3 support for nine months of first grade, even though the district typically referred students for evaluation after eight weeks of unsuccessful Tier 3 intervention. The Court determined that holding off on an evaluation for special education services was a child find violation, resulting in the student not having access to special education services for the entirety of first grade. Thus, the child find violation resulted in a denial of FAPE.

In *K.W. v. Tuscaloosa County School System* (2018), a district was found to have followed Alabama's child find procedures when it did not refer a first-grade student for evaluation and instead attempted classroom-level interventions. Although parents may request an evaluation at any time, Alabama's child find procedures require districts to attempt general education interventions for at least eight weeks. If the interventions are unsuccessful, then the district can initiate an evaluation.

The child was experiencing difficulties with reading and attention, and the district addressed these issues through individual and small group reading instruction as well as preferential seating to minimize distractions. The RTI team viewed the interventions as successful based on progress monitoring data. Additionally, the parent did not request an evaluation until after due process was initiated, and the student was not found eligible for IDEA services.

In a Sixth Circuit case, *M.G. v. Williamson County Schools* (2018), the court determined that a district met its child find obligations for a student in Tennessee. The student with speech and motor difficulties was evaluated in kindergarten and found ineligible for special education services. When the child continued to struggle, the district used general education interventions through the RTI process to address ongoing deficits. The Court found that general education interventions may be used after a student is found ineligible for special education services.

Minnesota requires districts to include a medical evaluation by a licensed physician if a student meets at least three of eight criteria for special education eligibility under the Other Health Impairment (OHI) category. These criteria include excessive absenteeism linked to a health condition, heightened or diminished alertness resulting from impaired abilities, and impairment in following directions. In Independent School District No. 413, *Marshall v. H.M.J.* (2015), an eight-year-old girl missed 35–39 days of school each year from kindergarten through the second grade. She had a history of cancer treatment-related illnesses, anxiety, frequent infections, and somatic complaints that impacted her attendance. A teacher reported that directions had to be repeated numerous times and that the student's anxiety distracted her from her schoolwork. The parent provided a private neuropsychological report that made a connection between the student's anxiety and her ability to attend and focus in school.

The district was aware that the student had asthma and a diagnosis of generalized anxiety disorder, so the District Court determined that the IDEA evaluation should have included a medical evaluation. The district unsuccessfully argued that it had no reason to suspect that the absences were the result of an acute or chronic medical condition. A child find violation was found in this case.

In another child find case in the Urbana School District in Illinois (2021), a teenage boy emailed his teachers in December 2019 and informed them of his diagnosis of Henoch-Schönlein Purpura (HSP). This disorder is now known as IgA vasculitis and is characterized by inflammation of small blood vessels, which cause a rash, joint pain, abdominal issues, and sometimes kidney problems. The teen was hospitalized and requested an extension on assignments and changes to grades. Some of his requests were denied.

The parent asserted a child find violation and contacted the Office for Civil Rights (OCR). While the district subsequently referred the student for an evaluation, OCR opined that the referral should have happened sooner. When the district first became aware of his diagnosis in 2019, it did not refer the student for an evaluation. The student reported continued struggles related to his diagnosis and medical treatments in December 2020. The district initially requested medical information in January 2021, but it did not initiate an evaluation until May 2021. None of the teachers notified the administration of the student's medical concerns for over a year.

Consider the case of *N.N. v. Mountain View-Los Alton Union High School District* (2022). A parent notified the school in October of a tenth grader's private diagnoses of anxiety and depression. A significant decline in academic performance was noted. The district responded by developing a Section 504 plan for the student. Even with a 504 plan in place, academic decline continued. While the district argued that it had no cause to evaluate the student for special education services prior to the mother making such a request, the California District Court disagreed and found that circumstances existed that should have triggered a referral due to the student's mental health needs. The district's decision not to evaluate the student for another seven months was viewed as unreasonable given the circumstances. The child find violation resulted in a denial of FAPE.

The case of *R.B. and S.R.B. v. North East Independent School District* (2022) involved a gifted student and the need for special education services in addition to gifted support services. This case reflects a District Court decision from Texas. A tenth-grade student was identified as gifted and was academically successful. The student advanced from grade to grade. In April, her parents reported increased anxiety. This was followed by reports of self-injurious behavior and suicidal ideation. The student was placed in an outpatient treatment facility in August. When she returned to school, her parents filed for due process; however, further decline resulted in the student entering a residential treatment facility. The student's status as gifted and her prior record of academic success did not relieve the district's child find obligation when academic decline and the need for residential treatment were noted.

Emotional needs also served as the basis of a dispute in the case of *Mr. P and Mrs. P v. West Hartford Board of Education* (2018). This case comes from a district in Connecticut. Parents requested an evaluation of their child following psychiatric hospitalization and a sudden refusal to attend school. At the time of the request, the student had only recently stopped attending school, had many friends, and had previously earned good grades. At a meeting to talk about the evaluation request, parents reported that medication was starting to help. The district did not seek permission to evaluate the student, but it continued to monitor the student and provided home tutoring as a temporary measure. When the school learned of a second psychiatric hospitalization a month after the parents requested an evaluation, it requested permission to evaluate the student. The district's evaluation was completed within the 60-day timeline. This was within three months of the parents' initial request for an evaluation. The multidisciplinary team found that the student was eligible for special education services.

While the parents viewed the district as violating child find and delaying the evaluation, the school argued that it was reasonable to wait a month to seek consent for an evaluation because the IDEA's definition of emotional disturbance requires that a student must exhibit characteristics over a long period of time to qualify for services. The Court agreed with the district and found that it complied with its child find obligations.

Behavioral issues can rise to a level that warrants more immediate action. A 2020 Fifth Circuit ruling in *Spring Branch Independent School District v. O.W.* involved a fifth-grade boy who had been diagnosed with oppositional defiant disorder. Behaviors of concern in the school setting included drawing violent pictures of murder and death, as well as anti-Semitic images. He used vulgar language, refused to follow directions, left the classroom, threw crayons at his teacher, climbed the gym walls, and engaged in other behaviors that led to his removal from class on a daily basis. The school initiated a behavior chart as a pre-referral intervention. No impact on student behavior was noted. The District Court ruled that a child find violation occurred, and the Fifth Circuit agreed that the severity of the behaviors made it unreasonable to attempt intermediate measures before initiating an evaluation.

Courts have also decided cases specific to a district's child find responsibilities under the IDEA for students receiving 504 accommodations. In California, the Ninth Circuit upheld a District Court decision in *Legris v. Capistrano Unified School District* (2021). Private evaluations resulted in diagnoses of ADHD, reading comprehension difficulties, and visual impairment. The student earned good grades in general education classes with 504 accommodations. While the student continued to perform well academically, the parents arranged for her to receive private individualized tutoring services. When the district was informed of this, it initiated an evaluation for IDEA services even though the student was a high school senior. The district completed the evaluation and found the student ineligible for services. She continued to qualify for 504 accommodations. The Ninth Circuit found that no child find violation occurred and that the district's assessment was thorough and supported the decision that the student was ineligible for special education services.

There are some best practices related to child find that can help school districts avoid due process.

- Be aware of the policies and procedures relevant to your local education agency (LEA) related to child find.
- Develop pre-referral intervention and progress monitoring procedures through Response to Intervention (RTI) and/or a Multi-Tiered System of Supports (MTSS) and identify IDEA referral criteria. Consider expanding these procedures beyond academics to address all areas of need.
- Conduct school-wide screenings to identify student needs.
- Engage in professional development with all school staff to understand child find obligations.
- Share information related to child find with parents, nonpublic schools, and other stakeholders.
- Remember to refer within a reasonable period of time when reasonable suspicion is triggered.

Violating Procedural Requirements for IEP Teams

Many procedural requirements exist for IEP teams. These are specified in multiple sections of the IDEA and relate to the provision of a Free Appropriate Public Education or FAPE (§300.17), the definition of an Individualized Education Plan or IEP (§300.320), membership of the IEP team (§300.321), parental participation (§300.322), timeline of when IEPs must be in effect (§300.323), and the development, review, and revision of the IEP (§300.324).

Examples of procedural violations include failing to meet timelines for notice, failing to address a student's needs, failing to implement a student's IEP, and failing to provide proper notice. Other examples include failing to provide parents with a meaningful opportunity to participate in the IEP process, failing to include required members, or failing to address transition planning.

It is important to distinguish between *procedural issues* and *substantive issues*. A procedural violation occurs when a district fails to follow a specific rule or procedure set forth in federal or state law. As an example, an evaluation must be completed within 60 calendar days. Suppose that an evaluation is delayed due to school cancellations because of snow and student absences. The evaluation is completed on day 63, and the report is then forwarded to the parent. The team finds the student eligible for services. At this point, a procedural violation has occurred because the evaluation timeline was violated by three days.

A substantive issue is something different. Substantive issues focus on the adequacy and appropriateness of an educational program and whether it provides meaningful educational benefit to the student. Substantive issues are focused on the outcome or the content of the IEP and the services provided, and whether a Free Appropriate Public Education (FAPE) was provided.

For a parent to prevail in a due process hearing on an issue related to a procedural violation, the parent usually has to show that the violation impeded the child's right to FAPE, significantly impacted the parents' opportunity to participate in the special education decision-making process, or resulted in the denial of educational benefit. This is articulated in the IDEA as noted below:

§ *300.513 Hearing decisions*

(a) *Decision of hearing officer on the provision of FAPE.*

  (1) *Subject to paragraph (a)(2) of this section, a hearing officer's determination of whether a child received FAPE must be based on* ***substantive*** *grounds.*

  (2) *In matters alleging a procedural violation, a hearing officer may find that a child did not receive a FAPE only if the procedural inadequacies –*

(i) *Impeded the child's right to a FAPE;*

(ii) *Significantly impeded the parent's opportunity to participate in the decision-making process regarding the provision of a FAPE to the parent's child; or*

(iii) *Caused a deprivation of educational benefit.*

In other words, a procedural violation occurs when the rules are not followed. A substantive issue results when that failure results in a denial of FAPE.

Referring to the previous example of violating the 60-day timeline to complete an evaluation, completing the evaluation in 63 days does not necessarily constitute a substantive issue. If the district has 30 calendar days to develop and implement an IEP and takes the entire 30 days to do so, services are delayed by three days beyond the 90-day timeline from signed consent to delivery of services for a student who qualifies. Because the district has denied services for three days, it could be required to provide compensatory services. If the district worked to develop and implement the IEP within 27 days or fewer, no denial of FAPE would occur. It is possible that a procedural violation, while certainly something to avoid, would not result in harm to the student or a denial of FAPE.

While the distinctions between procedural and substantive violations in the IDEA seem simple enough, they are not so easily pulled apart in actual cases. There are many conflicting examples of what constitutes a substantive violation, and the procedural requirements are intertwined with the substantive guarantees in the language of the IDEA itself.

The IDEA does not articulate the difference between procedural and substantive issues. There is, however, a seminal case that helps to clarify this distinction. The case is *Hendrick Hudson Central School District v. Rowley* (1982).

The Rowley case was the first case heard by the United States Supreme Court related to the Education for All Handicapped Children Act, which is now known as the Individuals with Disabilities Education Act (IDEA). Amy Rowley was a student with a hearing impairment at Furnace Woods School in the Hendrick Hudson Central School District in Peekskill, New York. Amy had minimal residual hearing, but she was described as an excellent lip reader.

Prior to her kindergarten experience, her parents and school administrators decided to place her in a regular kindergarten classroom. Preparations included some administrators attending a course in sign language interpretation and installing a teletype machine in the principal's office to communicate with Amy's parents, who were also deaf.

The trial period went well. A sign language interpreter was placed in the class for a two-week experimental period, but it was reported that Amy did not need this service. This determination was made by the school district's Committee on the Handicapped after reviewing expert evidence on the importance of an interpreter from the Rowleys and considering information from her teacher and others familiar with Amy's academic and social progress. The team also visited a class for the deaf. Amy continued in the general education kindergarten classroom, where she successfully completed kindergarten using an FM transmitter.

At the start of first grade, an IEP was prepared that outlined Amy's inclusion in general education, the use of the FM device, daily instruction from a tutor for the deaf for one hour per day, and speech therapy for three hours per week. The parents agreed with parts of the IEP but also wanted Amy to have a qualified sign language interpreter in all of her academic classes, in lieu of the assistance proposed in the IEP.

The school denied the request for an interpreter, and the parents requested an administrative hearing. The hearing officer ultimately agreed with the district's determination that an interpreter was unnecessary based on the fact that Amy was achieving "educationally, academically, and socially" without an interpreter. The decision was appealed to the New York Commissioner of Education, where it was affirmed. The Rowleys then brought the case to the United States District Court for the Southern District of New York, arguing that the denial of the interpreter constituted a denial of FAPE.

The Supreme Court articulated two questions in its analysis:

1. Has the State complied with the procedures set forth in the Act?
2. Is the individualized education program developed through the Act's procedures reasonably calculated to enable the child to receive educational benefit?

The Court argued that "the legislative conviction that adequate compliance with the procedures prescribed would in most cases assure much if not all of what Congress wished in the way of substantive content in an IEP." At the same time, the Rowley decision noted, "We do not attempt today to establish any one test for determining the adequacy of education benefits conferred upon all children covered by the Act."

Amy received substantial specialized instruction and related services. She was performing above average in regular education classes without a sign language interpreter within a public school system. She also received passing grades and was promoted from grade to grade; therefore, the Court found that she was not entitled to the services of a sign language interpreter as her parents requested. The education provided to her was deemed sufficient to confer some educational benefit to the student with a disability. Amy was still eligible for services as a student with a hearing impairment, and she continued to receive special education and related services through an IEP, but the district was not required to provide a sign language interpreter.

The Rowley case established a standard typically applied in FAPE cases. The two-prong Rowley test focuses on procedural compliance and substantive benefit. More specifically, it determines if the school followed IDEA procedures and if the student's IEP was "reasonably calculated to enable the child to receive educational benefits." The question of the educational benefit of FAPE requires more than a trivial or de minimis benefit, but it does not require an education that maximizes potential.

The Rowley standard was considered in another often-cited case that raised the standard. This is the case of *Endrew v. Douglas City School District* (2017). When he was two years old, Endrew was diagnosed with autism. From preschool through the fourth grade, Endrew attended a public school in the Douglas County School District and received services through an IEP. His goals changed very little over time, and the Court interpreted this as stalled progress. His challenging behaviors of screaming, climbing over furniture, and running away from school were largely unchanged over time as well. Before his fifth-grade year, the district offered an IEP essentially the same as the prior one, and his parents opted to enroll him in Firefly Autism House, a private school for children with autism.

A behavior plan was implemented in this program. Within months, Endrew made some academic progress. The parents then approached his public school for a new IEP, but they felt the second IEP was no better than the previous one. They filed a due process complaint with the Colorado Department of Education requesting tuition reimbursement because the public school failed to provide FAPE. An administrative law judge (ALJ) ruled on the matter and denied tuition reimbursement. The ALJ's decision was affirmed on appeal at the District Court of Colorado and by the Tenth Circuit Court of Appeals.

The case made its way to the Supreme Court, where a decision was issued in March 2017. The decision in Endrew raised the bar previously established by the Rowley case and required progress ***appropriate in light of the child's circumstances*** rather than the *de minimis* test that had been used in the Tenth Circuit decision. The United States Department of Education provided further guidance about the FAPE standard following the Endrew decision in *Questions and Answers on Endrew F. v. Douglas County School District.*[3] The guidance reminds districts that IEPs must include individualized and ambitious goals. IEP teams must revisit the IEP through the lens of the Endrew standard when students are not making expected progress.

There are many cases in which procedural violations have resulted in the denial of FAPE. One such case is *T.K. v. New York City Department of Education* (2016). This case involved L.K., a third grader who was severely bullied by her peers in the general education setting. A special education teacher verified that L.K. was subjected to constant bullying and a hostile environment. L.K.'s parents indicated that L.K. returned home after school in tears most days and dreaded going to school. Her parents raised the bullying issue at three separate IEP meetings, but they were told that the meetings were to discuss the IEP, not bullying. Parents requested incident reports, but the school did not provide them. The parents rejected the district's IEP and enrolled L.K. in a private school. The parents argued that IDEA violations occurred because the school refused to discuss bullying.

The parents lost at the initial hearing. When appealed, a State Review Officer agreed with the hearing officer. When appealed to the United States District Court for the Eastern District of New York, the parents prevailed. It was concluded that students have the right to be secure in school. The district denied FAPE because it refused to discuss the bullying, and this substantially impacted L.K.'s learning opportunities. The parents demonstrated that the private school was an appropriate placement for L.K. and that the equities were in their favor (i.e., the parents cooperated with the IEP process and acted reasonably), and they were awarded tuition reimbursement. When further appealed to the United States Court of Appeals for the Second Circuit, the decision of the District Court was upheld.

In *School District of Philadelphia v. Williams* (2016), the School District of Philadelphia argued that it did not deny FAPE to a student when it failed to provide a tablet to a student for seven months. The student had a communication disorder, and the student's IEP listed the tablet as an assistive technology device, referencing it seven times in the IEP. The district argued that the failure to provide a tablet did not amount to a denial of FAPE because the student was verbal and did not need the tablet to communicate. The parent argued that the student relied on the tablet at home and at school in prior school years because he struggled with word-finding difficulties. The hearing officer ruled against the school, finding that the failure to provide the tablet resulted in a denial of meaningful educational benefit for the student. The decision was appealed to the United States District Court for the Eastern District of Pennsylvania, where the decision was affirmed. This is an example of a clear-cut case. Services listed in an IEP must be provided.

Another case in which a procedural violation resulted in a denial of FAPE is the case of *Leggett v. District of Columbia* (2015). This case was not as clear-cut, and the decision was overturned upon appeal. The Leggett case involved a parent request for an IEP after her daughter did not successfully complete her junior year of high school. The District of Columbia Public Schools did not develop an IEP by the start of the school year. The parent enrolled her daughter in a private boarding school where she was successful, then the parent turned to the school to reimburse her for the cost of the residential program. The school argued that the student did not need a residential program. The hearing officer for the due process hearing found that the district violated the IDEA by failing to have an IEP in place by the start of the school year, but tuition was not reimbursed because the student did not require a residential program. Upon appeal to the United States Court of Appeals for the D.C. Circuit, the decision was reversed. The Circuit Court argued that the district failed to offer an IEP, "identified no suitable alternative, and failed even to challenge Leggett's claim that the residential school was the only available placement."

Of course, there are also numerous examples of procedural violations that did not result in the denial of FAPE. One example is *J.H. v. New York City Department of Education* (2009). J.H. was eligible for special education services as a student with a speech or language impairment. He repeated kindergarten, but he continued to struggle in school. Before his IEP meeting, his parent paid a nonrefundable fee and enrolled J.H. in a private school. She then rejected the district's IEP and requested a hearing to recover tuition.

There were procedural errors in this case. The district failed to have a special education teacher at the IEP meeting, and the IEP did not address an identified need of distractibility. The district's IEP was viewed as appropriate overall, similar to the program J.H. was receiving at the private school, and less restrictive (i.e., closer to the general education setting). It was clear that the parent unilaterally made the decision to send her son to the private school before attempting to work with the school to develop an acceptable IEP, which resulted in the equities not favoring the parent. Tuition reimbursement was denied because the parent did not intend to enroll her child in the public school program.

Another case, *C.H. v. Cape Henlopen School District* (2010), involved a student who was diagnosed with a specific learning disability as a second grader. When the student was in fourth grade, the parents argued that the district was not providing FAPE and the educational program was inadequate. The child was unilaterally enrolled in a private school, and the parents requested a hearing to seek tuition reimbursement. The hearing panel from the Delaware Department of Education denied the request. The hearing panel found that the District provided FAPE through an appropriate IEP. The parents appealed the decision to the United States District Court for the District of Delaware, which agreed with the hearing panel. The parents then took the matter before the United States Court of Appeals for the Third Circuit, where the prior decisions were affirmed.

Parents left the private school and returned to the district. They agreed on an IEP but disagreed on placement. They subsequently made a unilateral decision to enroll their child in a private residential school and again sought reimbursement for tuition. The district entered into a settlement agreement with the parent and agreed to pay the tuition for the year.

The following summer, the district completed an evaluation and held an IEP team meeting in August. The team adjourned before the IEP could be developed, but team members agreed to meet on September 11 to complete the IEP. This date was the first date the parent and other members were all available; however, the first day of school was September 5. While members agreed on the follow-up meeting time and place, a procedural error occurred when the district failed to send the parent an invitation to the meeting. The student did not attend school on the first day and instead returned to the private residential school on September 5. The mother refused to participate in any additional meetings and filed a request for a due process hearing on September 7. The meeting scheduled for September 11 was not held because the parent would not attend. Records ultimately revealed that the parent committed to the residential school in March of the same year.

The hearing panel determined that procedural errors were made. The invitation to the meeting was not sent to the parent, and there was no IEP in place for the first day of school. Despite these procedural errors, the panel determined that these errors did not result in a denial of FAPE. When appealed to the United States District Court in Delaware, the decision was affirmed. The District Court noted that no educational opportunity is lost in a situation in which no IEP is in place at the start of the school year when this is due, in part, to a lack of cooperation by the parents.

Another case involved a disagreement between parents (T.P. & S.P.) and the Mamaroneck Union Free School District (2009) surrounding a student with autism. While both parties agreed that the student qualified for services under the disability category of autism and needed special education services, they could not agree on the services. Parents wanted 25 hours per week of applied behavioral analysis (ABA) in the home and a full-time aide at school. They also felt that the IEP was pre-determined by the district staff before the IEP meeting.

The parents requested a hearing and reimbursement for the additional services they believed were needed. The Impartial Hearing Officer denied the parents' request. The decision was appealed and affirmed by a State Review Officer. The parents appealed to the United States District Court for the Southern District of New York. The District Court found that the school had violated both the procedural and substantive requirements of the IDEA and ruled in favor of the parents. Parents were awarded tuition reimbursement, attorneys' fees, and costs. The case proceeded to the United States Court of Appeals Second Circuit, which reversed the District Court's decision and ruled in favor of the school district. The Second Circuit found that pre-meeting discussions among school staff did not deny parents meaningful participation in the IEP process, noting that the IDEA allows districts to engage in *preparatory activities* and to develop proposals for later discussion without including parents. The district's actions were consistent with the IDEA regulations. The Circuit Court also reasoned that there was no predetermination by the school. Although the parents' request for placement was denied, many of their other requests were incorporated into the IEP.

A final case related to procedural violations involved issues of substance abuse. In *P.K. v. Bedford Central School District* (2008), P.K. was admitted to a Partial Hospitalization program as an eighth-grade student due to symptoms of depression, such as loss of appetite, irritability, sleep difficulties, and decreased concentration, resulting in academic decline. When discharged, his parents referred him to the district for an evaluation, and he was found to qualify for services as a student with an emotional disturbance. An IEP was developed that included five hours of resource room support and one individual counseling session per week.

P.K. was hospitalized at least three more times. P.K. also had issues with substance abuse. He attended a six-week wilderness program in another state. His parents agreed to a recommended residential program for P.K.'s ninth-grade year. The staff at the residential program recommended a second year at the treatment facility; however, district staff recommended that P.K. return to the district. P.K. subsequently returned to his home school for the tenth grade, but problems were noted by November of the school year. His parents resumed psychiatric treatment to include mood-stabilizing medication. By the spring, P.K. was suspended for a day in March and again in April. Substance abuse increased over the summer months, and he was hospitalized before being transferred to a partial program.

P.K. returned to school in November of his junior year with a plan in place. In January, he had several behavioral incidents, including a knife fight that led to felony charges. Another hospital stay was completed for substance use and suicidality. P.K. was then enrolled in a wilderness program for a month before his parents placed him in an out-of-state residential treatment program. The parents requested reimbursement for the program from the school, but the school viewed their educational program as appropriate for the student if he could gain control of his substance abuse.

The impartial hearing officer (IHO) ruled in favor of the district. She found that the district's proposed program was appropriate during the time periods in question and that other programs suggested by the parent were inappropriate. Upon appeal, the State Review Officer agreed with the IHO.

The parents appealed to the United States District Court (Southern District of New York). The parents argued that P.K.'s disability was intertwined with his substance abuse. Thus, the parents wanted to hold the district responsible for substance abuse treatment. They wanted the district to pay for the substance abuse program in addition to P.K.'s educational program. The District Court saw nothing in the IDEA that suggested Congress wanted school districts to pay for substance abuse treatment programs for students with disabilities. While the court acknowledged that a professional disagreement had occurred, it determined that such a disagreement was not an IDEA violation. The court noted that "meaningful participation does not require deferral to parent choice." The school district ultimately prevailed.

Suggestions to improve compliance and avoid due process related to procedural violations follow:

- Make sure staff are trained in procedural requirements.
- Use some type of tracking system with alerts.

- Adhere to timelines.
- Make sure all required members attend IEP meetings.
- If a procedural error occurs, strive to ensure it does not result in a substantive denial of FAPE.
- Give parents the opportunity to participate.
- Include necessary components and content in the IEP.
- Implement the IEP as written or convene the team to modify it.

Failing to Support Students' Behavioral Needs

The IDEA requires that positive behavioral interventions and supports be considered when students' behavior impedes their learning or the learning of others. This could include addressing behavior through annual IEP goals, modifications to the special education program, implementing an individualized behavior intervention plan, or adding other related services necessary to achieve goals.

A functional behavioral assessment (FBA) is often conducted to gain some insight into a student's problem behaviors. An FBA is an approach to assessment rather than a specific test. Information is collected through informants and could include interviews with parents, teachers, and other individuals, as well as the completion of rating scales. Observations of the student in the school environment are also conducted. Behavioral incident reports, disciplinary records, and any relevant medical information are typically reviewed. The FBA process operationally defines the problem behaviors, provides baseline data regarding the targeted behaviors, and offers some hypotheses about the conditions under which the behavior is more likely to occur, as well as the consequences that may be maintaining the behavior. This provides some insight to the IEP team when developing a behavior intervention plan.

For example, suppose that a fifth-grade student, Stew Dent, rips up his math assignment almost every day. When Stew does not rip it up, he scribbles on it or ignores it. There are many reasons why he may engage in these behaviors. Maybe he is frustrated by the task and rips it up so he can look bad instead of stupid. Maybe he can do the task but does not like to do long division, and ripping up the paper allows him to avoid or postpone the task. Maybe he really dislikes this teacher and refuses to do any work he assigns. Maybe the math worksheets use a small font that he can't see very well. He often makes errors because he confuses numbers, like threes and eights, due to farsightedness. He hates his glasses and refuses to wear them, so he rips up his paper rather than get them out.

Although the behavior of ripping up the math paper is the same, the same interventions would not work across scenarios. In one case, math skills need remediation. In another case, a student lacks motivation to complete the task, so remediation is not needed. A motivator would likely be an appropriate intervention. A personality conflict with a teacher and poor vision are unlikely to be resolved by remediation of a math skill. The FBA helps to identify the function of the behavior and increase the chances that an appropriate behavior intervention plan can be developed.

The IDEA does not describe the steps required to complete an FBA; however, state law or local procedures may articulate a specific process. FBAs help IEP teams define problem behaviors, the antecedents to the behavior, and the consequences that may be maintaining the behavior. Based on the collected information, a behavior intervention plan (BIP) is developed to control antecedents, teach replacement behaviors, and/or modify consequences. FBAs and BIPs may also be used proactively as determined by the IEP Team.

A functional behavior assessment (FBA) and a behavior intervention plan (BIP) are required when it is determined that students' behavior is a manifestation of their disability for disciplinary purposes. If the behavior is viewed as a manifestation of the student's disability, the school can adjust support for the student, modify antecedents, and/or teach replacement behaviors instead of relying on punishment to curtail the behavior. Specific disciplinary procedures may also be outlined in the IEP.

There is a lot of room for disagreement when behavior problems occur. Behavior may only occur at school or only at home. Home and school may agree that a particular behavior is present, but they may not agree that it is a problem. There may be disagreement about an appropriate intervention plan. Members of the team may also disagree when it comes to the findings of a manifestation determination. Parents may feel that a problem behavior is related to their child's disability and resist any type of punishment for a behavior that they feel the child cannot control. The school may view the situation differently. Thus, it is no surprise that issues related to students' behavioral needs can lead to due process proceedings.

Behavior and Appropriate Assessments

In a case from Nevada, *Clark County School District* (2022), a district was aware of a student's private diagnosis of ADHD for more than two years. Teachers noted difficulties with distractions and escalating behaviors, leading to suspensions. Despite these indicators of behavioral problems, the school did not initiate an FBA or conduct updated evaluations. The impartial hearing officer (IHO) found that the lack of updated assessment information prevented the IEP team from identifying appropriate present levels of academic achievement and functional performance, thereby impeding the decision-making process in developing the IEP. The IHO awarded the parent 60 hours of compensatory education. Upon appeal, a State Review

Officer (SRO) agreed with the IHO and found that a denial of FAPE occurred; however, the SRO increased the compensatory education award from 60 hours to 263 hours.

Another case, *C.F. v. New York City Department of Education* (2014), revolved around a six-year-old student found eligible for services as a student with autism. The district's behavior intervention plan was found to be vague and failed to align specific interventions and strategies with the student's behaviors. The district failed to complete an FBA, and the behavior intervention plan was viewed as deficient. This adversely impacted the IEP team's placement recommendation. The parents unilaterally placed their child in a private school because the district failed to offer an appropriate placement. The Second Circuit found the district violated the IDEA both procedurally and substantively, but it noted that failure to conduct an FBA does not automatically amount to an IDEA violation. Tuition reimbursement was awarded to the parents.

A Georgia case also focused on the adequacy of an FBA in determining if FAPE was provided. In this case, *Cobb County School District v. D.B.* (2015), a five-year-old boy exhibited aggressive behavior and outbursts. The FBA adequately defined the target behavior and provided sufficient data on behavioral antecedents; however, the data collected on the consequences of the behavior were deemed inadequate. The Court also noted other problems with the FBA. For example, the student's removals from the general education setting, as well as the lack of interviews and personal observations, were also deemed inadequate. The District Court noted that the function of the student's behavior could not be determined without information about the consequences maintaining the tantrums. This undermined the conclusions drawn by the evaluator and resulted in an FBA that lacked adequate support. The district was ordered to reimburse the parents for an independent behavioral assessment.

Behavior Intervention Plans

The absence of a behavior intervention plan (BIP) in an Individualized Education Plan was the issue at the center of the New York case of *R.K. v. New York City Department of Education* (2011). A five-year-old with autism could not focus, made inappropriate vocalizations, and engaged in self-stimulatory behaviors. While acknowledging these behavioral difficulties, the school did not feel a BIP was needed. The district's school psychologist argued that a behavior plan was not necessary for the student because the behaviors she exhibited were typical of students on the autism spectrum. New York law states that the determination of the necessity of an FBA and BIP is not based on whether the behaviors of concern are typical. That determination is based on whether the behaviors impede learning. Because the student required constant and direct supervision to learn, a BIP was necessary. The Court ruled against the district and ordered it to reimburse the parents for their child's private program.

The behavioral needs of a student with autism were also at issue in the Missouri case of *Lathrop R-II School District v. Gray* (2010). A middle school student with autism engaged in problem behaviors such as finger biting, hand flapping, loud outbursts, and sexual behaviors. The district conducted an FBA and subsequently developed a BIP. In addition to addressing target behaviors through the implementation of a BIP, the district also provided staff training and consultation, speech therapy, a sensory diet, and a personal aide.

The IDEA requires that positive behavioral interventions and supports be considered in the IEP if a student's behavior impedes learning. The Eighth Circuit Court found that the district complied with this requirement. The IDEA does not require specific goals to be established for behaviors. While not required, the district included baseline data for many of the IEP goals and included the required components, such as present levels of educational performance, measurable annual goals, and benchmarks for short-term objectives. The court ruled that the district provided FAPE to the student.

The implementation of a BIP was the central issue in the Alabama case of *Guntersville City Board of Education* (2006). A 17-year-old student was arrested for threatening to assault his English teacher. The student withdrew from school as part of a plea bargain. While the student had a BIP, the district did not conduct an FBA or document the nature of counseling provided to the student. The district also failed to follow the system of rewards and punishments that was outlined in the BIP. An impartial hearing officer (IHO) determined that the inconsistent implementation of the BIP impeded the student's success and resulted in a denial of FAPE. The district was ordered to develop a new BIP or provide homebound instruction as well as compensatory reading instruction and counseling services.

Behavior and Least Restrictive Environment (LRE)

When addressing behavioral needs, schools must educate students in the regular education classroom settings to the maximum extent appropriate. To be moved to a more restrictive placement, the nature or severity of the student's disability must be such that education cannot be satisfactorily provided within the general education setting with supplementary aids and services.

The least restrictive environment (LRE) will provide the student with needed special education services in a setting with other students who do not have disabilities to the maximum extent possible, as close as possible to the student's home. There must be a balance between the two legal requirements of placing a student in the LRE and providing an appropriate program that addresses the student's needs. When students present with behavioral challenges, LRE can be a point of disagreement between parents and schools. A Fifth Circuit case, *H.W. v. Comal Independent School District* (2003), addressed the issue of LRE for a student with behavioral needs.

H.W. had diagnoses of Down syndrome, ADHD, and speech impairment. Supplemental aids provided included a modified curriculum and special education support within the general education classroom. An FBA and BIP were completed, extended school year services were provided, and the IEP was revised in response to the student's lack of progress. The district subsequently recommended a blended placement for H.W. in which she would receive academic instruction in a special education class. The parent argued that the student mastered 11 of 17 IEP goals, demonstrating that progress had been made in general education. While this factor was an important consideration, the school noted that H.W. rarely interacted with peers and engaged in disruptive behaviors in the general education setting. Additionally, the student was showing regression in some areas and falling behind in standardized assessments. The district argued H.W. failed to make meaningful academic and nonacademic gains within the general education setting. The court found that the district adequately implemented supplemental aid and support in the general education setting before recommending a more restrictive placement. The court agreed with the district that H.W. could not receive a FAPE in the general education setting and that a more restrictive placement was required.

The district did not prevail in another case specific to LRE and behavioral needs. In *L.B. and J.B. v. Nebo School District* (2004), a school district recommended a preschool program composed mostly of students with disabilities for a student with autism. The student presented with behavioral, social, and language needs. The parents disagreed with the district's proposed program and opted to unilaterally enroll their daughter in a mainstream preschool program with an aide and Applied Behavior Analysis (ABA) at home. The student made satisfactory progress. Experts for the parents argued the student would have regressed in the self-contained setting recommended by the district because she would have emulated the maladaptive behavior of other students and received insufficient intervention for her own behaviors. The Tenth Circuit ruled in favor of the parents. It was determined that the district failed to exhaust supplemental aids in the less restrictive setting before refusing a parent's request for a more inclusive program. The district was ordered to reimburse parents for the ABA services and aide that were provided to the student.

Restraint and Seclusion

The Office for Civil Rights (OCR) issued a Dear Colleague Letter (U.S. Department of Education, 2016)[4] on the restraint and seclusion of students with disabilities on December 28, 2016. In the letter, it warned that inappropriate restraint and seclusion may result in discrimination against students with disabilities under Section 504. OCR advised that a school's use of restraint and seclusion could be evidence that the student's current supports and services do not address identified needs, prompting the need for a reevaluation. Restraint and seclusion should be used with a student with a disability only if they would be used with a nondisabled student under similar circumstances. The inappropriate use of restraint or seclusion with a student with a disability could result in a FAPE denial. For example, the student could be traumatized by the restraint or seclusion, which could result in new academic or behavioral difficulties that, if not addressed promptly, could constitute a denial of FAPE.

OCR further defined restraint and seclusion:

- *Restraint: personal restriction that immobilizes or reduces the ability of a student to move his or her torso, arms, legs, or head freely.*
- *Mechanical restraint: the use of any device or equipment to restrict a student's freedom of movement. The term does not include devices implemented by trained school personnel, or utilized by a student that have been prescribed by an appropriate medical or related services professional and are used for the specific and approved purpose for which such devices were designed, such as: (a) adaptive devices or mechanical supports used to achieve proper body position, balance, or alignment to allow greater freedom of mobility than would be possible without the use of such devices or mechanical supports; (b) vehicle safety restraints when used as intended during the transport of a student in a moving vehicle; (c) restraints for medical immobilization; or (d) orthopedically prescribed devices that permit a student to participate in activities without risk of harm.*
- *Seclusion: the involuntary confinement of a student alone in a room or area from which the student is physically prevented from leaving.*

In the case of *Weber (UT) School District* (2017), OCR found that a district in Utah failed to consistently and completely document its use of seclusion and restraint as emergency behavioral interventions for students with disabilities. The district agreed to resolve the matter by drafting policies, developing and implementing a data collection system for accurate reporting, and training relevant staff on the use of restraint and seclusion in accordance with the updated policies. OCR opined, "inadequate recordkeeping makes it difficult for the district to satisfy its ongoing obligation to determine whether a student's IEP or Section 504 plan is effective with respect to the use of restraint or seclusion."

Another case involving restraints was pursued by the mother of a seven-year-old boy with autism. In this case, *J.V. and M.Q. v. Albuquerque Public Schools* (2016), the student engaged in disruptive behavior for a period of two hours. His disruptive behavior included eloping and kicking staff.

The mother provided permission for the school safety officer to restrain the child during the behavioral incident, and the student was briefly handcuffed. The parents filed a discrimination claim based on the child's disability against the school. The Tenth Circuit determined the parents did not meet the three elements required for a discrimination claim. They did not prove the district discriminated against the student or that the student was discriminated against because of his disability. The court held that the use of the mechanical restraint was based on the student's conduct rather than his disability; therefore, the actions were not discriminatory. The parents enrolled their child in another district elementary school after the event, so they were unable to demonstrate a denial of any educational benefit. The parent also did not provide evidence to support the claim that the district failed to accommodate the child or that it disregarded an obvious need for staff training. The Tenth Circuit found in favor of the district.

In the case of *P.T. v. Jefferson County Board of Education* (2006), the Eleventh Circuit ruled that an Alabama district did not deny FAPE to an 11-year-old nonverbal student with autism when it used a harness on a bus due to behavioral outbursts that posed a serious risk of bodily injury to passengers. Interventions such as an aide and a lap belt were not effective. The district then used an H-type harness, which was effective in preventing the student from leaving her seat or removing and throwing her shoes. The court noted that the district appropriately considered student safety when it determined that the use of a safety harness was necessary.

Behavior and Interim Alternative Educational Settings (IAES)

In general, a district must conduct a ***manifestation determination*** review before removing students with disabilities from their current educational placements for more than 10 days. However, the IDEA (§ 300.530) allows school personnel to remove a student to an interim alternative educational setting for up to 45 school days, without regard to whether the behavior is determined to be a manifestation of the child's disability, under special circumstances.

Special circumstances. School personnel may remove a student to an interim alternative educational setting for not more than 45 school days without regard to whether the behavior is determined to be a manifestation of the child's disability, if the child –

(1) *Carries a weapon to or possesses a weapon at school, on school premises, or to or at a school function under the jurisdiction of an SEA or an LEA;*
(2) *Knowingly possesses or uses illegal drugs, or sells or solicits the sale of a controlled substance, while at school, on school premises, or at a school function under the jurisdiction of an SEA or an LEA; or*

(3) *Has inflicted serious bodily injury upon another person while at school, on premises, or at a school function under the jurisdiction of an SEA or an LEA.*

A student may also be placed in an IAES through a due process hearing initiated by the school district when the district demonstrates that the student's behavior is likely to result in injury. The placement in an IAES may be for up to 45 school days and is unrelated to any disciplinary action related to the student or the outcome of a manifestation determination review.

A disagreement regarding the placement of a child in an IAES led to a due process hearing in Arkansas. In *Booneville School District* (2022) in Arkansas, the district requested a hearing to place a nine-year-old student in an IAES because of multiple school staff members being injured and requiring minor medical treatment as a result of the student's behavior. The IDEA defines serious bodily injury as *bodily injury that results in a substantial risk of death, extreme physical pain, protracted or obvious disfigurement, or protracted loss or impairment of the function of a bodily member, organ, or mental faculty.* The impartial hearing officer (IHO) determined that the injuries sustained by staff were minor and did not reach the threshold of serious bodily injury. The IHO did not agree that an IAES was warranted but recognized the student was likely to injure himself or others if he returned to school. The district was subsequently ordered to provide services in the student's home until an FBA could be conducted and an IEP meeting held to determine placement.

In a similar case in Michigan, *G.D. and R.D. v. Utica Community Schools* (2023), a kindergarten student with an unspecified disability threw supplies, books, pieces of a broken thermometer, and a phone base at district staff. The district sought to suspend the student. A manifestation determination concluded that the behavior was a manifestation of the student's disability, but the student was removed to an IAES because the school believed that the student used dangerous weapons. The parents challenged the removal, and an administrative law judge determined that the removal to an IAES was not warranted. Upon appeal, the court acknowledged that an object could be used as a weapon, but it determined that the objects thrown in this scenario were not likely to cause a substantial risk of death when thrown by a kindergarten student. Because the student did not possess a dangerous weapon, his removal to an IAES was found to be inappropriate.

In Sacramento City Unified School District (2023), an ALJ found that placement in an IAES was appropriate for a 15-year-old student with a specific learning disability and conduct disorder. The student threatened to physically harm female students, the vice principal, and other staff. He also had a history of shoving other students into lockers. The ALJ found that the student was likely to injure others due to difficulties with self-regulation and a lack of behavior support at school. Thus, the ALJ granted the district's request to remove the student to a behavior-based IAES program for 45 days. While in placement in the IAES, the student then described additional violent behaviors in a journal entry, including a dream in which he raped and murdered a classmate. He also told his therapist that he wished he had punched his vice principal in the face. The district filed for due process and asked the ALJ to extend the IAES for another 45 days as the student continued to pose a risk. The parents argued that the student was simply describing a nightmare in his journal and just venting to his therapist, but the ALJ was not persuaded by the parents and disagreed. The ALJ continued the student's IEAS placement.

Some suggestions for avoiding due process related to student behavior are provided.

- Be aware of any state-specific laws (or local requirements) related to procedural requirements for managing student behaviors, including FBAs and BIPs.
- Be proactive by addressing student behaviors as they arise.
- Exhaust all supplemental aids and services within the student's current placement prior to moving to a more restrictive setting due to behavior.
- Thoroughly document student behavioral needs and interventions.
- Ensure staff are appropriately trained and aware of relevant legal requirements and procedures.
- Conduct updated evaluations as students' needs change.
- Keep parents informed and involved in decision-making.

Failure to Support Students' Mental Health Needs

Students with mental health needs are often identified as eligible for IDEA services under the eligibility category of emotional disturbance (ED). ED is defined as:

(1) *Emotional disturbance means a condition exhibiting one or more of the following characteristics over a long period of time and to a marked degree that adversely affects a child's educational performance:*
   (A) *An inability to learn that cannot be explained by intellectual, sensory, or health factors.*
   (B) *An inability to build or maintain satisfactory interpersonal relationships with peers and teachers.*
   (C) *Inappropriate types of behavior or feelings under normal circumstances.*
   (D) *A general pervasive mood of unhappiness or depression.*
   (E) *A tendency to develop physical symptoms or fears associated with personal or school problems.*

(2) *Emotional disturbance includes schizophrenia.*

(3) *term does not apply to children who are socially maladjusted, unless it is determined that they have an emotional disturbance under paragraph (c)(4)(i) of this section.*

Note that the IDEA does not require that a student have a specific diagnosis to be eligible for services due to mental health needs. This is apparent in the due process hearing involving the *Los Angeles Unified School District* (2007). This California case involved a 17-year-old student who began to experience behavior and academic difficulties in the eighth grade when his parents separated. Poor attendance and grades were noted in ninth grade, and he discontinued his involvement in organized sports. He enrolled in various private schools, then he returned to the public school. At that time, the parent referred the student for evaluation due to diagnosed depression and truancy problems. The parent also noted that the student was seeing a private therapist.

Despite poor attendance and grades, the school team found the student to be well-adjusted socially and happy in school. He was found not eligible for services. The parent enrolled the student in a therapeutic residential school and initiated due process for tuition reimbursement.

The State Education Agency found that nothing in the assessments or testimony indicated that the student exhibited inappropriate behavior at school. The student's depression was not observed in school, so there was no indication that the student exhibited a general pervasive mood of unhappiness or depression. The evidence demonstrated that the student received educational benefit despite poor attendance, as his standardized achievement scores were in the average range. Thus, a diagnosis of depression was not sufficient to warrant eligibility for special education services. The district completed the evaluation at the parent's request and made an appropriate determination that the student was not eligible for services. Because the student was ineligible for an IEP, the parent was not entitled to tuition reimbursement.

"Over a Long Period of Time"

The definition states that symptoms must be present *over a long period of time* to warrant an ED classification. It is commonly accepted that the symptoms should be present for at least several months and that the classification is not provided for a temporary problem (e.g., an adjustment disorder). The classification criteria do not define the minimum time period; however, some states include definitions within their criteria. The Office of Special Education Programs (OSEP) opined that a range of two to nine months could qualify, provided preliminary interventions were implemented and proven ineffective.

In *R.B. v. Napa Valley Unified School District* (2007), the court found that a California district did not deny a student FAPE by determining the student was not a student with ED. The district demonstrated that the student's improvement in behavior suggested the student's needs did not persist over a long period of time. The judge noted that the testimony demonstrated the student's inappropriate behaviors were not to a marked degree over a long period of time.

"To a Marked Degree"

The IDEA does not define *to a marked degree.* In general, the IEP team must identify whether the student's needs represent a significant normative deviation from peers. In *Letter to Anonymous* (1989)[5], the Office of Special Education Programs (OSEP) opined that *to a marked degree* generally refers to the frequency, duration, or intensity of a student's needs compared with the student's peers. Terms such as *acute, continuous,* and/or *pervasive* are sometimes used for clarification purposes.

"Adversely Affects Educational Performance"

To warrant an ED diagnosis, the student's emotional/behavioral struggles must significantly hinder learning, social skills, and overall school functioning. Grades, social relationships, task completion, or access to the curriculum could be impacted. This goes beyond academics and includes any area of school life in which the disability prevents students from fully benefiting from their education without targeted support.

Academically, a student could be earning failing grades, unable to focus, or failing to complete tasks. Adverse impact could include difficulty learning new material or significant gaps between ability and achievement. In the social/emotional area, impairments could present as an inability to form friendships, inappropriate behavior, persistent sadness, severe anxiety, excessive withdrawal, or physical symptoms associated with stress. A student may also miss class and not be able to access educational programming due to behavioral outbursts, extreme difficulty managing emotions in the classroom, or an inability to follow directions.

The issue of adverse impact on educational performance was the basis for a due process hearing in the Minnesota case of *Independent School District No. 382 v. E.M.D.H.* (2020). The Eighth Circuit found that the district violated the IDEA by delaying an initial evaluation, then conducting an improper evaluation, and finding the student ineligible based on her academic ability. The student had a history of mental health issues that prevented her from attending school. However, the district argued that the student did not have a disability-related need for special education, given her above-average test scores and exceptional performance when she was in attendance. While the school argued that her mental health issues did not adversely affect her educational performance, the court held that the student qualified for an emotional disturbance classification.

In a similar case, *M.M. and I.F. v. New York City Department of Education* (2014), a District Court found that a New York district erred in finding a student diagnosed with an emotional disability ineligible for IDEA services. The district argued that the student's disability did not affect her learning, as evidenced by her good grades. The court, however, disagreed and pointed out that the more fundamental question was whether the student could attend school. The student missed several weeks of school, and the district provided home instruction for multiple months. In addition, the student's grades declined during this period, and she was unable to earn enough credits to move on to the next grade. The court ruled that all of this pointed to the student's need for IDEA services. The district was subsequently ordered to reimburse the parents for the student's residential placement.

In a due process decision in *Adams County School District* (2019), a Colorado district evaluated a student and found her ineligible for an IDEA classification, but the school implemented a Section 504 plan to address the student's anxiety, depression, and Post-Traumatic Stress Disorder (PTSD) after she was sexually assaulted. The parent argued that this decision denied the student a FAPE. The ALJ disagreed as a diagnosed condition alone does not make a student eligible for IDEA services. In this instance, the student successfully completed grade-level courses and benefited from general education with her Section 504 accommodations. The ALJ sided with the school.

The case of *Devon L. v. Clear Creek Independent School District* (2016) also centered on the issue of *adversely affecting educational performance.* The Fifth Circuit held that a Texas district did not violate the IDEA when it found an eleventh-grade student with anxiety, depression, and ADHD ineligible for services. The student earned As and had strong interpersonal skills at the time of the eligibility determination, indicating he did not have an educational need for special education. The parents argued that the student's prior classification in ninth and tenth grades, along with their concern that he would not be able to maintain his current level of performance, should make him eligible. The Court observed that eligibility could not be decided based on concerns that a student might require special education at some point in the future. The district prevailed.

Social Maladjustment

The IDEA definition has an exclusion for social maladjustment. It notes that ED does not apply to students who are socially maladjusted unless it is determined that they are also emotionally disturbed. This exclusion was present in the Education for All Handicapped Children's Act (PL 94–142), which is the predecessor of the IDEA. The social maladjustment exclusion was maintained to clarify that special education services were not intended for court-supervised, adjudicated youth. While the term social maladjustment has been used in special education legislation since 1975, it has not been defined.

At the time PL 94–142 was passed, the Diagnostic and Statistical Manual of Mental Disorders II (DSM-II) described social maladjustment as a cultural conflict resulting from difficulties in adjusting to or adapting to another cultural standard or norm. There was no reference to conduct disorder, oppositional defiant disorder, or delinquency. The diagnosis of social maladjustment is not included in the current DSM-5.

Social maladjustment is currently thought of as a persistent pattern of violating societal norms and/or a perpetual struggle with authority that involves willful, deliberate, antisocial, or delinquent behaviors. For example, theft, defiance, and chronic truancy are examples of behaviors associated with social maladjustment. Key characteristics include the notion that these behaviors are deliberate and under the student's control. The student understands right and wrong but chooses to violate rules. Students with social maladjustment often lack empathy and remorse. While the behaviors break the rules of the majority culture, they may be acceptable within certain subcultures.

Students who are socially maladjusted may be excluded from special education services unless they have other needs that otherwise qualify them for special education. Students who are only socially maladjusted do not receive the benefit of special education protections. These students are likely to be dealt with in the school setting through disciplinary actions, such as suspension and expulsion, rather than through the provision of support services.

In contrast, emotional disturbance includes a broader range of issues like anxiety, depression, and schizophrenia, in which mental health issues impair learning. The problem behaviors are not necessarily willful.

Given the difference in how problem behaviors may be addressed for students with social maladjustment versus emotional disturbance, this determination can greatly impact a student. Since there is no clear guidance in the IDEA regarding the distinction, subjective decisions are made that can lead to due process.

In *W.G. and M.G. v. New York City Department of Education* (2011), a District Court held that a minor episode of depression in a previous grade did not make a student eligible as a student with an emotional disturbance. The Court found that the student's drug and alcohol abuse, truancy, defiance, and refusal to participate in school were based on social maladjustment. Without sufficient evidence of an emotional disturbance as the root of the problem, the Court upheld a State Review Officer's determination that the student was ineligible for IDEA services.

In a similar case, *Springer v. Fairfax County School Board* (1998), the Fourth Circuit concluded that a student's stealing, skipping school, and substance abuse were the result of social maladjustment and not from ED. The Court disagreed with the parents that the student qualified for special education due to an emotional disturbance and pointed out that the student maintained satisfactory relationships with teachers and peers and did not manifest pervasive unhappiness or depression. Furthermore, evaluations conducted by psychologists and the parents' expert did not conclude that the student had an emotional disturbance.

In *H.M. v. Weakley County Board of Education* (2015), a Tennessee District Court found that the district incorrectly determined a student was ineligible for IDEA services as a result of being socially maladjusted. In this case, the Court found that the student's history of sexual abuse and severe major depression, along with medical and educational evaluations stating the student had Post-Traumatic Stress Disorder combined with her performance issues at school, all pointed to eligibility for IDEA services as a student with ED. This case demonstrated that a socially maladjusted student may still be eligible for classification as a child with an emotional disturbance when one of the five criteria for ED is met. Therefore, the presence of social maladjustment is not a total rule-out for classification; rather the IEP Team should explore whether the student exhibits other needs that would entitle the student to an IEP.

In an Eighth Circuit case, *Hansen v. Republic School District (*2011), a student was found eligible for IDEA services under the categories of ED and Other Health Impairment (OHI) as a result of his bipolar disorder, ADHD, and inability to build or maintain satisfactory interpersonal relationships. This Missouri school district chose not to submit its own evidence. Instead, the district argued that the parent's evidence was inadequate and that a diagnosis of ADHD alone did not entitle a student to special education services. The Court ruled that while that may be the case, the district's failure to submit evidence meant it could not conclude that ADHD *was not* adversely affecting the student's educational performance, especially considering the student's multiple disciplinary referrals and academic struggles. The parents prevailed.

Mental Health Needs and Therapeutic Placements

Due process hearings for students with emotional disturbance are sometimes related to placement issues. Therapeutic placements may be the least restrictive setting for some students. These placements typically provide a specialized environment for students with emotional, behavioral, learning, or mental health issues that interfere with their education. In addition to academic instruction, there is a focus on counseling and emotional well-being. Therapeutic placements typically offer smaller class sizes and individualized pacing of instruction.

Placement in a therapeutic program was at issue in a hearing in *Boston Public Schools* (2008). The district determined that a 12-year-old boy with depression could not return to a school for gifted students after assaulting a classmate. Instead, the school recommended a therapeutic day school. The parents argued that the therapeutic school recommended by the district offered academic services well below the student's ability. The student's private therapists testified that the student could be successful in a general education setting with services and support to ensure he did not harm himself or others. Although the IHO agreed that the student could not be returned to his gifted placement, the therapeutic setting was not viewed as an appropriate placement either. The IHO determined that an IEP Team must consider the full continuum of placements when addressing a student's mental health needs, including whether placements that are less restrictive than therapeutic placements may be appropriate.

In *Wood Dale School District No. 7* (2008), a student with ADHD and a mood disorder previously required a therapeutic placement; however, it was determined that the student did not require a current therapeutic placement to receive FAPE. The Illinois hearing officer found that the most recent evaluations indicated that the student no longer required such a restrictive setting. Moreover, the student received counseling in the intervening months since the last evaluation. None of the evaluators recommended a therapeutic placement, and there was no indication that the student required a therapeutic setting to meet her needs. The district's rejection of less restrictive settings due to a lack of counseling and psychiatric services was inadequate to justify the restrictive placement. The IHO ordered the student's placement in a self-contained classroom.

A District Court Judge in New York agreed with the school that a student with autism was appropriately placed in a therapeutic setting in *Yeger v. East Ramapo Central School District* (2022). The parents' chosen out-of-district residential program was too restrictive, and the court noted that the student regressed behaviorally while there. The court agreed with the SRO's decision that the district's therapeutic day setting could meet the student's disability-related needs while allowing the student to remain in his community, thus representing the LRE.

Mental Health Needs and Section 504

If a student has mental health needs but does not need specially designed instruction, eligibility for a Section 504 service agreement may be considered.

Due process hearings have arisen related to 504 eligibility determinations and service delivery.

In *Farmington (MO) R-VII School District* (2021), a student presented with behavioral and mental health issues and received treatment at a private medical center. The Missouri school district transferred the student to an alternative school without conducting a comprehensive evaluation. The Office of Civil Rights found the transfer inappropriate and determined that the district violated its child find duty by failing to assess the student's needs for a Section 504 plan.

In the case of *D.M. v. East Allegheny School District* (2023), a student experienced anxiety and depression as a result of peer bullying. The student had difficulty concentrating and struggled in class; however, the district argued that anxiety and depression were not disabilities. The school district opted to place the student in a cyber program that offered no direct instruction. A District Court in Pennsylvania pointed out that anxiety and depression were conditions that substantially impaired the student's daily life. The court ruled that the cyber placement supported the parents' claims of disability discrimination against the student based on her mental health needs. The District Court agreed with the parents' claims of disability discrimination because the district failed to address the student's mental health issues.

The cases presented in this section, specific to students' mental health needs, provide guidance for schools seeking to avoid due process.

- Build the capacity of staff members to identify and respond to the mental health needs of students.
- Have an adequate number of school mental health professionals on staff, including access to a psychiatrist when possible.
- Provide a continuum of services that target students based on their individual needs.
- Regularly assess the mental health needs of students to determine whether students are responding to interventions.
- Refer students who do not have an adequate response to interventions to the IEP or Section 504 Team. Consider expedited referrals for students with more significant needs.

Issues Surrounding English Learners with Disabilities

According to the federal definition, an English learner (EL) is a student who *has sufficient difficulty speaking, reading, writing, or understanding the English language and whose difficulties may deny such individual the opportunity to learn successfully in classrooms where the language of instruction is English or to participate in society due to the following reasons: was not born in the U.S. and native language is not English, Native American or Alaska Native, is migratory and native language is not English* (PL 103–382).

The Equal Protection Clause of the 14th Amendment prohibits discrimination based on ethnicity or language, and it prohibits discrimination based on disability. Other laws may also apply to English learners with disabilities, including Title VI of the Civil Rights Act of 1964, Section 504 of the Rehabilitation Act of 1973, the Equal Educational Opportunities Act (EEOA) of 1974, and the Individuals with Disabilities Education Act (IDEA) of 2004.

The *Supreme Court decision of Plyler v. Doe* (1982) invalidated a Texas law that denied state funding to schools that educated undocumented students and authorized schools to deny enrollment to such students. The Supreme Court held that the Constitution guarantees equal protection under the law for undocumented children. The Court determined that denying education to undocumented students would "deny them the ability to live within the structure of our civic institutions, and foreclose any realistic possibility that they will contribute in even the smallest way to the progress of our nation." While not specific to students with disabilities, this decision made it clear that students in the United States, whether undocumented or citizens, have the right to an education in public schools.

There are two main areas in which due process hearings occur with respect to English learners. These relate to the identification of English learners as eligible for special education services and to the provision of a FAPE. Identification encompasses child find, evaluation, eligibility determination, and misidentification.

Child Find

K.A.B. v. Downingtown Area School District (2013) is an example of a case that centered on the issue of child find. A due process hearing was initially filed by the parents, Susan B. and John B., in 2010.

K.A.B. was adopted from an orphanage in Russia when he was four years old. A month after his arrival, his parents requested an evaluation for Early Intervention services; however, results were inconclusive because he was not conversant in English. His parents placed him in Occupational Therapy (OT), but the therapist noted no problems. His parents also enrolled him in a private preschool. Six months later, he was enrolled in kindergarten. His parents requested OT and speech evaluations. These evaluations were completed, but he was found ineligible for services. Another speech evaluation was completed at the parents' request in August, before first grade, with inconclusive results due to his limited English proficiency. He received Instructional Support Team (IST) and English as a Second Language (ESL) services. In November of second grade, he was found eligible for services as a student with a specific learning disability. An IEP was developed and implemented for learning support services in language arts. ESL services were continued. In April, another speech evaluation found him eligible for speech/language support, and speech therapy was added to his IEP. In January 2010, during his third-grade year, his parents filed for a due process hearing, alleging the district failed to identify their child in a timely manner and failed to provide FAPE. In September of 2010, the parents placed him in a private school for fourth grade. His parents requested compensatory education, attorneys' fees, and costs.

The hearing officer concluded that the district, for the most part, had adequately met its child find obligation and provided K.A.B. with a FAPE. However, the hearing officer found the district's November 2008 evaluation was deficient because it lacked a speech/language assessment. Therefore, K.A.B. was entitled to 11 hours of compensatory speech/language services. Furthermore, the hearing officer found that K.A.B.'s various IEPs had improperly failed to address his difficulties in attention and focus. Therefore, K.A.B. was entitled to 68 hours of compensatory education to develop his self-regulation abilities. This decision was affirmed on appeal.

Evaluation

In *B.G. ex rel. J.A.G. v. Board of Education of Chicago* (2018), the central issue was the reevaluation of a seventh grader who had received services as a student with a specific learning disability since the second grade. His mother spoke only Spanish. The student had significant attendance issues related to family problems and health issues. B.G. was diagnosed with morbid obesity, hypertension, severe obesity-related hypoxia syndrome, Type 2 diabetes, and obstructive sleep apnea. He also experienced the death of his father. His reevaluation was initiated by a bilingual school psychologist, with testing conducted in English, because she concluded that he was proficient in English and that English was his preferred language. The school psychologist went on maternity leave, and a second bilingual school psychologist completed the reevaluation report.

The parent disputed the findings of the reevaluation, which determined the student was eligible for services as a student with SLD and ED. The parent requested an Independent Educational Evaluation at public expense in seven areas: psychology, speech-language, physical therapy, occupational therapy, nursing, social work, and assistive technology. The Hearing Officer's decision, issued in March 2015, found that the parent was not entitled to an IEE.

Two experts (a psychologist and a speech therapist) were presented by the parent. They did not have any direct involvement with B.G., nor did they observe him. Although they were credible witnesses, they were not persuasive. On appeal, the court upheld the decision.

In a 2014 California case, *Celerity Educational Group v. Parent on Behalf of Student*, the evaluation was also in dispute. This case involved a second-grade charter school student with primary languages of Portuguese and

Spanish. He was classified as an English learner, and his overall English development was at the intermediate level. He demonstrated fluency in spoken English. As English appeared to be his dominant language, he was assessed in English by a bilingual school psychologist. A bilingual intern completed the achievement testing but was directly supervised by an educational specialist assigned to oversee academic testing. The student was found ineligible for special education services. The parent requested an Independent Educational Evaluation, which was denied. When the parent did not respond to the denial of her request, the charter school requested a due process hearing. The Hearing Officer found that the multidisciplinary assessment met all legal requirements, so the parent was not entitled to an IEE at public expense.

Eligibility

The eligibility determination for a student was in dispute in the Ninth Circuit case of *E.M.v. Pajaro Valley Unified School District* (2011). E.M. was from a bilingual household; however, it was unclear if he was bilingual. Spanish was listed as his first language on his school enrollment form; however, his mother chose a structured English Immersion Program rather than the mainstream English program or a bilingual program. In a psychological report secured for immigration purposes, it was noted that E.M.'s family should not be deported to Mexico because Spanish purportedly was E.M.'s second language. While the record was unclear on this point, there was sufficient evidence to suggest that E.M. remained bilingual, as demonstrated by the fact that he informed an evaluator that he dreamed in both English and Spanish.

E.M. struggled in school with homework completion and inattention. Grade retention was considered, but he attended summer school to improve his skills. Before the start of fifth grade, his parents paid for an evaluation by a psychologist. He had an average IQ (Wechsler Intelligence Scale for Children – Third Edition, Full Scale Intelligence Quotient = 95). Scores on the Woodcock-Johnson Tests of Achievement – Third Edition were average in all areas, although mild impairment was noted in Oral Language. The private psychologist diagnosed a specific learning disability in oral language based on the DSM-IV criteria, which require a discrepancy of at least one standard deviation. The primary purpose of this evaluation was for immigration proceedings and included statements about how moving to Mexico would present issues because of E.M.'s disability and apparent preference for English over Spanish. The evaluation was suggested by the family's immigration attorney because proof of a learning disability can impact the child's ability to stay in the United States and receive services. Because of the statements indicating that the child was an English-only speaker, the Hearing Officer found the private psychologist not credible.

The student's mother shared the outside report and requested an evaluation. The district completed an evaluation. Results on the Kaufman

Assessment Battery for Children (KABC) were inconsistent with prior results (IQ = 111); therefore, the Test of Nonverbal Intelligence was also administered, yielding a score of 98. Believing the KABC results to be inaccurate, the district's school psychologist relied on prior WISC-III results and chose the performance score based on his bilingual background. Based on these results, no discrepancy existed. Conners ratings were average by the teacher but elevated by the parent. The school found the student to be non-exceptional and offered a 504 plan.

The parent disagreed. The private psychologist submitted a letter stating that a discrepancy occurred if the KABC score were used. The parent accused the district of cherry-picking results to support a predetermined conclusion. The Hearing Officer ruled that the district could choose how to interpret valid but contradictory scores. The district prevailed, and the decision was supported on appeal.

Misidentification

Issues related to the misidentification of English learners have also led to due process hearings. The case of ***Mumid v. Abraham Lincoln High School*** (2010) is one such case.

At the time of the due process hearing, Abraham Lincoln High School (ALHS) was an alternative public high school in Minneapolis serving Somali and Ethiopian refugees receiving EL services. The students had very little to no formal schooling and ranged in age from 14 to 20. Thirteen former students filed the suit. Five of these students had graduated, while eight did not because they could not pass the state-required exam. Students lodged a complaint with the Minnesota Department of Education (MDE) claiming that the school was not meeting their needs. The MDE found it highly probable that the school had failed to identify some special education students. The state average for the special education population was 12.5%, while the rate at ALHS was less than 1%. The school did not evaluate students for special education until they had been in the system for three years. This delay in evaluation was viewed as impermissible.

With a ruling in their favor, the students filed a complaint under Title VI and the Equal Education Opportunity Act. Intentional discrimination could not be demonstrated because there was no similarly situated comparison student whom the school treated better, and deficient programming alone was not sufficient to establish intentional discrimination based on national origin. No monetary damages were awarded.

Free Appropriate Public Education (FAPE)

Marple Newtown School District v. Rafael N. (2007) is a Pennsylvania case involving a 17-year-old Spanish-speaking student with an intellectual disability and epilepsy. The student immigrated to the country after the death of his family members. Language was impaired in both Spanish and English. The parent spoke another language and was illiterate. The student initially attended a life skills classroom; however, seizures and medications affected his ability to participate in programming. Pull-out ESL services were removed because the IEP team determined that he was not benefiting. It was recommended that his needs be addressed by integrating ESL into the classroom. A bilingual evaluation of the student was ordered by a Family Court judge in proceedings unrelated to the district or Intermediate Unit. The district agreed to complete the evaluation. Push-in ESL was recommended along with monthly consultation with an ESL teacher. The Notice of Recommended Educational Placement (NOREP) was rejected because the parent did not feel that the student's language needs were being accommodated. The parent had two private evaluations completed. Although there was agreement on eligibility for services, there were some differences in recommendations for programming.

The parent requested an extension of the two-year limit for seeking a due process claim. The parent showed that almost all correspondence between the district and the parent was in English, and the district did not always provide translation services. Based on the "disturbing pattern of insensitivity to the fact that the Parent is monolingual [redacted] speaking and illiterate," the hearing officer found that the parent should be permitted to present evidence to support his claims for compensatory education beyond the two-year period prior to his request for a due process hearing. However, the parent could not present evidence that any departures from proper procedures resulted in a denial of a FAPE to the student. No compensatory education was awarded on this basis.

The decision was appealed. The appeals panel found that the district denied the student FAPE because the student's IEP was not reasonably calculated to address his language needs and ensure he received a meaningful educational benefit. The IEP services were almost exclusively in English, and ESL instruction had been replaced with speech and language therapy in a group setting for 30 minutes per week. The review panel ruled that the IEPs were not appropriate, and the United States District Court affirmed that ruling. Remediation included bilingual special education instruction.

Another Pennsylvania case related to FAPE for English learners was *A.G. v. Philadelphia City School District* (2015). In the decision, 30 hearing dates were listed. The student moved to Philadelphia from another country in January 2011 but initially attended a parochial school and resided with a relative. He returned to his native country from March 2011 to November 2012, where he did not attend school. He then enrolled in a Philadelphia high school for 57 days and was late or absent 28 times. He received ESL services and was not referred for an evaluation. He returned to his home country for about a year before re-enrolling in another Philadelphia high school in October 2013. He was enrolled for 148 days and was absent or late 97 days. In March of 2014, the parent submitted a letter and a court order that was tantamount to a request for an evaluation. The parent was sent a permission to evaluate (PTE) form in English. The parent requested due process in June 2014. The district agreed to an Independent Educational Evaluation (IEE) that was completed in July 2014. The student also had surgery in July 2014 due to Blount's disease. The IEE and NOREP were provided to the parent in both English and Spanish.

A primary issue was related to meaningful parental participation. The IDEA's regulations require the translation of only the procedural safeguards notice and prior written notices (NOREPs). The IDEA does not explicitly require the translation of other documents. IDEA does, however, require meaningful parental participation, and without key documents being translated, it was determined that the parent could not meaningfully participate. Thus, although the district complied with the IDEA requirement for translated documents, the hearing officer found that it did not meet the meaningful parental participation requirement. The district's IEP was viewed as appropriate. The student was not entitled to any compensatory education because the district did not fail to offer an appropriate program. The district's failure to include the parent in a meaningful way constituted a substantive violation, remedied by compensatory education. For the three IEP meetings that the parent attended but could not fully participate in, three hours of compensatory education were awarded. The guardian was to determine how the hours were used.

Another case, *T.R. et al. v. School District of Philadelphia* (2015), is a federal class action suit alleging that thousands of parents and their children were illegally denied the opportunity to participate in the special education process due to their limited English proficiency. The complaint alleged that the School District of Philadelphia failed to adequately interpret or provide translated documents to parents in a timely manner. Ultimately, claims were dismissed in April 2020 due to failure to exhaust administrative remedies.

The following suggestions are offered to assist schools in meeting the needs of English learners with disabilities and to avoid due process hearings.

- Do not have practices or policies of systematically delaying the evaluation of ELs for a specified period of time.
- Translating required documents (PSN, Invitation) does not guarantee meaningful parent participation.
- Translating other key documents, such as the IEP, may be necessary to ensure meaningful parent participation.
- Build capacity by developing culturally and linguistically sensitive general and special education classrooms.
- Consider alternative dispute resolution procedures such as mediation and facilitated IEP meetings.

- Recruit and retain competent bilingual school psychologists and other SPLED personnel (teachers, speech therapists, OTs, PTs, supervisors).
- Include ESL teachers in IEP and other team meetings.
- ESL and SPLED services are not mutually exclusive; students can receive both.

Notes

1 Supreme Court Cases Heard. https://www.uscourts.gov/about-federal-courts/educational-resources/about-educational-outreach/activity-resources/about
2 Zirkel, P. (2020). Child Find Under the IDEA: An Updated Analysis of the Judicial Case Law. *National Association of School Psychologists. Communique*, 48(8), 14–16.
3 *Questions and Answers on Endrew F. v. Douglas County School District Re-1*, 71 IDELR 68 (DOE 2017).
4 U.S. Department of Education, Office for Civil Rights. (2016, December 28). *Dear Colleague Letter: Restraint and Seclusion of Students with Disabilities* [Letter]. https://www.ed.gov/media/document/colleague-504-restraint-seclusion-ps-2016-35076.pdf
5 U.S. Department of Education, Office of Special Education Programs. (1989, February 15). Letter to Anonymous, 213 IDELR 247 [Policy Letter]. Individuals with Disabilities Education Act (IDEA).

List of Cases

Adams County Sch. Dist. #27J, 76 IDELR 28 (SEA CO 2019).
A.G. v. Philadelphia City School District, ODR File No. 15166-13-14 (Pa. ODR May 26, 2015).
A.P. ex rel. Powers v. Woodstock Bd. of Educ., 572 F. Supp. 2d 221 (D. Conn. 2008).
Avaras v. Clarkstown Cent. Sch. Dist., 73 IDELR 50, 118 LRP 37050 (S.D.N.Y. September 28, 2018).
B.G. ex rel. J.A.G. v. Bd. of Educ. of Chi., 906 F.3d 632 (7th Cir. 2018).
Booneville Sch. Dist., 82 IDELR 145 (SEA AR 2022).
Boston Pub. Schs., 50 IDELR 55 (SEA MA 2008).
Celerity Educational Group v. Parent on Behalf of Student (OAH Case No. 2014050842) Decision: September 19, 2014.
C.F. v. New York City Dep't of Educ., 62 IDELR 281 (2d Cir. 2014).
C.H. v. Cape Henlopen Sch. Dist., 606 F.3d 59 (3d Cir. 2010).
Clark County Sch. Dist., 122 LRP 45275 (SEA NV 07/29/22).
Clinton County R-III School District v. CJK, 896 F. Supp. 948 (W.D. Mo. 1995).
Cobb County Sch. Dist. v. D.B., 66 IDELR 134 (N.D. Ga. 2015).
Devon L. v. Clear Creek Indep. Sch. Dist., 70 IDELR 32 (5th Cir. 2017), aff'g 68 IDELR 166 (S.D. Tex. 2016).
D.M. v. East Allegheny Sch. Dist., 82 IDELR 171 (W.D. Pa. 2023).
E.M. v. Pajaro Valley Unified Sch. Dist., 652 F.3d 999 (9th Cir. 2011).
Endrew v. Douglas Cty. Sch. Dist., 137 S. Ct. 988, 996 (2017).
Farmington (MO) R-VII School District, 79 IDELR 20 (OCR 2021).
G.D. and R.D. v. Utica Cmty. Schs. 83 IDELR 12 (E.D. Mich. 2023).
Guntersville City Bd. Of Educ. 47 IDELR 84 (SEA AL 2006).
Hansen v. Republic R-III School District, 632 F.3d 1024 (8th Cir. 2011).

Hendrick Hudson District Board of Ed. v. Rowley, 458 U.S. 176 (1982).
H.M. v. Weakley County Bd. of Educ., 119 F. Supp. 3d 873 (W.D. Tenn. 2015).
H.W. v. Comal Independent School District, 344 F.3d 462 (5th Cir. 2003).
Independent Sch. Dist. No. 283 v. E.M.D.H., 960 F.3d 1073 (8th Cir. 2020).
Indep. Sch. Dist. No. 413, Marshall v. H.M.J., 123 F. Supp. 3d 1100 (D. Minn. 2015).
J.H. v. New York City Department of Education, 652 F. Supp. 2d 297 (N.D.N.Y. 2009).
J.V. v. Albuquerque Public Schools, 67 IDELR 55 (10th Cir. 2016).
K.A.B. v. Downingtown Area Sch. Dist., 966 F. Supp. 2d 456 (E.D. Pa. 2013).
K.W. v. Tuscaloosa County Sch. Sys., 73 IDELR 157 (N.D. Ala. 2018).
Lathrop R-II School District v. Gray, 54 IDELR 276 (8th Cir. 2010).
L.B. and J.B. v. Nebo School District, 41 IDELR 206 (10th Cir. 2004).
Leggett v. Dist. of Columbia, No. 14-7021 (D.C. Cir. July 10, 2015).
Legris v. Capistrano Unified Sch. Dist., 79 IDELR 243 (9th Cir. 2021).
Los Angeles Unified Sch. Dist., 107 LRP 27850 (SEA CA 2007).
Marple Newtown Sch. Dist. V. Rafael N., 48 IDELR 184, (E.D. Pa. 2007).
M.G. v. Williamson County Schs., 71 IDELR 102 (6th Cir. 2018).
M.M. and I.F. v. New York City Dep't of Educ., 63 IDELR 156 (S.D.N.Y. 2014).
Mr. P and Mrs. P v. West Hartford Board Of Educ., 71 IDELR 207 (2nd Cir. 2018).
Mumid v. Abraham Lincoln High School, 618 F.3d 789 (8th Cir. 2010).
N.N. v. Mountain View-Los Alton Union High Sch. Dist., 81 IDELR 161 (N.D. Cal. 2022).
Perez v. Sturgis Public Schools, 143 S. Ct. 859 (2023).
P.K. v. Bedford Cent. Sch. Dist., 569 F. Supp. 2d 371 (S.D.N.Y. 2008).
Plyler v. Doe, 457 U.S. 202 (1982).
P.T. v. Jefferson County Board of Education, 46 IDELR 3 (11th Cir. 2006).
R.B. v. Napa Valley Unified Sch. Dist., 48 IDELR 60 (9th Cir. 2007).
R.B. and S.R.B. v. North East Indep. Sch. Dist., 80 IDELR 162 (W.D. Tex. 2022).
R.K. v. New York City Dep't of Educ., 56 IDELR 212 (E.D.N.Y. 2011).
Sacramento City Unified Sch. Dist., 123 LRP 6993 (SEA CA 2023).
Sch. Dist. of Phila. v. Williams No. 2:14-cv-06238 (E.D. Pa. 2014).
Spring Branch Indep. Sch. Dist. v. O.W., 76 IDELR 234 (SEA Tex. 2020).
Springer v. Fairfax County School Board, 134 F.3d 659 (4th Cir. 1998).
T.K. v. New York City Department of Education, 810 F.3d 869 (2nd Cir. 2016).
T.P. & S.P. ex rel. S.P. v. Mamaroneck Union Free School District, 554 F.3d 247 (2nd Cir. 2009).
T.R. v. School District of Philadelphia, 115 F. Supp. 3d 509 (E.D. Pa. 2015).
Urbana (IL) Sch. Dist. #116, 121 LRP 36494 (OCR 08/11/21).
Weber (UT) Sch. Dist., 71 IDELR 109 (OCR 2017).
W.G. and M.G. v. New York City Dep't of Educ., 801 F. Supp. 2d 142 (S.D.N.Y. 2011).
Wood Dale School District No. 7, 51 IDELR 260 (SEA IL 2008).
Yeger v. East Ramapo Cent. Sch. Dist., 82 IDELR 24 (S.D.N.Y. 2022).

Laws Cited

Civil Rights Act of 1964, Title VI, 42 U.S.C. §§ 2000d–2000d-7.
Education for All Handicapped Children Act, Pub. L. No. 94–142, 89 Stat. 773 (1975).
Equal Educational Opportunities Act of 1974, 20 U.S.C. § 1701 *et seq.* (1974).

Improving America's Schools Act of 1994, Pub. L. No. 103-382, 108 Stat. 3518 (1994).
Individuals with Disabilities Education Act, 20 U.S.C. § 1400 (2004).
Rehabilitation Act of 1973, § 504, 29 U.S.C. § 794 (1973).
U.S. Const. amend. XIV, § 1.

6 Section 504

Shirley A. Woika

What Is Section 504?

Section 504 of the Rehabilitation Act of 1973 (PL 93–112) was signed into law on September 26, 1973, by President Richard M. Nixon. This act replaced the Vocational Rehabilitation Act. The main purpose of Section 504 was to extend and revise the authorization of grants to states for vocational rehabilitation services. The regulations implementing Section 504 for educational institutions are found at 34 C.F.R. Part 104.

Section 504 applies to all elementary and secondary public schools, school districts, state educational agencies, private schools, and juvenile justice facilities that receive Federal financial assistance from the United States Department of Education. It prohibits these entities from discriminating against qualified individuals with disabilities based on their disabilities. Schools cannot discriminate against students with disabilities in their programs and activities. For example, if a school sponsors a bus to an away football game, and a student who requires wheelchair-accessible transportation signs up, the school must provide transportation for all students.

The Act contains several subparts:

Subpart A – General Provisions
Subpart B – Employment Practices
Subpart C – Accessibility
Subpart D – Preschool, Elementary, and Secondary Education
Subpart E – Postsecondary Education
Subpart F – Health, Welfare, and Social Services
Subpart G – Procedures

Section 504 is widely recognized as the first civil rights statute for people with disabilities. It prohibits discrimination on the basis of disability in programs conducted by Federal agencies, in programs receiving Federal financial assistance, in Federal employment, and in the employment practices of Federal contractors. It is an unfunded mandate.

DOI: 10.4324/9781003728993-7

504 Requirements

Each Federal agency has its own set of 504 regulations that apply to its programs. Common requirements include reasonable accommodation for employees with disabilities, program accessibility, effective communication with people with hearing/vision disabilities, and accessible new constructions and alterations.

Section 504 is actually only one sentence long. It reads:

> *No otherwise qualified individual with a disability ... shall solely by reason of her or his disability, be excluded from the participation in, be denied the benefits of, or be subjected to discrimination under any program or activity receiving federal financial assistance.*

Section 504 paved the way for the Americans with Disabilities Act (ADA) in 1990. The ADA is similar to Section 504; however, it applies to entities that do not receive federal funds. Section 504 applies to recipients of federal funds.

The definition of a disability is broad under Section 504.

A person is considered to have a disability if that person:

(1) *has a physical or mental impairment which substantially limits one or more of such person's major life activities*
(2) *has a record of such an impairment, or*
(3) *is regarded as having such an impairment*

A physical or mental impairment is defined as:

(a) *any physiological disorder or condition, cosmetic disfigurement, or anatomical loss affecting one or more of the following body systems: neurological; musculoskeletal; special sense organs; respiratory; including speech organs; cardiovascular; reproductive; digestive; genito-urinary; hemic and lymphatic; skin and endocrine; or*
(b) *any mental or psychological disorder, such as mental retardation, organic brain syndrome, emotional or mental illness, and specific learning disabilities.*

An exhaustive list of impairments is not provided due to the difficulty of ensuring its comprehensiveness. The definition of a "physical or mental impairment" does not specify that a formal diagnosis is required. Therefore, there is no legal requirement for a student to have a formal diagnosis to qualify for Section 504 accommodations; rather, the Section 504 Team is tasked with identifying, typically through an evaluation, whether the student requires accommodations due to having a physical or mental impairment that substantially impacts at least one major life activity. Conversely, a student having a formal diagnosis does not, on its own, entitle that student to Section 504 accommodations. Rather, the Section 504 Team would need to determine whether that diagnosis (which we would assume is a physical or mental impairment) substantially limits a major life activity.

As noted in the definition of disability, the physical or mental impairment must substantially limit one or more major life activities. Major life activities include functions like caring for one's self, performing manual tasks, walking, seeing, hearing, speaking, breathing, learning, reading, concentrating, thinking, communicating, and working. Again, the list is not exhaustive.

Note that learning is one of many life activities listed. Thus, learning need not be affected to warrant consideration for eligibility under 504. If learning is impacted, it may be evident by performance on standardized tests, grades, attendance rates, or other indicators.

Section 504 requirements as they apply to schools include:

- Evaluating students believed to have a disability.
- Providing periodic reevaluation of students with disabilities.
- Providing education to students with disabilities in the least restrictive environment.
- Providing established standards and procedures in the identification and evaluation process.
- Providing equal access to parents who have a disability.
- Providing students with disabilities equal access to nonacademic services.
- Ensuring behavior in question is not a manifestation of the student's disability during disciplinary proceedings.

School districts must provide a free appropriate public education (FAPE) to each qualified student with a disability, regardless of the nature or the severity of the disability. FAPE consists of the provision of regular or special education and related aids and services designed to meet the student's needs as adequately as the needs of nondisabled students are met at no cost to the student. An example might include providing curb-to-curb transportation for a student who lives within walking distance of the school but cannot walk the distance due to dwarfism. Another example might involve administering medication to a student who cannot self-administer if the service is needed to meet the student's educational needs. If a student cannot toilet and needs assistance with a catheter, the school district must provide a trained individual to assist.

There is an exception to the no-cost mandate. If fees are imposed on nondisabled students and their parents, they may also be imposed on protected students and their parents. For example, if all students have to pay $25 for a field trip, the fee may also be assessed to students with disabilities. However, students with disabilities cannot be required to pay a higher fee than their nondisabled peers – even if those students with disabilities require accommodations that result in an increased cost to the school.

Procedural safeguards must be established for the identification, evaluation, and educational placement of students who are believed to be in need of special education or related services due to a disability. This information must be communicated to parents, and parents must be notified of evaluation or placement actions. School districts are required to develop Section 504 procedural safeguards that comply with the legal requirements.

504 versus IDEA

It is important to understand the relationship between students who qualify for special education services under the Individuals with Disabilities Education Act (IDEA) and those who qualify for services under Section 504. All students who are eligible for special education services under the IDEA are also eligible for services – and entitled to disability discrimination protections – under Section 504; however, an IEP provides greater protection for such students than a 504 service agreement. Thus, an IEP must address the need for accommodation. This is typically documented under *Special Considerations the IEP Team must consider before developing the IEP* and/or under *Special Education/Related Services/Supplementary Aids and Services/Program Modifications.* If a student qualifies for an IEP, there is no need to write a separate 504 service agreement. Further, if a 504 student is identified as eligible under IDEA, the 504 service agreement is discontinued in favor of an IEP.

The Venn diagram on the following page illustrates the relationship between eligibility under the IDEA and under Section 504 for the student population (Figure 6.1).

While both the IDEA and Section 504 address the needs of students with disabilities, there are also distinctions between the two. While the IDEA is an *education* law, Section 504 is a *civil rights* law. The IDEA focuses on ensuring that children with disabilities receive a free appropriate public education or FAPE. Section 504 of the Rehabilitation Act is focused on ensuring an equal opportunity for individuals with disabilities to participate with nondisabled peers. It ensures that individuals with disabilities are not discriminated against.

To be eligible for services under the IDEA, students must be between the ages of 3 and 21 years (with some states providing such protections until a student turns 22) and have a disability that adversely impacts their educational performance and/or their ability to benefit from general education. There are 13 disability categories under the IDEA, and individuals must meet the definitional criteria and demonstrate a need for support services to qualify for services.

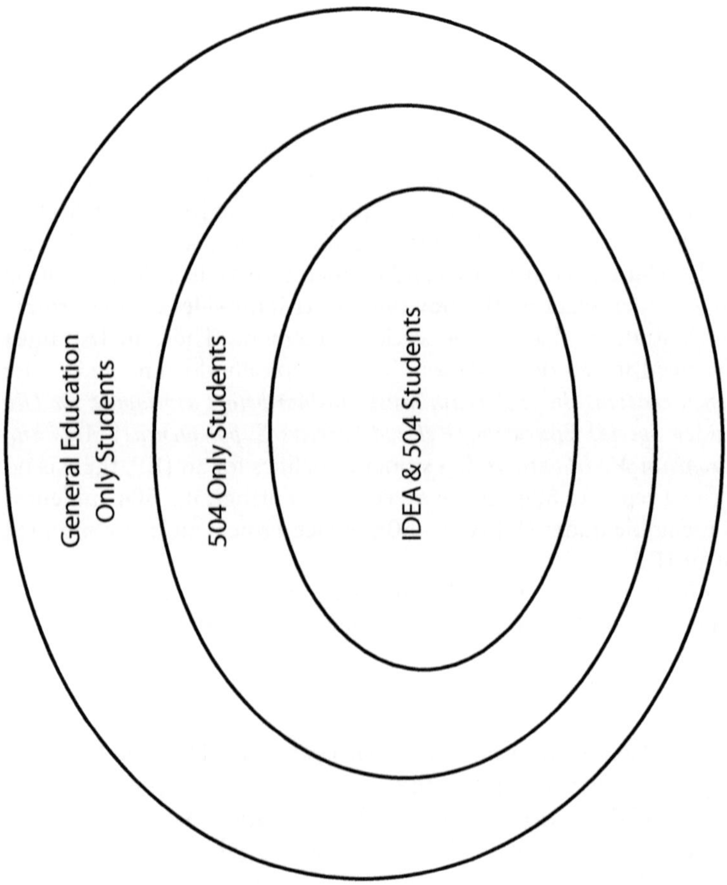

Figure 6.1 Venn diagram showing the relationship between students receiving IDEA, 504, and/or General Education services.

Section 504 is not limited to school-age students. It also applies to adults in the workplace of any entity that receives federal funding. Thus, a teacher in a school setting with a disability may be entitled to workplace accommodation as an employee. Section 504 has a much broader definition of disability than the IDEA. There is not an exhaustive list of disabilities. Any physical or mental impairment that limits a major life activity is needed for eligibility. Individuals also receive disability discrimination protections under Section 504 if they have a record of impairment or are regarded as having an impairment.

Students who qualify for services under the IDEA receive individual supplemental services and supports at no cost. These services might include learning support, autistic support, emotional support, or vision support, as well as related services like physical therapy or speech/language therapy. Special education services are documented in an Individualized Education Program (IEP).

Section 504 focuses on removing barriers that prevent a student from participating fully in the general education program. For example, if a student has asthma and needs to use an inhaler in the event of an attack, the 504 plan would allow the student to carry an inhaler on his person, even if the district policy requires all medications to be kept in the nurse's office. Similarly, a student who uses a wheelchair and needs wheelchair-accessible transportation to get to school and toileting assistance during the school day would be entitled to those services. Although there is no legal requirement to have a written plan, most schools document their services in some type of written service plan or service agreement. When complaints are filed and investigations are completed by the Office for Civil Rights, investigators are interested in seeing related documents.

The IDEA is federally funded, and schools receive additional funding to offset the costs of special education and related services. In contrast, Section 504 is an unfunded mandate. There is no funding associated with implementing 504 requirements.

Evaluations for special education services under the IDEA involve a multidisciplinary team (MDT) evaluation, and the parent must provide signed authorization to proceed. The members of an MDT – also called IEP Teams – are prescribed. The properly comprised team includes a parent, a teacher, a representative of the school that can commit resources, and others. For many situations, a school psychologist is a required member of the team as well. A variety of assessment tools are used to assess a student in all areas of suspected disability. A student suspected of an intellectual disability might be assessed with an intelligence test and an adaptive behavior measure. A student suspected of an emotional disturbance would likely have a functional behavioral assessment completed, and students suspected of being visually impaired might be given a functional vision assessment. If a parent disagrees with the school's multidisciplinary evaluation, an independent educational evaluation (IEE) can be requested. The school district must pay for the IEE or initiate due process to deny the request.

To be eligible for a 504 Service Plan, a team of knowledgeable individuals may review information from a variety of sources in the area of concern. Schools are required to have a designated 504 Coordinator. Team membership varies by disability area. A nurse would likely be included for medical concerns such as a seizure disorder or diabetes. A physical therapist might be included for students with mobility impairments. Notice of the evaluation is required. Although written consent is not required in the law, most states and schools have a process in place that includes securing written consent for the evaluation. While a school would not diagnose conditions such as spina bifida, seizure disorder, or diabetes, the team would review medical records, consult with doctors, and focus on how the condition affects the student in the school environment. This would help to identify the student's needs. If the parents do not agree with the findings of the 504 evaluation team, there is no recourse for an independent evaluation at school district expense.

Should a dispute arise between parents and schools regarding a student who is eligible or thought to be eligible for services under the IDEA, due process procedures exist to resolve such conflicts. These include meetings aimed at resolving the issue and can continue to a due process hearing. These procedures can address differences of opinion related to the evaluation and identification of a student, IEP implementation, or the student's placement. There are no monetary awards through the due process procedures. If a parent prevails at a hearing, the remedies are limited to compensatory education, tuition reimbursement for a private placement obtained by the parent, substantive changes to the student's IEP (including placement, program, related services, accommodations, etc.), or other equitable relief (such as staff training, conducting evaluations, etc.). For example, if a student should have been receiving an hour of speech therapy but was receiving only 30 minutes per week, the resolution could include compensatory services of 30 minutes per week for each week missed. Compensatory education is not always a 1:1 make-up of missed or owed services; rather, it is calculated based on the services required to place students in the position they would have been in had they received the services. All remedies must be exhausted through due process before filing appeals in the legal system, such as state or federal courts. This is called the exhaustion of administrative remedies.

Section 504 requires that a grievance procedure be established and followed to resolve disagreements between parents and the school. A complaint can be filed with the Office for Civil Rights (OCR), or an action can be filed in federal court without going through the due process procedures. It is also possible to receive compensatory damages and substantive modifications to the Section 504 accommodations through this process. Courts are increasingly awarding parents monetary damages through Section 504 claims, as decided in a recent Supreme Court decision, *A.J.T. v. Osseo Area Schools*, Independent School District Number 279 (2025).

These key differences between the IDEA and Section 504 are summarized in Table 6.1.

Table 6.1 IDEA and Section 504 Comparison Chart

Area	*IDEA*	*Section 504*
Purpose	Ensure FAPE for children with disabilities who fall within one of the specific disability categories listed in the IDEA	Civil rights law aimed at preventing discrimination by ensuring individuals with disabilities have opportunities to participate with non-disabled peers
Who?	Eligible students age 3–21 whose disability adversely affects educational performance and/or ability to benefit from general education	Covers all people with a disability from discrimination in settings that receive federal funds based solely on their disability. 504 defines a person with a disability as having a physical or mental impairment that limits one or more major life activities; having a record of such an impairment; or being regarded as having an impairment
Services	Individual supplemental services and supports at no cost	Requires schools to eliminate barriers that would prevent the student from participating fully in the programs and services offered in the general curriculum
Requirements for service delivery	IEP	Does not require a written plan as part of legislation, but OCR looks for a documented plan, typically referred to as a service plan or service agreement
Funding	Federal funds provided	No additional funds are provided
Evaluation Procedures	Multidisciplinary evaluation using a variety of assessment tools, including information from parents, to assess in all areas of the suspected disability	Evaluation draws on information from a variety of sources in the area(s) of concern, and a decision is made by a group of knowledgeable individuals

(*Continued*)

Table 6.1 (Continued)

Area	*IDEA*	*Section 504*
Permission	Parental permission required for evaluation	Written consent is not required, but notification is required
Independent Evaluation	Parents may request an IEE if they disagree with the district's evaluation	No allowance for IEE at district expense
Due Process	Requires districts to provide resolution sessions and due process hearings for parents who disagree with identification, evaluation, implementation of IEP, or student's LRE placement. Resolution is limited to compensatory education	A grievance procedure must be established and followed. Due process is not required before OCR involvement or court action unless the student is also covered by IDEA. Compensatory damages are possible

Section 504 and Service Animals

Picture yourself at work in a school. You are just getting settled when you are called to the office by the building secretary. She tells you that the building administrator is out of the building, and she is not sure what to do in this situation. She was hoping that you would have some guidance.

A third-grade student and his mother arrived at the office with a miniature horse and stated that the animal will now assist the child throughout the school day. Does the student have the right to bring a horse to school? What is an appropriate response from the school?

Although an unlikely scenario, knowing what the federal government says about service animals will guide an appropriate response. We will return to this scenario later in the chapter.

Similar to the Rehabilitation Act of 1973, the Americans with Disabilities Act (ADA) is a civil rights act that protects the rights of people with disabilities. The ADA ensures that places like stores, public transportation, healthcare facilities, and public housing are accessible. The ADA and Section 504 of the Rehabilitation Act are distinct pieces of legislation; however, Section 504 applies only to entities that receive federal funds, while the ADA applies broadly to other entities beyond those that receive federal support.

Title II of the Americans with Disabilities Act (ADA) applies to both public and private schools. Public schools from preschool to higher education are covered under Title II, while private schools are covered under Title III. In the Code of Federal Regulations, service animals are addressed under Title 28, Part 35, Section 136 (28 CFR 35.136). Section 504 definitions are largely aligned with the ADA. Both the ADA and Section 504 apply to schools and prohibit discrimination against students with disabilities.

The ADA Amendments Act of 2008 went into effect on January 1, 2009. It amended the ADA of 1990 and included a conforming amendment to the Rehabilitation Act of 1973; however, it did not require the United States Department of Education to amend its Section 504 regulations. The existing Section 504 regulations were valid as written. These regulations are enforced by the Office for Civil Rights (OCR). The OCR has determined that Section 504 applies to playgrounds, band programs, special programs and assemblies, field trips and off-site programs, clubs, after-school and summer programs, late bus transportation, and graduation.

The ADA Amendments Act requires that episodic impairments or impairments in remission be assessed when active, and the eligibility determination be made *without regard to the ameliorative effects of mitigating measures.* A list of mitigating measures is provided and includes medication, mobility devices, low-vision devices (except eyeglasses and/or contacts), hearing aids, prosthetic devices, cochlear implants, assistive technology, reasonable accommodations, and others. The ADA also noted that an individual with a minor impairment that has an expected duration of six months or less would not be regarded as a person with a disability as minor impairments are considered "temporary impairments." Such temporary needs could be addressed through the school, but a formal 504 plan would not be required.

The ADA has a rather narrow definition of a service animal. A service animal is defined as a dog that is individually trained to do work or perform tasks for a person with a disability, including a physical, sensory, psychiatric, intellectual, or other mental disability. Note that the definition is limited to dogs that are trained to take a specific action to assist the person with a disability. Additionally, the work or task the dog has been trained to perform must be directly linked to the person's disability.

Service animals are not pets. Service animals are working animals. They perform tasks like guiding individuals who are blind, alerting people who are deaf to sounds, alerting diabetics that their blood sugar is too low or too high, detecting the onset of a seizure, keeping someone safe during a seizure, or reminding individuals with mental health concerns to take prescribed medications.

The ADA specifically notes that dogs whose sole function is to provide comfort or emotional support are not service animals. Therefore, emotional support, therapy, comfort, or companion animals are NOT service animals under the ADA because they have not been trained to perform a specific job. They provide comfort just by being present.

It can sometimes be difficult to determine if an animal is a service animal or a comfort animal. If an animal has been trained to sense an anxiety attack and take a specific action to reduce it, it would be considered a service animal. If the mere presence of the dog reduces anxiety, it would not qualify as a service animal under the ADA.

Section 504 and the IDEA have broader definitions of service animals. Section 504 and the IDEA allow students to use an animal that does not meet the definition of a service animal in schools if the IEP or Section 504 team determines that the animal is necessary for the student to receive FAPE (in practice, this is an exceedingly rare accommodation recommended by the IEP or Section 504 team). In this sense, Section 504 and the IDEA provide broader coverage than the ADA; however, the opposite is not true. If the Section 504 or IEP team determines that a service animal is not necessary for FAPE, students are still permitted to use a service animal (and not another type of assistance animal) based on their rights under the ADA. These rights are not dependent on the determination of need by the Section 504 or IEP team. Remember that if a dog is required as per the IEP/504 team, all responsibility for the dog lies with the school district. This would include the cost of the dog, the cost of maintaining it, and the responsibility for controlling it.

Once it is determined that an animal is a service animal, it must be permitted to accompany the individual with a disability in all areas of the school that the public is generally able to access. This is not limited to students and includes any staff or visitors who are accompanied by a service animal.

To determine whether an animal is a service animal, two specific inquiries are permitted. These include:

1. Is the animal required because of a disability?
2. Has the animal been trained to perform a specific task?

If the answer to these questions is obvious, they should not be asked. For example, if the dog is guiding an individual who is blind or pulling a wheelchair user, there is no need to ask these questions. Individuals cannot be asked about the nature or extent of their disabilities. Schools cannot demand documentation or evidence that the dog is trained or licensed as a service animal. Note that dogs in training are not covered under the ADA. It must already be trained before the ADA applies.

If there is a no pets policy, an exception must be made for service animals. If there is a local restriction against a specific type of dog, an exception must be made for a service animal. The school cannot require the animal to wear identification, such as a vest or harness, that identifies it as a service animal. No additional fees can be charged because an individual is accompanied by a service animal; however, individuals may be charged for any damage caused by their service animal. Owners of service animals must comply with local laws regarding animal control and public health requirements. Typically, local laws require dogs to be licensed and vaccinated.

Schools are not required to assume responsibility for the care and supervision of a service animal. This responsibility is designated to the handler. The handler is the person who is responsible for caring for and supervising the service animal. This includes feeding, toileting, and grooming the animal, as well as providing veterinary care. Handlers are usually the student with the disability or a third party who accompanies the student if the student is unable to act as the handler. A handler must control the service animal at all times. The service animal must be harnessed, leashed, or tethered in public; however, it may be unleashed to complete a specific task.

Service animals can be excluded if they pose a threat to the health or safety of others or cause substantial property damage. They can be removed if they are out of control or not housebroken. If they interfere with the operation of the school, they can be removed. If the presence of the animal causes a fundamental change in a school program, service, or activity, it may be removed or excluded.

A school may have concerns about allergies or a fear of dogs by other students. These concerns do not overshadow the rights of the individual with a disability. Schools are advised to find a way to make it work. If there is a student with an allergy, assign the students to different rooms or find some other way to accommodate both.

While the ADA definition of a service animal specifically references only dogs, a separate provision in the revised ADA regulations references miniature horses. A miniature horse ranges in height from 24 to 34 inches at the shoulders and weighs between 70 and 100 pounds. If a miniature horse has been trained to perform a task for a student with a disability, it is considered to be a service animal. Schools would therefore be required to modify their policies regarding animals to permit the use of miniature horses where reasonable. Of course, if the animal is not house trained or if any of the other permitted exclusions apply, the horse could be removed from the school. Factors to consider when determining whether a miniature horse can be accommodated at the school include whether it is housebroken, under the owner's control, and whether the facility can accommodate the horse safely.

Because the ADA and Section 504 overlap in schools, there are different paths to resolve any conflicts. If a parent of a student files a complaint under Section 504, the Office for Civil Rights would oversee the complaint process. The parent would also have the option to file a private lawsuit under the ADA with the Department of Justice.

An Office for Civil Rights (OCR) Decision in 2008 focused on the issue of service animals in the Bakersfield City School District in California. The OCR found that the district violated the ADA and Section 504 by excluding a student's dog from the school setting by unilaterally determining that the dog posed a health and safety risk to students and staff. The district did not attempt to determine whether the dog was a service animal or trained to provide a service to a student with a disability. Even if the dog was not a service animal, the district should have conducted the inquiry and determined whether the dog's presence was needed to ensure that a student with a disability received FAPE.

In a 2016 federal court case in Pennsylvania (*A. P. v. Pennsbury School District*), the district tried to exclude a dog from school. The dog was a service animal, but it had growled, lunged, and nipped at others. It did not follow commands and caused disruption. When it bit another student on the upper leg, the animal was excluded. The district felt the animal posed a direct threat to others because the handler was unable to control it. The parents sued the district, arguing that the dog had been taunted and provoked. Given the history of incidents, the district prevailed in this case.

Keep in mind that issues with service animals in schools are not limited to students. Staff and school district employees with disabilities also have rights under the ADA and Section 504 (not the IDEA) regarding the use of animals. In *Clark v. School District Five of Lexington & Richland Counties*, an elementary teacher sued her employer, the elementary school, for failing to accommodate her disability. The teacher wanted her dog Pearl to come to work with her to mitigate her symptoms related to PTSD and panic disorder. She had her psychiatrist's recommendation that Pearl be allowed to accompany her to work. The district considered the request but denied it. In a preliminary report from the Magistrate, the judge noted that employees have the right to reasonable accommodation if it allows the individual to perform the essential function of the job and to enjoy equal benefits and privileges of employment. The judge concluded that Ms. Clark could perform her essential job function of teaching without the service animal. Further, the school allowed Ms. Clark a trial period with the dog, but it did not seem to relieve her anxiety and panic attacks. Thus, it did not appear to be successful.

The case proceeded to the United States District Court for the District of South Carolina, where the question regarding Ms. Clark's ability to teach without accommodation was given further consideration, along with whether the dog was the only accommodation. A court date was set for June 15, 2017, but no further judicial action could be found.

Let's return to the scenario at the start of this chapter. What can a school district employee do if someone arrives with a miniature horse?

There are only two questions that can be asked.

1. Is the animal required because of a disability?
2. Has the animal been trained to perform a specific task?

If the answer to both questions is yes, the horse stays unless its presence poses a threat to the health or safety of others or causes substantial property damage or otherwise violates the requirements for service animals.

Schools should be prepared for this scenario. An approved school board policy could outline a process for submitting a request for a service animal.

The policy should be consistent with ADA requirements. For example, parents could be asked to voluntarily have the service animal wear a vest to indicate that it is a service animal, but they cannot be required to do so. Schools cannot require any type of training certificate for the dog, nor can they require the animal to demonstrate the tasks it was trained to perform. If the student requesting the animal is not an identified student with a disability, the student would be considered a thought-to-be-eligible student. The district may wish to pursue an evaluation to determine whether the student has a disability and, if so, develop a plan to address the student's needs within the school setting.

Testing Accommodations

Under the IDEA, testing accommodations are often included in IEPs as part of specially designed instruction. A Section 504 plan is another means to attain testing accommodations. Such accommodations are designed to ensure that a student with a disability has the opportunity to demonstrate knowledge and skills in a way that levels the playing field. For example, it would not be fair to assess a student with a visual impairment using a standard print version of a social studies test. An appropriate test accommodation might include a large-print version of the test, a magnifier, or having the test read aloud with answers dictated. Such accommodations would allow the student to demonstrate knowledge of social studies content without relying on vision to read the questions. The accommodations should compensate for the disability without giving the student an advantage on the test.

A testing accommodation allows a student with a disability to complete the same test as others, with changes in timing, format, setting, schedule, presentation, response, or a combination of these. A change to timing might allow a student additional time due to high anxiety. A change in format could involve having the test read to the student rather than having the student read the items. Setting changes allow the student to take the test at a different location, which may be free of distractions. A change in schedule may be appropriate for a student with diabetes who struggles to control blood sugar at certain times of day, or it may allow breaks in the testing schedule. A change in presentation and response might involve providing a braille version of the test to a student who is blind and allowing him to use a braille writer to record his responses.

In December of 2022, a settlement agreement was reached between the United States Department of Justice and the Educational Testing Service (ETS) regarding testing accommodations. Although this settlement focused on the requirements of the ADA, the ADA also applies to schools. Section 504 specifically applies to entities that receive federal funds, including schools, but it is part of a related body of legislation.

ETS is a private, nonprofit organization based in New Jersey that develops, administers, and scores high-stakes tests, such as the GRE General Test used for graduate school admissions and the Praxis exams used for teacher certification. The settlement was preceded by multiple complaints filed between October 2017 and April 2020, alleging that ETS violated the ADA's testing accommodation procedures.

These claims were investigated. Some complainants were required to attain a costly updated evaluation before accommodation was provided. Insufficient documentation was a common reason for denials, even when qualified professionals provided statements regarding the disability. Another had a documented learning disability questioned by ETS personnel who had never met with or evaluated the complainant and denied any accommodation. A student was granted additional time and a large-print test booklet, but scheduling the exam took months.

As a result of the investigation, it was determined that ETS failed to give weight to the determination of qualified professionals who supported requests for accommodations, failed to consider the history of testing accommodations provided on other high-stakes tests, and failed to consider accommodations that had been previously provided through IEPs and 504 plans. Additionally, the process ETS had in place for such considerations was not timely. As a result of these issues, ETS denied accommodation requests that were not consistent with its legal obligations.

While ETS denied the violations, it entered into a settlement agreement that required results to reflect aptitude or achievement rather than the individual's impairment. ETS also agreed that requests for documentation would be reasonable and that responses to requests would be timely. Importantly, ETS agreed to give considerable weight to testing accommodations provided in an IEP or 504 Plan. Monetary relief ranging from $2,500 to $10,000 was paid to various complainants, and ETS agreed to reporting requirements.

Schools should give serious thought to student needs and any related testing accommodations. Test integrity should be maintained. If a test measures math calculation skills, the use of a calculator undermines the integrity of the test. If math problem-solving is being assessed, then the use of a calculator may be appropriate. Similarly, a spell checker would not be an appropriate accommodation for a spelling test but might be fine if the assessment focuses on written expression.

Additional time is the most common accommodation, but not all students benefit from it. A highly impulsive student with ADHD who is always the first one done and who struggles to maintain attention for 10 minutes is not likely to perform better when given more time. A student with low vision who uses a magnifier, which significantly slows reading, may benefit greatly from extended time because it takes the student longer to read with a magnifier. While extended time is often provided to students with anxiety, there are studies that suggest avoidance-based interventions, such as extra time and separate rooms for testing, may actually exacerbate anxiety.[1] Avoidance can increase anxiety, while exposure can lessen it. Even if an accommodation generally works with similar students, it may not work for a particular student. It is advisable for 504 Teams to trial testing accommodations and collect data on their effectiveness when determining whether a student requires a given accommodation.

Substance Abuse

Section 504 can be utilized for a student recovering from substance abuse because drug addiction can be viewed as a disability that substantially limits a person's major life activities. Therefore, a student returning to school following drug and alcohol treatment may trigger an initial evaluation under Section 504. Note that current users of illegal drugs are excluded from the definition of a person with a disability under Section 504 and the ADA. There is no obligation to evaluate current drug users.

Possession of drugs does not automatically result in the loss of 504 protections. The student with a disability must be using drugs and/or alcohol to be excluded from protections. If the school cannot show that the student is currently using, the student must be provided the procedural protections to determine if the behavior is a manifestation of the disability for disciplinary purposes.

Alcohol is not specifically referenced under 504, but OCR addressed the issue in a 1991 Staff Memorandum.[2] OCR agreed with parents of a student with alcoholism that the student's misconduct was related to his disability; however, OCR also determined that a student who is currently using alcohol can be disciplined in the same way as nondisabled students. OCR upheld the district's decision to expel a student for alcohol-related offenses that occurred on school grounds in the case of *Pinellas County School District* in Florida. Thus, when code of conduct violations occur for students protected under 504 who are currently using drugs or alcohol, those students may be subject to the same disciplinary actions as their nondisabled peers. The OCR defines *current use of drugs* as *illegal use of drugs that occurred recently enough to justify a reasonable belief that a person's drug use is current or that continuing use is a real and ongoing problem.*[3] A manifestation determination is not required for such disciplinary actions, and the parent does not have the right to challenge the disciplinary consequences based on the argument that the student's drug or alcohol-related misconduct was related to the student's disability.

Schools may struggle to identify ways to support students in recovery from substance abuse through a 504 plan. Consider a hypothetical female named Maryjane Jones, a high school junior. Maryjane spent 30 days in an intensive inpatient program due to cocaine addiction. While a 90-day placement is recommended, her parents' insurance only covers 30 days, so she will be returning to school after the winter break, as this is a logical break in programming. Her parents are paying out of pocket for an additional 12 days of treatment, so her total treatment will consist of 42 days. A summary from the facility states that she no longer experiences the physical symptoms of withdrawal, but she is experiencing psychological dependence and depression. She has difficulty sleeping and struggles to wake up and function in the mornings. She will be participating in outpatient therapy after discharge. Recommendations from the facility include severing ties with former friends who continue to use, establishing a safe space at school, a modified academic workload, scheduling the most rigorous courses in the afternoons, regular contact with parents regarding performance, and other supports deemed appropriate by school personnel.

Assuming the 504 evaluation team finds her eligible due to her standing as a recovering addict, Maryjane's 504 plan could include the following:

1. The school counselor has set up a schedule for Maryjane that avoids identified past associates and includes her main academic courses in the afternoon. Additionally, she arranged a first-period study hall so Maryjane could take advantage of a later start to her school day. Alternatively, Maryjane may choose to take advantage of tutoring services in the learning support classroom during the first period to catch up on missed assignments.
2. Given the cumulative nature of instruction in math and science courses, Maryjane has been deliberately scheduled in classes taught by teachers who hold tutoring sessions after school two days per week. Trigonometry tutoring occurs on Tuesday and Thursday. Chemistry tutoring occurs on Monday and Wednesday.
3. Maryjane's teachers will be advised of Maryjane's return to school. They will be instructed to eliminate any graded assignments that are not critical to continued progress in the course. Maryjane will have six weeks to make up any critical assignments she missed during her six-week absence from school.
4. If teachers determine that the six-week absence has resulted in a gap in critical knowledge, learning support services may be used for the remainder of the marking period to remediate any deficiencies. Specific objectives and critical course assignments will be coordinated between the learning support teachers and the regular classroom teachers. Parents will be informed of any short-term change in assignment to learning support via email.
5. Mr. and Mrs. Jones are encouraged to sign up for Parent Connect so that they may check Maryjane's grades in all classes at any time.

6. Maryjane will participate in a drug and alcohol support group run through the Student Assistance Program once a week on Fridays. This group is run by an external certified drug and alcohol counselor.
7. A release of information has been signed by Mr. and Mrs. Jones to allow the exchange of information between Maryjane's outside counselor and her school counselor. The school counselor's office has been designated as a "safe space" for Maryjane, and she will be permitted to use it as needed during her transition back to public school.
8. Maryjane will automatically be included in the school's random drug testing program in place for student athletes as a potential deterrent to relapsing into drug use. She will be tested every two weeks for the remainder of the school year at no cost to the parent.

Sample Cases

Because all students who qualify for special education services are also protected by Section 504, the legal cases that are often cited specific to Section 504 include both students who only receive accommodations through a 504 service plan, as well as students who receive accommodations in addition to specially designed instruction through an IEP.

Recall that the Individuals with Disabilities Education Act (IDEA) provides federal funding to states for providing a free appropriate public education (FAPE) to students with disabilities. The IDEA also established a process for resolving disputes related to the provision of FAPE. The Americans with Disabilities Act (ADA) and Section 504 of the Rehabilitation Act of 1973 also protect the rights of individuals with disabilities. These laws were considered together in the Handicapped Children's Protection Act of 1986, which mandates that any suit brought under the ADA, Section 504, or similar laws seeking relief also available under the IDEA must first exhaust the IDEA's administrative dispute resolution procedures. More specifically, the provision of the statute from the Handicapped Children's Protection Act of 1986 states:

> *Nothing in [the IDEA] shall be construed to restrict or limit the rights, procedures, and remedies available under the Constitution, the [ADA], title V of the Rehabilitation Act [including §504], or other Federal laws protecting the rights of children with disabilities, except that before the filing of a civil action under such laws seeking relief that is also available under [the IDEA], the [IDEA's administrative procedures] shall be exhausted to the same extent as would be required had the action been brought under [the IDEA].*
>
> (20 U.S.C. 1415(*l*))

This requirement became the focus of an often-cited 504 lawsuit. The *Fry v. Napoleon Community Schools* case was ultimately heard by the Supreme

Court. According to court documents, this case involved a girl named Ehlena Fry. Ehlena was born in India and adopted by the Frys just before she turned one. Ehlena was diagnosed with a severe form of cerebral palsy known as spastic quadriplegic cerebral palsy. Cerebral palsy is a group of neurological conditions caused by damage to the developing brain. A common cause of cerebral palsy is anoxia (lack of oxygen) during the birth process. The motor cortex is typically the part of the brain that is initially affected, disrupting the ability to control movement. Symptoms can range from mild to severe and impact mobility, balance, posture, swallowing, and speech.

In the fall of 2009, Ehlena enrolled in Ezra Eby Elementary School in Napoleon, Michigan. She was five years old and about to enter kindergarten. The Frys believed Ehlena's service dog would be welcome in the building based on their discussions with the principal; however, in October of 2009, after just one day in the school, the principal reported that some students were afraid of the dog. The school wanted more time to research the issue.

Court records show that the district believed Ehlena did not need a service animal because her IEP included a one-on-one aide who could provide any needed assistance. The school was also concerned about student or staff allergies to dogs, classroom disruptions, and some students' reported dog phobias. There were questions about how a student as young as Ehlena could control a service animal. The district was also concerned that kindergarten students could be distracted by an animal in the classroom, potentially affecting their education.

School personnel refused the request to allow Ehlena's service dog, a white goldendoodle named Wonder, to attend school with her. The service dog was prescribed by her pediatrician to help Ehlena gain more independence. Wonder was trained to perform tasks such as opening doors, turning on lights, removing her coat, steadying her when she used her walker, and picking up dropped items. To this point, the Frys had felt supported by the community. The local community had raised about $13,000 to cover the cost of 10 days of training that Ehlena and Wonder completed together, and the dog was actually donated to the Frys by the organization 4 Paws for Ability. Wonder had been trained for more than a year to function as a service animal.

Soon after Ehlena enrolled, the Frys were told that Wonder was not permitted to accompany Ehlena in school. The American Civil Liberties Union (ACLU) intervened on Ehlena's behalf, and in April of 2010, Wonder was permitted to attend school with Ehlena on a trial basis. Wonder was not acknowledged as a service dog, and there were restrictions on where the dog could go. For example, the dog could not be with Ehlena at lunch or recess, could not assist her in the restroom, and had to stay in the back of the classroom with a handler. The trial period lasted from mid-April until the end of Ehlena's kindergarten experience.

The school argued that Ehlena already had a personal care aide assigned to her as part of her Individualized Education Program (IEP); thus, her needs were already being addressed through services provided by the district. At the end of the year, the Frys were told that Wonder would not be allowed back in the school the following year.

Shortly after receiving this news, the Frys filed a complaint with the Office for Civil Rights (OCR), an office of the United States Department of Education. While they waited for their complaint to be resolved, they opted to homeschool Ehlena using an online curriculum. In May of 2012, the OCR determined that Ehlena's rights had been violated by the school under the Americans with Disabilities Act (ADA) and the Rehabilitation Act by failing to modify its policies, practices, or procedures to permit Ehlena to be accompanied by her service animal. Napoleon Community Schools subsequently agreed to let Wonder attend school with Ehlena for the second grade, but his role was restricted.

The Frys opted to leave the district. Ehlena and her two older brothers initially attended Klage Elementary School in Manchester, Michigan, about 20 minutes away, through Michigan's school choice program. The family eventually moved into the district with their five children. Ehlena enrolled in a new school district in which Wonder was permitted to attend school with her. Wonder was seemingly welcomed into the new school. He was given his own identification badge, and his picture was even included in the school's yearbook alongside the staff.

The Frys, with representation from the ACLU of Michigan, filed a lawsuit against their former school district. In 2015, the case was dismissed by the lower courts and the Sixth Circuit of Appeals in Cincinnati, Ohio. These decisions noted that the Frys had failed to exhaust all available administrative remedies under the Individuals with Disabilities Education Act (IDEA) before filing for damages under the ADA and Section 504 of the Rehabilitation Act of 1973. In legal briefs filed regarding the case, the district argued that Congress balanced the IDEA and other laws established to protect the rights of students with disabilities. The district acknowledged that the IDEA did not limit students' rights under the ADA or the Rehabilitation Act. It required that if parents seek relief also available under the IDEA, they must attempt to obtain that relief through the procedural safeguards that exist under the IDEA (through a due process hearing) before pursuing other avenues, like filing a lawsuit against the district.

The Frys argued that the dispute was never about Ehlena's education. It was about the school's refusal to accommodate her use of a service dog at school to help her gain independence.

The case made its way to the Supreme Court. In a unanimous 8–0 decision, the Supreme Court ruled in Ehlena's favor. The primary holding was that a person bringing a claim under the IDEA does not have to exhaust administrative procedures if the claim is based on something other than the denial of FAPE.

Ehlena was 13 years old and in sixth grade when the case was heard. Wonder retired after seven years of service, and Ehlena no longer needed a service dog. Nonetheless, she was grateful for the decision and for the attention it focused on the rights of individuals with disabilities. The Supreme Court justices decided that if a lawsuit does not claim that a proper special education under the IDEA is being denied, then exhausting the IDEA's administrative remedies through local and state dispute resolution and due process procedures is not required.

The Court established a two-part test for determining the core issue of a lawsuit. The first part focused on determining if the plaintiff could have filed suit if the incident had occurred in a public place other than a school. If so, the requirement to exhaust remedies under the IDEA is likely not applicable. The second part focused on determining if an adult could have filed the same claim in the same public setting. If so, the exhaustion requirement likely does not apply.

The case was remanded back to the lower appeals court for resolution. The decision, rendered on February 22, 2017, allows families to take legal action against schools for possible discrimination under the ADA and the Rehabilitation Act without having to go through the time-consuming and sometimes costly IDEA administrative process. The IDEA exhaustion requirement applies only to claims that, at their core, focus on the provision of a free appropriate public education (FAPE). If the issue in dispute is not FAPE, then other legal recourse is available for families.

Irving Independent School District v. Tatro (468 U.S. 883) is an earlier United States Supreme Court case, decided on July 5, 1984, that brought claims under the Education for All Handicapped Children Act of 1975 (EHA, now known as the IDEA) and under the Rehabilitation Act of 1973. The primary question for the court was whether catheterization services were included as a related service under the EHA and, if so, whether the family could seek attorney's fees under the Rehabilitation Act. A main focus of the case was on differentiating between required related services and medical services that did not have to be provided by schools.

This case involved three-and-a-half-year-old Amber Tatro, the daughter of Henri and Mary Tatro, who resided in the Irving Independent School District in Texas. Amber had been born with spina bifida, a neural tube defect in which the spinal column does not fully close during the prenatal period. It creates an opening in the spine that can damage the spinal cord and nerves. Severity varies, and it often leads to physical disability, learning challenges, and problems with bowel and bladder control.

In Amber's case, she experienced a neurogenic bladder, a condition that prevents the bladder from working properly due to nerve damage that disrupts the nerve signals that control bladder function. Complications of this condition can lead to frequent and repeated urinary tract infections and kidney damage or failure. Therefore, Amber required catheterization every three or four hours every day to avoid complications. Clean intermittent catheterization (CIC) was the preferred method of catheterization. As a preschooler, Amber was unable to perform CIC independently; however, a layperson could easily be taught to perform the procedure.

In 1979, an IEP was developed for Amber that outlined her attendance in an early childhood development class, along with the provision of physical and occupational therapies. There was no provision for CIC services during school hours.

At that time, Texas law required schools to provide a FAPE, including related services; however, medical services had to be provided only for the purpose of diagnosis or evaluation. The school viewed catheterization as a medical service and did not believe that it had an obligation to provide medical services to students. The Tatro family attempted to resolve the conflict through administrative remedies available to them; however, they were unsuccessful.

By October 1979, the Tatros took legal action against the school district, the Texas State Board of Education, and others. They wanted the court to order the district to provide CIC services to Amber and to award damages and attorneys' fees under the Rehabilitation Act. Their claim under the Rehabilitation Act focused on the fact that programs receiving federal funds could not exclude individuals with disabilities from participating in their programs and allowed prevailing parties to recover attorneys' fees.

The district court determined that CIC was not a related service. This decision was based on the fact that CIC did not arise from an effort to educate. Therefore, the court denied the Tatros' request for a preliminary injunction to provide CIC.

The Tatros appealed to the United States Court of Appeals in the Fifth Circuit. The appeals court reversed the district court's decision and held that CIC was, in fact, a related service under the EHA. Related services were viewed as services needed for a student with a disability to access public education. Since Amber could not attend school without the provision of CIC, this was related to the provision of FAPE. It was not viewed as a medical service because it did not require a licensed medical professional to provide it.

The case was sent back to the district court. The district heard the case again and ruled that CIC was not a medical service under the EHA because it did not have to be administered by a physician. The district court directed the school district to modify Amber's IEP to include CIC as a related service. Finally, the district court held that the Tatros had shown a violation of the Rehabilitation Act. When appealed to the Fifth Circuit, both decisions were upheld.

The case was then heard by the United States Supreme Court. In a unanimous decision, the Supreme Court ruled that the CIC provision was a related service, not a medical service, under the EHA. In the EHA, a related service was defined as a service required for a child with a disability to benefit from special education. Without CIC, Amber would not be able to attend school and benefit from her special education programming. The justices found that CIC was necessary to carry out Congress's intent under the EHA by ensuring meaningful access to public education.

It was further determined that CIC was not a medical service because, under the Department of Education's own regulations, medical services were defined as those services provided by a licensed physician. In contrast, CIC could be performed by a trained layperson. The justices determined that CIC was a related service because it met the requirements of a related service as defined by both the Department of Education and Congress, and the service was required for the student to attend school.

The second legal question posed in this case involved the awarding of attorneys' fees under the Rehabilitation Act. In a 6–2 decision, the Court reversed the holding from the Fifth Circuit that the Tatros were entitled to attorneys' fees. Because relief was available under the EHA, attorney's fees were not awarded. The Tatro decision is viewed as a precedent-setting case on how medical services should be interpreted in public school settings.

The 1999 Supreme Court case of *Cedar Rapids Community School District v. Garret F.* (U.S. 66) relied on the precedent set in Tatro in its decision. This case from Iowa focused on the needs of a student named Garret.

When Garret was four years old, his spinal column was severed in a motorcycle accident, and he was subsequently paralyzed from the neck down. His mental capacities were not impacted by the accident. He could speak. He used a motorized wheelchair controlled by a puff-and-suck straw. He used a computer with the use of a device that responded to head movements. Garret was successful in the general education setting in a typical school program. He was dependent on a ventilator and could not breathe without assistance. Someone had to pump an air bag attached to his tracheostomy tube when the ventilator was being maintained. He required a responsible person nearby to address physical needs at school. For example, he needed to have his tracheotomy tube suctioned at least once every six hours. He also needed assistance with urinary bladder catheterization once per day and help with food and drink at lunch. He was also to be placed in a reclining position for five minutes each hour. An individual who could perform emergency care in case he experienced autonomic hyperreflexia (uncontrolled visceral reaction to anxiety or a full bladder) was needed.

The family provided Garret's physical care throughout the school day during his early school years. His 18-year-old aunt served as his attendant during his kindergarten experience. Settlement money received after the accident, insurance money, and other resources were used by the family to cover the cost of a licensed nurse for the next four years. In 1993, the family requested that the District assume financial responsibility for Garret's services during the school day. The district did not believe that it was legally obligated to pay for continuous one-on-one nursing services at school, so it denied the parent's request.

Garret's mother sought a hearing through the Iowa Department of Education, which was reviewed by an administrative law judge (ALJ). The ALJ determined that about 2,200 of the district's 17,500 students required some form of special education services. While Garret was the only student who was ventilator-dependent, the other services were already being provided to other district students. The ALJ clarified that the services were not medical services as they did not require a licensed physician to provide them. Instead, they were school health services which could be provided by a qualified school nurse or other qualified individual. The ALJ concluded that the District had the responsibility to pay for the needed services to include continuous nursing care.

The District appealed to the Federal District Court. The court relied on the two-step analysis established in *Irving Independent School District v. Tatro*. The services were needed and did not meet the definition of medical services. The district argued that the cost presented an undue burden and that the services, while performed by a nurse, were medical in nature. In its decision, the appeals court supported the ALJ's determination. The district had to assume financial responsibility for the continuous, one-on-one nursing care needs of Garret during the school day as long as the services could be provided by someone other than a physician. The cost of the service was not a valid reason to deny the service, thereby denying the student FAPE. This case was viewed as a major win for students with disabilities.

A more recent Supreme Court case, *A. J. T. v. Osseo Area Schools*, was decided on June 12, 2025. In this case, A. J. T. had a rare form of epilepsy that severely limited her physical and cognitive functioning. She needed help with everyday tasks like walking and toileting because her seizures throughout the day created safety concerns. She experienced frequent and severe seizures in the morning, but she was alert and able to learn from noon until about 6:00 p.m.

When she first started school, A. J. T.'s needs were met in her school district by allowing her to avoid morning activities and by providing instruction at home in the evening. In 2015, the ten-year-old moved with her family to Minnesota and enrolled in the Osseo Area Public Schools. The school repeatedly denied parental requests for evening instruction as part of A. J. T.'s IEP. As a result, she received only 4.25 hours of daily instruction, while her peers received 6.5 hours from 2015 through 2018.

As A. J. T. prepared for her transition to middle school, the district proposed further reducing the length of her school day. Her parents objected and requested that she have a school day of comparable length to her non-disabled peers. The district refused to lengthen her day and rejected a proposal to at least maintain the instructional hours she had received at the elementary level.

The parents responded by filing a special education due process complaint with the Minnesota Department of Education. The hearing lasted five days, and the administrative law judge (ALJ) found that the district violated the student's rights. Several hundred hours of compensatory education were awarded, and at-home instruction from 4:30 – 6:00 p.m. was ordered to be added to her program. The district appealed to the Federal District Court. The ALJ's decision was upheld. The Eighth Circuit agreed with the District Court, and the decision was affirmed.

With these victories through administrative procedures, A. J. T. and her parents sued the school district and the school board in federal court for violations of the ADA and Section 504 of the Rehabilitation Act. They sought an injunction, reimbursement for some costs, and compensatory damages. The district made a motion for summary judgment, which was granted by the trial court on the basis that the plaintiff had failed to show that school officials "acted with bad faith or gross misjudgment."

An appeal to the Eighth Circuit upheld the lower court's decision. Under a precedent in the Eighth Circuit, alleged failures to provide reasonable accommodations for students with disabilities under the ADA and Section 504 were not sufficient to trigger liability. In the Eighth Circuit, the plaintiff had to show that the school officials acted with bad faith or gross misjudgment, not merely noncompliance with a federal statute. The panel noted that the parents did not show that the school's actions reflected bad faith or gross misjudgment. While this higher standard set a higher bar for claims based on educational services, the panel noted that it remained the law and thus was bound to abide by it.

In its unanimous decision, the Supreme Court vacated the Eighth Circuit ruling and held that schoolchildren bringing claims related to their education under the ADA and the Rehabilitation Act do not have to show bad faith or gross misjudgment. Instead, they are subject to the same standards that apply in other disability discrimination contexts. More specifically, claims outside of education allow plaintiffs to establish violations and seek relief without proving intent to discriminate. Compensatory damages generally accept the deliberate indifference standard rather than a higher bad faith or gross misjudgment standard.

A redacted version from a hearing officer's final decision dated January 31, 2020, offers some insight into disagreements between parents and school districts regarding 504 services. This closed hearing involved the

Owen J. Roberts School District in Pottstown, Pennsylvania, and a student whose identity was redacted in order to preserve his/her anonymity.

In this case, the seventh-grade student had a Section 504 Agreement that was reviewed and modified in August of 2017. The parents did not approve of the proposed agreement, so the district informed parents that it would continue to implement the previously agreed-upon agreement from March 2017. This agreement included 18 accommodations, such as the use of an agenda book, verbal reminders, reduction of visual distractions, prompts to use dictation applications, allowing the student to stand to complete work, transition meetings at the start of each school year, occupational therapy, breaks, and extended time to complete assignments.

The student was found eligible under the IDEA as a student with autism. An IEP was developed in early September of 2017 that included goals for organization, speech/language, literacy in science and technical subjects, and social skills. The IEP also included 43 SDIs (specially designed instruction), speech therapy, and nursing services. A Notice of Recommended Education Placement (NOREP) was issued on September 13, 2017, which offered autistic support, nursing services, participation in regular education classes, and speech and language support. On September 25, 2017, the parent was informed that if she did not approve the NOREP or the Section 504 Agreement, the student would be deemed a regular education pupil. The Section 504 plan would be discontinued, and the IEP would not be implemented. The parent requested additional time to review the documents. On October 3 and again on October 11, the parents were notified in writing that 504 services would be discontinued without approval of a plan, and the IEP would not be implemented without their consent. Procedural safeguards were provided to the parents in the written notices. Another meeting was held on October 12.

The student was admitted to the Children's Hospital of Philadelphia from October 12 to October 18, 2017. The staff at CHOP provided a letter describing medically necessary services to address the student's Qualitative Platelet Function Disorder. On October 24, all parties met to revise the student's health plan and addressed the platelet disorder, asthma, use of an epi-pen, medication administration, and directions to monitor fluid intake and to take frequent bathroom breaks. Another letter was provided by the mother on October 25, 2017, stating that the student was hospitalized at an acute behavioral health care facility for seven days. A two-sentence letter from CHOP was provided on October 26, directing the school nurse to follow a series of concussion protocols with no explanation for the directions or identification of a new Section 504 disability.

On October 27, the mother did not approve of the NOREP, nor did she approve the proposed 504 Agreement. Instead, the parent asked to have the prior 504 Agreement from March of 2017 updated and reinstated. The parent filed a complaint with the Office for Civil Rights in November of 2017, alleging discrimination, retaliation, and a denial of FAPE. The parent emailed to state her agreement with speech support, but she disagreed with the pull-out autistic support services outlined in the IEP. On December 6, CHOP sent a letter to the district informing them that the student had a history of multiple concussions and suggesting academic accommodations. In March, CHOP updated student protocols for gastrointestinal issues and listed 22 medical conditions. Neither traumatic brain injury nor recurring concussions were listed. In April of 2018, the mother requested an evaluation under the IDEA to determine if her child qualified as a student with an Other Health Impairment (OHI). On May 5, 2018, the Section 504 Agreement was reinstated. On May 10, CHOP sent a letter to the district that listed vestibular/oculomotor dysfunction as a medical condition. This had not been previously diagnosed.

The parties met again in September 2018 to develop a new 504 plan. On October 2, 2018, the district denied the parent's request for a one-on-one aide or one-on-one personal nursing services. The letter from the district also stated that, based on their observations, these services were not needed to provide FAPE.

CHOP then provided updated assessment information on October 11, 2018. Based on parent responses to an adaptive behavior measure (Adaptive Behavior Assessment System – Third Edition), CHOP recommended daily instruction on living skills, social skills, and occupational awareness and exploration. Forty hours per week of community-based in-home applied behavioral analysis (ABA) training was also recommended. In December, the mother shared that the student was receiving outpatient physical therapy services. In February of 2019, the mother requested an Independent Educational Evaluation (IEE), and the school district agreed; however, the parent then filed a due process complaint. The district then withdrew its offer to pay for an IEE, as it had hoped to avoid litigation by agreeing to the IEE. The district then filed its own due process complaint defending its 2017 IDEA evaluation.

In March 2019, CHOP forwarded a doctor's statement that the student was experiencing a gastrointestinal flare and should be excused from school for one week. The mother then requested immediate in-home tutoring on April 2. The parties met on April 3 and on April 17, 2019, but no agreement was reached. On April 8, 2019, *intermittent homebound instruction* was requested in a letter from CHOP. On April 29, the School Board approved homebound services. Homebound instruction was provided; however, the instructor refused to return to the home after the student threw a remote, which struck her. Homebound at an alternate location was proposed in May 2019. The student later returned to school with a private one-on-one nurse. The private nurse could not provide documentation of proper clearances, so the district had her remain in the office and provided a district-funded nurse to support the student. On May 28, the district emailed the mother, indicating that it would fund a one-on-one nurse.

After five days of attendance with a private-duty nurse selected by the parents, the services abruptly ended on September 9, 2019, both at home and at school. The district offered to provide a one-on-one nurse, but the parents refused to send the student to school. The district reached out about the absences, but the reasons for them were unclear. A behavioral specialist working in the student's home provided a letter describing emotional concerns and requested homebound instruction. CHOP also requested homebound instruction but noted that staff were not authorized to discuss the basis for the request. The district determined that the absences were not related to a medical condition or disability and denied the request for homebound. Thus, truancy notices were issued, but the parents refused to develop a truancy elimination plan or engage in any discussion about attendance. On November 1, 2019, the student and parents moved out of the district.

In his decision, the hearing officer noted that Section 504 applies to public schools. He explained that in order to prevail in a 504 discrimination claim, the parents had to show that the student had a disability, was otherwise qualified to participate in a school program, and was denied the benefits of the program as a result of his disability. To prove a denial of benefits, deliberate indifference must be established. To prevail on the retaliation claim under 504, the parent must show that the parents and the student each engaged in a protected activity, that the district's alleged retaliatory action deterred them from exercising their rights, and that there was a causal connection between the protected activity and the retaliation. The hearing officer also addressed the associational discrimination claim.

The hearing officer opined that the district's unilateral decision to discontinue the 504 plan constituted a procedural violation; however, the parents failed to establish whether the student was excluded from or suffered a loss or denial of benefits as a result of that procedural violation. He reasoned that Section 504 does not require a written document, and the teachers all testified that they continued to accommodate the student even after the 504 plan was discontinued. Because the student excelled in regular education, earning high grades in honors math, the hearing officer concluded that he received an equal opportunity to access the benefits of the district's educational program, even though there was no written 504 plan. The error was harmless.

The parents also filed a Section 504 FAPE claim, which was rejected. The parents would not sign a consent for the school to communicate with CHOP. They would not consent to a reevaluation and refused to sign a release of information so that the district could obtain existing medical and behavioral health data. The parents also prevented the district-funded one-on-one nurse from talking to CHOP's staff by phone. These actions blocked testing and evaluation protections. Letters from CHOP requested significant changes to the content and method of instruction, OT, PT, and one-on-one supports for a student with above-average intelligence enrolled in honors classes, without linking the accommodations to updated assessment data or to a new or existing disability. As the hearing officer wrote:

> *Under these facts, the Parents cannot expect to prevail on a claim that the District failed to provide a substantive offer of a FAPE when they withheld consent for all that they now complain about. Accordingly, for all of the following reasons, the Parents' substantive Section 504 FAPE claims are rejected.*

In his order dated January 30, 2020, the hearing officer found in favor of the District and against the parent and student on all five claims (discrimination and/or associational discrimination, retaliation, failure to provide FAPE with regard to Section 504, failure to provide FAPE specific to gifted education, and for all other violations under the IDEA, Chapter 16, and Section 504).

Let us apply principles covered in this chapter to a hypothetical case. A seventeen-year-old high school student was placed into a residential treatment center for drug addiction and alcoholism by his mother over the summer vacation. The student completed the program and returned to school as a regular education student in the fall. During a meeting held the first week of school to discuss taking the SATs and completing college enrollment applications, the student informed his school counselor of his treatment during the summer vacation. The school counselor believes the information is confidential under HIPAA and tells no one else about the discussion, including the Director of Special Education.

During the first marking period, the student was caught under the influence of drugs and in possession with intent to sell controlled substances at a school-sponsored activity, where the student was acting in the capacity of a student mentor to younger students. The student was selected as a mentor due to his outstanding academic performance and to pad his college applications.

The Superintendent concludes that the student's actions constitute a violation of the school district's drug and alcohol policies and suspends the student initially for three days, followed by seven more days pending a Board hearing on the Superintendent's recommendation that the student be expelled. At the expulsion hearing, the student testifies in his own defense and tells the Board of his treatment for drugs over the summer and that he intends to return to rehabilitation due to his relapse. The Board expels the student permanently.

Should the student have been evaluated to determine eligibility for a 504 Plan? If so, when?

The student should have been evaluated following his disclosure to the school counselor. This should have triggered the referral for an evaluation under Section 504. The student and/or his parents could have declined the evaluation (and if they declined, the school's obligations to refer would have been satisfied), but it should have been offered.

Was the student likely eligible for a 504 plan? If so, under what definitional criteria?

Given the student's status as an individual in treatment for addiction, he likely would have been eligible for a 504 plan.

What discipline should be imposed upon the student?

Even if the student had been eligible for a 504 plan, any protections offered regarding discipline would not have applied once he began to use illegal substances. Therefore, typical disciplinary procedures would apply, and the student would not be entitled to manifestation determination protections.

What liability issues does the school district have, if any?

The district has to consider whether the student would have begun to use substances if he had been identified as a student with a disability and if appropriate supports had been put in place. If this implies negligence on the district's part, the district will want to consult its solicitor for guidance on how to proceed.

Let us examine another hypothetical case involving a school district employee. A third-grade teacher at a small elementary school is a lactating mother of a four-month-old son. She lives very near the school and leaves during lunch and midday recess to nurse her baby, as she has no assigned duties. In her district, teachers are permitted to leave the school over lunch. Therefore, she did not need to request any formal accommodation.

A field trip for her class is coming up. This is an all-day field trip that includes a hike to a location where fossils are often found. She recognizes that there will be no private space for her to pump breast milk during the field trip. She shares her concerns with the second-grade teacher, who understands the situation and offers to swap assignments with her for the day. When the teacher approaches her male principal with this suggestion, he says that he does not like the idea of disrupting the other class or imposing on the other teacher. He subsequently denies the request. Instead, he suggests that the teacher stay home that day and use a sick day. A substitute teacher can handle the field trip.

The teacher objects, noting that she has limited sick days remaining after using her accumulated days for paid childbearing leave. She does not want to use a sick day for this purpose and feels that her solution will work. The other teacher knows all of the students in the class as they had her as their teacher the previous year. The other teacher volunteered to make the switch and is actually looking forward to the day with her prior students. The principal still objects. He argues that if she does not want to use a sick day, she should go on the field trip as per her job assignment and "just not pump that day." The teacher is not sure what recourse she may have.

Is this a possible 504 issue warranting reasonable accommodation?

Remember, the 504 definition of a disability is quite broad. Lactation involves the lymphatic and endocrine systems. Any condition affecting a body system, including the lymphatic and endocrine systems, is included in the definition of a disability under Section 504. A condition that does not last for at least six months is not considered a disability under 504. The teacher's baby is four months old, and she anticipates breastfeeding him until he is at least one year of age. Therefore, lactation will continue for more than six months. Based on this information, the teacher appears to qualify as an individual with a disability under Section 504.

As a lactating woman, it is clear that she just cannot forego pumping during lunch on the day of the field trip. It is also not appropriate for her to pump in the presence of her students. While the principal thinks it is reasonable for her to use a sick day when she is not sick, the teacher does not want to do this. Her proposal to switch job assignments voluntarily with another teacher seems reasonable. She may wish to make a formal request to the principal through the lens of a 504 accommodation and see what happens. This would give her access to internal dispute resolution options if the request is denied.

This chapter provided an overview of Section 504 requirements and compared them to IDEA requirements. Sections on service animals, testing accommodations, and drug and alcohol addiction were also addressed as they apply to Section 504. Finally, actual cases and hypothetical cases were presented to illustrate how these concepts apply in practice.

Notes

1 Lovett, B. J., & Fienup, D. M. (2023). Using Interventions to Increase Test Access: An Alternative to Accommodations? *Assessment for Effective Intervention*, 49(1), 41–49.
2 U.S. Department of Education, Office for Civil Rights. (1991). OCR Staff Memorandum, 17 IDELR 609.
3 U.S. Department of Education, Office for Civil Rights. (1992). OCR Staff Memorandum, 19 IDELR 859.

List of Cases

A. J. T., by and through her parents, A. T., et al. v. Osseo Area Schools, Independent School Dist. No. 279, 605 U.S. ___ (2025).
A.P., et. al. v. Pennsbury School District (C.A. No.16-02224 E.D. Pa).
Cedar Rapids Cmty. Sch. Dist. v. Garret F., 526 U.S. 66 (1999).

Clark v. Sch. Dist. Five of Lexington & Richland Cntys., No. 3:15-cv-02864-CMC-PJG, 2017 WL 1067649 (D.S.C. Mar. 29, 2017).
Fry v. Napoleon Cmty. Schs., 137 S. Ct. 743 (2017).
Irving Indep. Sch. Dist. v. Tatro, 468 U.S. 883 (1984).
OCR Case Resolution Letter, United States Department of Education, Office for Civil Rights. (2008, January 25). *Bakersfield School District, Bakersfield, California* (OCR Case No. 09-07-1220).
Pennsylvania Office for Dispute Resolution. (2020, January 31). *[C.C.] v. Owen J. Roberts School District*, ODR File No. 21838-18-19 [Decision].
Pinellas County (FL) School District, 20 IDELR 561 (OCR 1993).
United States Department of Justice. (2022, December 19). *Settlement Agreement between the United States and Educational Testing Service* [PDF]. https://content.govdelivery.com/attachments/USDOJUSAO/2022/12/19/file_attachments/2359254/ETS.Settlement.pdf

Laws Cited

ADA Amendments Act of 2008, 42 U.S.C. § 12101 et seq. (2008).
Americans with Disabilities Act of 1990, 42 U.S.C. § 12101 et seq. (1990).
Education for All Handicapped Children Act, Pub. L. No. 94–142, 89 Stat. 773 (1975).
Handicapped Children's Protection Act of 1986, Pub. L. No. 99-372, 100 Stat. 796 (1986).
Individuals with Disabilities Education Act, 20 U.S.C. § 1400 (2004).
Rehabilitation Act of 1973, Pub. L. No. 93-112, 87 Stat. 355 (1973).
Rehabilitation Act of 1973, § 504, 29 U.S.C. § 794 (1973).
- Regulations: 34 C. F. R Part 104.
Rehabilitation Act Amendments of 1974, Pub. L. No. 93-516, 88 Stat. 1617 (1974).
Rehabilitation Act Amendments of 1998, Pub. L. No. 105-220, 112 Stat. 1092 (1998).
Vocational Rehabilitation Amendments of 1954, Pub. L. No. 83-565, 68 Stat. 652 (1954).

Index

For Product Safety Concerns and Information please contact our EU representative GPSR@taylorandfrancis.com
Taylor & Francis Verlag GmbH, Kaufingerstraße 24, 80331 München, Germany

www.ingramcontent.com/pod-product-compliance
Ingram Content Group UK Ltd.
Pitfield, Milton Keynes, MK11 3LW, UK
UKHW022353190926
475702UK00015B/2266
* 9 7 8 1 0 4 1 2 1 7 7 2 5 *